FIFTY
SHADES OF
WHITE

FIFTY
SHADES OF
WHITE

HALF A CENTURY OF PAIN
AND GLORY WITH LEEDS UNITED

GARY EDWARDS

First published by Pitch Publishing, 2016

Pitch Publishing
A2 Yeoman Gate
Yeoman Way
Worthing
Sussex
BN13 3QZ

www.pitchpublishing.co.uk
info@pitchpublishing.co.uk

ISBN 978-1-78531-198-7

Typesetting and origination by Pitch Publishing
Printed by Bell & Bain, Glasgow, Scotland

Contents

This book is dedicated to Wub, who once again has supported me throughout. And is in fond memory of Reece Hopkins, who was truly one of our own. My old mates Haggis and Ray 'misjudged it' Beverley, Silver, Pete Conway and to Baz Starmore. We also lost my Uncle John who came off the bench alongside Uncle Ernie and my Grandma's chap, George, who tossed a coin between them to see who would take me to United's games in the 60s and early 70s, when Dad couldn't make it.

Acknowledgements

MANY, many thanks to: Neil Jeffries, Phil Hay, Neil Redfearn, Ken and Suzannah Bates, Massimo Cellino, Stix Lockwood, Ishmail Ghandour, Paul Gannon, Andy Starmore, Mac MacMichael, Big Tony, Bob and Andy Liddle, Cato Visdal Mikalsen, Les Rowley, Mary, Matt and Luke Hammond, Smithy, Dave Rawson, Rune Roalsvig, Basher, Slugger, Andy 'Monkey' Caunt, Kevin Blackwell, Trevor Cusack, Smiggy, Gary McAllister, Skippy, Frank Rounding, Para Dave, Geir Magne Fjellseth. The staff: Paul, Jane, Duncan, Graham, Barry and Dean.

Finally, considering what I've hurled at it over the years, huge thanks to my liver for so far staying by my side throughout those 50 years.

Introduction

THERE are approximately 2,607 weeks in 50 years of time. The following is an account of one man's dedication to one football club for the entirety of that 50-year timeline, taking him to five different continents. Obsession or passion? You decide.

Arthur Daley perhaps summed up the plight of Leeds United when, in a drunken stupor in the Winchester Club he said, 'Life is but a veil of tears, you soldier along trying your best then around the corner – fate – ever waiting with the old half brick; it is always the sunniest days that Dame Fortune chooses to mount her most vicious attack. You're walking along, spring in your step then, wallop! You're lying in the gutter spitting out your teeth.'

Foreword
by Neil Redfearn

MY first experience of professional football came at seven years old, when my Dad took me to my first Leeds United game. The journey was from Birkenshaw to Leeds on the 226 bus, then a walk down the snicket and under the flyover and round the back of the Gelderd Road end to queue for tickets in the West Stand. I remember walking up the stand stairs and seeing the lush Elland Road turf for the first time and being mesmerised by the 11 white-shirted players that carried such an air of confidence and surety as they stroked the ball about in the warm-up. Then how they stood in the middle of the pitch before the game and acknowledged the fans, waving in unison to all four stands. They were like gladiators accepting the adoration of the Elland Road faithful. I was hooked from that moment on...

My Dad, who had played professionally for the likes of Bradford PA, Bradford City and Blackburn Rovers, used to emphasise the fact that I was witnessing one of the greatest club sides ever to play in this country. He used to point out how players like Paul Madeley and Eddie Gray used to receive and caress the ball with effortless touch and appreciation; the pure theatre of Norman Hunter as he thundered into every tackle with the baying approval of the crowd and how Billy Bremner would cover every blade of grass and always be there when it mattered.

But there was one player in particular that I was taken by: Allan Clarke.

He did everything I wanted to do as an impressionable junior. He scored goals for Leeds United and England and although I never did either, those early days and great experiences shaped my football education and ultimately my career in professional football. I couldn't have wished for a better education than the team that Don Revie built, not only high quality footballers but it had a wholesomeness about it – I was part of the Leeds United family.

It's difficult to describe but the feeling of togetherness and will to win for the cause was so good to be part of as a supporter. Fast forward to 2009 and joining Leeds United's academy as under-18s coach, I was determined that the values and education of those early days and of my own experiences in football would shape the development of young players at the club and retain those core values that Don Revie had shown me as a youngster, sat in the West Stand with my Dad.

So there was no prouder moment when players like Sam Byram, Alex Mowatt, Lewis Cook, Charlie Taylor, Chris Dawson and Kalvin Phillips took to the Elland Road pitch as first-team players, and I knew from that moment those values were still alive. I was asked to do this foreword by Gary Edwards and to pass on my experiences from being a fan to being in charge of Leeds United.

I would say you never stop being a fan and that what matters the most to any manager matters that little bit more when it's something that you genuinely care about. I think I had an advantage because when you know what is expected and what has got to be 'a given' that forms the basis of what you expect from the players and that the bar is always that little bit higher than normal.

I knew the history and what it meant and how it shaped top class players down the years, the DNA of being a Leeds United footballer and the standards that needed to be set. What was needed was an influx of players that understood all this and how it mattered. It is no coincidence that all the young academy players that came through the ranks and into the first team carried this – they were moulded in it for the best part of seven years.

Into the first team came players that played with no fear and who revelled in the 'muck and bullets' of Championship football, but that DNA didn't stop there, it had to be an unwritten rule of how things were going to be, whether you were an overseas player or experienced pro that had been at the club a while.

This is what being 'Leeds United' meant and it was a start. My point being, is that only a supporter can understand that and what it means to represent your club and the fact that 'hurt' needs 'honesty' and all the strength that it carries. I think the proudest part of my time in charge of Leeds United was how close the people of Leeds had become with the players and what was trying to be achieved; even though it was far from being the finished article, it was on the right lines and everyone knew it.

I think it is only then that you truly understand how important unity and togetherness is within your club. There used to be a saying on the gym wall at Thorp Arch that read 'no one of us knows more than all of us', and I used to look at it every time I was in the gym, as the answer was staring everyone in the face. Confidence is a massive thing in any sport, and having the backing of a unified football club, with everyone all for the cause is a must to be successful, but this process is slow and built on trust and honesty and these core values are demonstrated by everyone.

Only a supporter can understand history well, Leeds United's history was built on 'side before self' and all the values that it incorporates. I'm sure that in years to come Leeds United will become successful and strong again but not until it is built on trust and honesty, but it will happen because there are too many supporters, like me, and like Gary Edwards, that understand this.

Now, enjoy the latest instalment of Gary's fascinating adventures watching this great club.

MOT (Marching on Together).

Neil Redfearn played over 1,000 games as a professional footballer and is a former head of academy and first-team manager at Leeds United.

Chapter 1

Divine White

I'VE never been a particularly religious person, attending church only for the odd wedding, funeral or the occasional midnight mass on Christmas Eve after consuming a couple of gallons of festive cheer. I did once visit my local church alone one afternoon in mid-April 2004 to make a desperate plea to the Almighty asking Him to intervene and prevent Leeds United from being relegated from the Premiership. I raised my eyes to the magnificent stained glass window facing the top end of Kippax High Street.

The bright sun shone through the array of many different colours; the window depicted the Risen Christ joining the two disciples on their way to Emmaus who thought him a stranger until he broke bread with them and revealed himself as their beloved master, when he vanished from their sight with this utterance, 'All things are possible.'

A fortnight later, Leeds got stuffed at Bolton and were relegated.

The sound of my local church bell-ringing practice was serenading through my open office window at the moment I received an email from the BBC early one spring Wednesday evening.

Belmont Abbey sits in the heart of the Herefordshire countryside and it is a Catholic Benedictine monastery, home to about 40 monks, one of which is Father Cadfan. The BBC thought it would be a good idea for me to escort this particular monk to his first ever football match as part of a series called *The Real World*.

So, in the very early hours of Saturday 22 April 2006, Father Cadfan attended morning prayers in the Abbey Church before leaving the Belmont Abbey monastery, from which confines he rarely departed. The Earl of Belmont had a few words with him before his journey.

'I wish you well on your expedition Father. One thought to take with you. Do you know why a football team has 11 players? It is because of the rule of St Benedict – senior monks in charge of ten others – everything is done according to the rule. When medieval monasteries played ball games, it was one dormitory against the other. It was 11-a-side – so there you have the link between football and monastic life.'

'Well,' said Father Cadfan, 'you learn something every day,' and with only a solitary call from a crow to send him on his way, he walked into town to board a train for the long journey north to Leeds and the unknown.

The Viaduct pub deep in the heart of the bustling city centre of Leeds was the meeting place for hundreds of Leeds United fans before a home game at Elland Road and it was where I was to meet up with Father Cadfan. The clientele in the Viaduct these days tend to favour size 12 high heels, have slight stubble, large hands and wear large flowery frocks as opposed to Doc Martens and Stone Island, but here in 2006 I arrived at the pub early to meet the crew of the BBC's Radio Four programme where I introduced them to the landlord Les Hince. A female member of the crew then briefed me on the arrival of Father Cadfan and I was asked to wait in a room at the far end of the pub where I would come face to face with the monk. I must admit to having expected your stereotypical monk, dressed in a brown cloak tied with string and a barnet resembling Friar Tuck, completed by a pair of old sandals and holding a tankard of mead. But when Father Cadfan walked through the door I couldn't have been more wrong.

For a start, he was wearing a dog collar, much like a vicar, and he was about 4ft tall. He wore glasses that looked like two transparent glass dinner plates and these were supported by the largest pair of ears I have ever seen, and in one of these ears he had a hearing aid that was as big as a 20 pack of cigarettes. I held out my hand and he shook it warmly. 'Hello,' he said, 'I'm Father Cadfan, I'm delighted to meet you.'

'Hello Father,' I replied. 'Great to meet you too. I'm Gary, welcome to Leeds.'

I got myself a pint of Tetley's bitter and half a pint of stout for my guest.

'Are you looking forward to this?' I asked.

'Yes,' Father Cadfan replied, 'I am indeed, very much.'

'Have you any questions?' I asked, picking up my first pint of the day.

'Well, where do you start? I've never been to a football match in my life; in fact, I've hardly ever left the abbey. You'll have to talk me through it. How did you start going to watch football?'

I told him how special it felt walking into Elland Road for the very first time. How, at that very first instance, I was hooked for life. I told him how my dad had tried to dilute my enthusiasm by taking me to watch Huddersfield Town when Leeds United were playing away. These days that would almost certainly result in a child cruelty charge.

'How did you start in your particular thingy?' I asked him clumsily.

'I took up my *vocation* many years ago,' said Father Cadfan. 'I had wanted to be a monk from the age of 17, but it took 30 years to do it. I've been a monk now for 25 years. I feel like your support of Leeds United is a *vocation* and I feel that my life as a monk is a *vocation* too.'

'Are there any restrictions in your way of life as monks?' I asked him.

'There used to be,' he said, but the days when we were forbidden to do certain things are pretty much over now. You're dealing with grown men who we hope know how to behave themselves. Much in the same way as we hope that your supporters do themselves.'

I told him more about today's game. 'It's the last game of the season at Elland Road so it'll be a bit of a carnival atmosphere, and it's against Crewe Alexandra, who unfortunately have already been relegated.'

'Like the *Last Night of the Proms*,' said Father Cadfan.

'Yes, but there will be some sympathy for Crewe from the Leeds fans. We've been there ourselves and we know how it feels.'

The pub was now full of Leeds fans as we moved out into the beer garden followed by the BBC crew. It has to be said, it's not the most picturesque beer garden, nestled beneath a railway viaduct and cut off from natural sunlight, but we liked it. I introduced my monk to a couple of friends of mine from Norway, Geir and Bjorn. He was astounded by the fact that people as far away as Norway came to support Leeds and that there were thousands of them, not just from Norway but from all across Scandinavia.

I told him that Leeds fans also came from all across the world including Europe, Ireland, Australia and America and Father Cadfan was genuinely shocked. Leeds fan Sean Ethrington joined us at our table and talked about how being a Leeds fan had changed his life and he spoke of his hatred of that team from Old Trafford and I gladly endorsed that. 'I haven't uttered their name for more than 40 years,' I said.

'Well, a man has to keep up his standards,' said the monk.

I then dropped in the fact that I used to drive to matches in a hearse, to which Father Cadfan remarked, 'Very laid back, I'd say.'

He obviously had a keen sense of humour, but our man of the cloth had a serious side too. 'I understand that fans have to be segregated and with respect, your view of non-Leeds fans is a little provocative'.

'No, not at all,' I replied.

'Did you know,' he said, 'That more people go to church than watch football over a weekend and we don't have police sorting the churchgoers out, now doesn't that say something?' I seized on the opportunity.

'I think that if you had a church split down the middle,' I said, 'with Christians down one side and say, Muslims or Islamists down the other, you would probably need the police.'

'Perhaps,' said Father Cadfan. 'Now I hadn't thought of that – that's an interesting thought, I'd never actually considered that.'

After a couple of hours in the pub, we left to travel the two or three miles to Elland Road. Father Cadfan still had half a glass of the stout he had when he first arrived.

I directed the two cars from the BBC as Father Cadfan and I sat in the back of a small saloon, with microphones and sound equipment laid across our legs.

'So we're off to Elland Road,' Father said into the mike. 'Gary is taking me to see this match between Leeds United and Crewe. He's hoping for a convert. And I'm hoping for a convert from him.'

Ten minutes into the game, Ray Beverley, a good friend of mine, who was two rows in front of us, passed back a large bottle of whisky. Ray had brought me it back as a gift from his recent holiday in Magaluf, but as I took hold of the bottle, the look on Father Cadfan's face told me quite clearly that he thought I was going to start drinking the whisky there and then. I pretended to unscrew the cap and said to him, 'Fancy a nip Father?'

As we chatted at half-time, I asked my guest what he thought of it so far, to which he replied, 'I'm enjoying it, but it's a bit like being in church, standing up, sitting down, standing up.'

After the game, Father Cadfan and I assembled with the rest of the crew in the concourse beneath the Kop for a final conversation before a parting of the ways.

Father Cadfan noticed my bottle of whisky was still unopened.

'You have shown remarkable restraint there Gary,' he said.

'Yes Father,' I replied. 'That and the alcohol restriction laws upstairs.'

He smiled and then said, 'I may have a small tankard of mead myself when I return to my fold.'

He was then asked by the BBC if he had enjoyed the experience, and what his thoughts were.

'Well, that's it, the match is over and Leeds have beaten Crewe 1-0 and I have to say that I have thoroughly enjoyed it, although I have to say that I'm going to need a bit of working on yet. I didn't think that there was sufficient sportsmanship. I do think that Crewe gave Leeds a run for their money but there was too much booing. The man in front of us, I wondered at times why he was there. It's the first time I've ever been to a soccer match and I wanted to watch where the ball was going, but he seemed interested in only seeing Leeds score.'

He continued, 'I was upset when those children ran on the pitch after the game. I thought that they were encroaching on somewhere that is sacred.' I had to agree with him there.

It was the last game of the season and one or two fans had ventured on to the pitch, but it was nothing more than mischievous, as the match announcer's words echoed around the ground.

'Please stay off the pitch. We require fans not to encroach on the playing surface. Please remain in your seats.'

Father Cadfan looked at me and said, 'I've never met anyone like you. Your passion for the club is overwhelming. But I do feel that you appear uneasy in the presence of rival supporters.'

'No, not at all,' I said. 'There is comparatively little trouble inside football grounds these days. However, despite this, the police can still be overpowering and sadly, on occasion, when there hasn't been any trouble, the police have been known to provoke some. It seems like they have to justify their presence and high wages.'

This comment clearly upset Father Cadfan. 'I do find myself very disturbed to hear you say that you find the police presence provocative, I do find myself amazed that I hear you say this – I think what we have to do here is to agree to disagree.'

'In the words of Dave Allen,' I said, 'May your God go with you.'

'I'll drink to that,' said Father Cadfan.

'It's a great feeling when you wake up the next morning having won, but it's horrible when we've lost,' I said. 'Nearly 50 years on and I still get that same hurt when we've lost and I still get that same joy when we've won. It never leaves you. I have to admit to you that first and foremost I'm a Leeds fan rather than a football fan and I would sooner see Leeds win than see a good game and us lose.'

It was time for Father Cadfan to deliver a sermon. 'There is a saying in religion that God has no hands, He has no feet – He has no mouth, except ours. We are God's representatives.'

I put my arm on the Father's shoulder. 'Well in that case, He wouldn't have to pay full whack to watch Leeds United. And I honestly think that if there had been a God we would have won the European Cup Winners' Cup in Greece in 1973 and the European Cup in Paris two years later.'

Father Cadfan and I then hugged and after shaking hands with the BBC entourage, we went our separate ways, almost certain never to meet again.

Listening back to the programme when it aired a week later, it was gratifying to hear Father Cadfan talking about his day.

'Well, I'm on the train on my way back to Belmont and it's been a very interesting day indeed. When Leeds United scored, Gary literally lifted me off my feet and almost threw me into the air. I was amazed at such enthusiasm – and it meant a lot.

'When I tell my congregation of my day out when I get back, I expect them to say, Halleluiah! Halleluiah! with the same passion and enthusiasm as the Leeds supporters shouted praise when their goal was scored.'

The programme played out with the Leeds fans chanting, 'Glory, Glory, Leeds United!'

Before ending with these words.

'Join us next week when a Buddhist nun will spend the day on the news desk of a Scottish national newspaper.'

Chapter 2

Blood, Sweat and Tears

AFTER being fortunate enough to see every Leeds United game, home and away, anywhere in the world since early 1968, the most frequent question I am ever asked is, 'What will you do when you miss a Leeds game?' The answer to that is simple.

It is inevitable that one day I will not get to a game, for whatever reason, and when that time comes, I will just go to the next one instead. Obviously this thought has crossed my mind, of course it has, but I can honestly say that when the time comes I will not be worrying about it or throwing myself off the nearest bridge. That said, once you have read this particular chapter you could be forgiven for thinking that what I have just told you is a complete load of bollocks.

I was sat watching telly late one Saturday night in October 2006, enjoying a nice glass of Shiraz. Leeds had won that afternoon and things were looking good in *Leeds United World* for a change, despite hovering in the lower regions of the Championship. Suddenly, I felt a trickle of blood run down from my nose on to to my top lip. Briefly, the thought occurred to me that it was Shiraz and that I was full up. I wiped it away but the blood started coming faster and thicker. I rushed to the sink and quickly realised that this was no ordinary nosebleed and it was showing no sign of slowing down – let alone stopping. Twenty minutes later, Wub was driving me to St James' Hospital – TV's *Jimmy's* – holding and wiping my nose with three towels. Upon arrival at A&E, I soon blended in with the usual Saturday night bloody noses, black eyes, missing teeth, bandaged limbs and such. I was then given a bowl to catch the torrent of blood and taken into my own cubicle for examination.

'Have you ever suffered from a nosebleed like this before?' asked the doctor as he shone a torch into my eyes. 'No, but Leeds beat Southend this afternoon and we've moved up two places in the league. Could that be the reason for my nosebleed?' I replied.

My comment went completely over the head of the doctor who clearly wasn't a football fan as he continued to find another reason for the red deluge. At around 3am the bleeding finally stopped and I was allowed home.

A year later, almost to the day, I was out walking our dogs, Jack and Jill, in the woods close to our home, it was 11am and I had arranged to go into Leeds for a lunchtime drink with some mates before heading north for Leeds' Johnstone's Paint Trophy second round tie – Northern Section, against Darlington. As I headed back to the house with the dogs, I felt a slight trickle coming down my nose and instantly knew that my dreaded nosebleed had returned.

Twenty minutes later, Wub was once again driving me to Jimmy's with me perched over a large plastic bowl oozing what seemed to be pints of blood, and which had to emptied three times en route. Once at the hospital, I was rushed into yet another cubicle and examined by a team of three doctors and two nurses. And I was given another large bowl.

The bleeding was far worse than the last time and I was worried – worried that I wouldn't get a pint with my mates before setting off for Darlington. The thought that I may even miss the game hadn't crossed my mind at this point. It was now 1pm.

The medical team tugged and probed at my nose and shoved all sorts of swabs up there, but it simply refused to stop bleeding. I looked at the clock over the doctor's shoulder at 3pm and although the bleeding had slowed down a bit, it was still bleeding quite profusely. I could tell the doctors were slightly puzzled and a bit worried – and so too was I when the clock clicked on to 4.30pm. A doctor then came in and said, 'We're just going to shove these pads up your nose Gary, and see if that has any effect.' They were actually called tampons and had a thin sharp wooden shaft running through the middle. It didn't half make my eyes water but I thought, 'Just get on with it and get me out of here'. An hour later they said that they were going to move me across town to the Leeds General Infirmary (LGI). They wouldn't let Wub take me in the car because I had lost so much blood and I had to wait for an ambulance. This took ages to arrive and even longer to transport me across Leeds in what now was the rush hour, and apparently I wasn't worthy of blue flashing lights just yet.

As I sat in the back of the ambulance, the medic looked at me and I could see that he was struggling not to laugh at my face. I looked like Blackadder in the episode where he shoves two pencils up his nose to try and avoid going to the Russian Front by claiming insanity. By now, my nose, eyes and face were swelling up too.

'How long will I be mate, I'm going to the Leeds match tonight?' I asked.

'You shouldn't be long now, what time is kick-off?' said the medic, still trying hard to keep a straight face. '7.30', I said.

'Oh, still plenty of time, you'll be at Elland Road in an hour,' said the medic.

'It's away,' I replied. 'Up at Darlington.'

He hitched up his sleeve, took a peak at his watch and remained silent.

At 6pm I was sat in the waiting room feeling like an exhibit from some sort of freak show as everyone stole a stare when they thought I wasn't looking. I was now wearing one of those rather unflattering hospital gowns. The clock was going round faster than Mo Farah and it was then that I was called to the desk and asked if I had any valuables or jewellery and to deposit it with them. It was also then that I realised that they planned to admit me. I returned to Wub who had arrived at the LGI and told her of my predicament. Before she had a chance to respond I whispered, 'Go get the car and bring it round the back… quick! I need to escape now.'

She was understandably reluctant, but against her better judgement she did as I asked. I gave it a few minutes and then I told the desk nurse I was just going to the toilet. Once I was out of sight, I ran for dear life towards the rear exit. But in my panic I couldn't find it. LGI is one of the largest hospitals in the world. The rear exit area is a grand affair with large wood panelled walls, old paintings, statues and busts. Majestic stone staircases with rich wooden bannisters dominate the entrance and I was running about like a mad man trying get out of the hospital with tampons stuck up my nose, a catheter stuck in each arm with needles and wires all over the place… and my arse hanging out of my hospital gown. I finally emerged from the somewhat spooky and gloomy Victorian rear entrance, and with the getaway car ticking over, jumped into the passenger seat, and just like in the films shouted, 'Go! Go!'

I have to admit, as we sped up the A1, with the wind and thunderous rain lashing the jeep and the full speed wipers struggling against the torrent, that I wondered, 'What the hell am I doing?'

I struggled in my seat to put my jeans and t-shirt on and remove my gown without dislodging all the equipment attached to me.

My nose was still bleeding and I was really beginning to feel light-headed but I didn't let on to my heroine driving the car.

We arrived at the Balfour Webnet Arena 15 minutes into the game.

'Are you coming into the match?' I asked Wub. 'No,' she said, 'I'll stay here and read my book. Be careful, and if you don't feel well come out straight away. Make sure your phone is on.'

I almost had her eye out as I leant across and kissed her and caught her with the small shaft from one of my tampons. 'I love you,' I said and hurried into the stadium.

The unimportance of this game was reflected in the crowd of 7,891, but had it not been for my dear wife, it would have been a '0' on the end of that attendance.

In the concourse beneath the stands I mingled with the Leeds fans, the vast majority of whom I knew, trying desperately to blend in unnoticed. But it didn't stop everyone I spoke to taking the piss out of my appearance and some even thought I'd been beaten up. 'It's just a nosebleed,' I'd say meekly. 'Yeah, right,' came the standard answer.

I tried in vain to start up a normal conversation with Gary Barass, the landlord at the Hope pub, but he couldn't get past the face. 'Sorry Gaz' he said, with his face creased up. 'You look hilarious.'

Ray walked past and mischievously tugged at one of my many wires.

'Nice fancy dress Gaz,' he smirked.

Smithy, one of the lads who I had arranged to travel up with, just kept staring at me.

I'd start talking about anything just to divert attention from my appearance. But that is extremely difficult when it's your face that is affected.

'Fuckin' 'ell mate,' Smithy said, almost crying, 'I've never seen owt as funny in my life!' He then took out his phone and took my picture and soon I was standing there surrounded by dozens taking my photograph. Once the photo shoot was over, I returned to my seat upstairs and encountered many more curious looks, photographs and comments. Even my best mates around me were sniggering and I swear, at times there were more people staring at me than watching the match, even though the Leeds team that evening contained such star-studded players as Mark De Vries, Ian Westlake, Filipe Da Costa, Curtis Weston, Tomi Ameobi and who could forget the dazzling skills of Wayne Andrews.

I wondered to myself how a nosebleed could attract so much attention. And strangely I began to wish that I *had* been beaten up, or involved in a crash or something – at least I could say something other than, 'It's just a nosebleed.'

One young lad who came out a winner that day though, was Leeds fan Carter Allwood. He'd had his face painted in the Leeds colours for the match and was spotted by Johnstone's sponsorship manager, Teresa Hardwick who said, 'Congratulations Carter, you looked fantastic on the night of the match and to show our appreciation we will be sending you a £100 voucher to spend at your local Johnstone's Decorating Centre. Who knows – if you ask your dad, Tony, nicely, you could have an early Christmas present by painting your room in Leeds colours!'

At least Carter took the attention away from my mug for a while. For the record, Paul Huntington scored the only goal of the game to send Leeds through to the next round.

I left the ground early and got back into the jeep, which had been parked outside the stadium all through the game. Wub looked across at me and gently closed her book.

'You okay love?' she asked.

'Yes ta,' I said bravely. 'It hurts though,' I added pathetically.

We pulled away and joined the A1 southbound. I got out my phone to discover about 20 texts all basically saying the same thing. 'What's up with your face mate?'

My phone rang as we were about halfway home; it was our friend and neighbour Ken.

'Where are you mate?' he asked, sounding really worried. 'Are you alright?'

'I've been to the match Ken, why?' I answered.

'The police have been to your house, twice. The second time they came, I asked if there was a problem. They didn't give me any details, but said that they needed to contact you urgently. I told them that you would be at the match. Are you sure everything is okay mate?'

I discovered later, that because I had lost so much blood and had disappeared, the police had to be routinely called in to trace my whereabouts.

I gave Ken a brief rundown of the day's events and told him that I was heading back to the LGI to give myself up. I thanked him for his concern and as he had a key for our house, asked him to look in on the dogs.

As we arrived at the back of the hospital, I looked up at the bleak and somewhat eerie facade of this Victorian building framed by a stormy, cloudy, dark sky. It was on the roof of this very hospital in 2006 that a Yorkshire Air Ambulance helicopter landed carrying the badly damaged body of *Top Gear* presenter Richard Hammond following his horrific crash at RAF Elvington airbase near York, when his Vampire Dragster overturned while doing 288mph. Then my thoughts moved towards what I was going to tell the nurse and the rest of the staff regarding my escape and whether they would still treat me. I had concocted a weak story that I had to go home and feed the dogs. I obviously wouldn't mention the match. As I crept into the waiting area where I had been sitting five hours earlier, I noticed that the nurse was different to the one I had spoken to earlier and I was greeted by a man who can only be described as the living double in every way of TV's Alan Carr. 'Well, look here. Here's the man who's been to the footy. You're a very naughty boy', he said, wagging his finger at me. I just stood there, head bowed and cut a very pathetic figure indeed.

'Let's get those clothes off and get you into bed,' said 'Alan'.

'Er, I'm okay thanks,' I said to him in the deepest voice I could muster. 'I'll keep my jeans on. I'll just lie on top of the bed if that's ok? I'll be fine like that.' 'Suit yourself sweet cheeks, follow me,' he replied.

I took a dog-eared cowboy paperback from the shelf nearby, climbed on to the bed, curled up and read it from cover to cover – little did I know that something else would be curled up the next morning. At 4am my nose finally stopped bleeding. It had slowed down considerably, but had been bleeding non-stop for 17 hours and it was at that point that I finally dropped off to sleep.

At 7.30am I was sat up enjoying a slice of toast and my early morning cuppa when a doctor came to see me to tell me that I would be taken down to surgery later that morning to have my nose 'seen to'. Wub arrived to see how I was going on at about 10-ish and shortly afterwards I was being pushed in a wheelchair to have my nose 'seen to'. My nose was to be welded to stop it bleeding again – in medical terms it was going to be cauterised. I was put in a chair rather like a dentist's chair and then this sadistic doctor, after talking to me really nicely, inflicted pain upon me that I had never witnessed before in my life. He cauterised my nose, ramming a poker-like instrument up to the very top of it, and then with a slight smell of burning, my toes curled up and tears streamed down my cheeks. All that was missing was a giant fork of lightning and the sound of thunder crashing against the window. Ten minutes later I was done. And – touch wood – I've not had a nosebleed problem since. Wub is an absolute hero, and since we met all those years ago, she has always supported me. I missed my engagement party to my first real girlfriend because I was late back from a match at Burnley, and my first marriage didn't last as long as the Argentina World Cup in 1978, so Wub and me trod carefully, and after being engaged for over 20 years we finally tied the knot at Elland Road in 2006.

I found out some time after my nosebleed that the great Don Revie had suffered a very similar experience to mine while a 21-year-old player for Leicester City in 1949. Leicester had beaten Sunderland in the FA Cup semi-final and two weeks before the final, during a home game against West Ham, Revie received a bad knock which resulted in a bloody nose. It was classed as an ordinary nosebleed but as a precaution and with the final against Wolves in mind, Leicester manager Johnny Duncan rested Don for the penultimate league game at Plymouth, although Revie travelled with the team. It was during the night after the game in his hotel room that Don's nose began to bleed again. The nose continued to bleed off and on for several days as Duncan stayed with Revie at the hotel before deciding to transfer him to a hospital nearer home. So, after an eight-hour taxi journey, several sips of brandy and countless ice packs, they arrived at Leicester Infirmary where Revie was given an immediate blood transfusion and told that if he had been on the road for another hour he may well have died. Sadly, Revie couldn't play in the final and so our similarities continued as Revie missed out on Wembley, just as Leeds did in the 2008 Johnstone's Paint Trophy.

Chapter 3

Cornish Tease

NEIL Warnock took over the managerial reins at Elland Road in February 2012 and his arrival immediately divided opinion amongst the fans. There were those who looked at Warnock's record of getting teams promoted from the Championship into the Premier League and hoped that he would gain his eighth promotion which would represent an all-time record. On the other hand, there were those who viewed his appointment with scepticism – claiming that Warnock had always hated Leeds and had never sought to hide the fact and that he was only here to destroy the club – or was he? Even Ken Bates had called him a 'gutter rat' before he appointed him. He constantly came out with comments of how much he respected Leeds United and how he hadn't realised the 'enormous passion and loyalty' of the Leeds fans until he arrived at Elland Road. The truth is, no one really knew of Warnock's intentions, but for the present there was a mouth-watering pre-season tour to look forward to.

Cornwall has long been a favourite destination for Neil Warnock (and me), he even owns a house in Stoke Climsland, in the south-east of the county, so this was the inevitable choice for preparations for the new season ahead. Warnock had brought his previous clubs – Sheffield United, QPR and Crystal Palace – down here. 'I've organised the sunshine to come out over Cornwall for our stay,' announced Warnock proudly.

A very good friend of mine, Billy Burton, had just been released from a Philippines jail after a 20-year sentence and this tour was his first real chance to resume his passion for Leeds United. He and his girlfriend from the Philippines, Mafe, stayed with Wub and I the night before we set off on the coach for Cornwall with (Big Mick) Hewitt Tours. Billy, Mafe, Wub and I sat at the back and were soon in holiday mode. It was glorious weather all the way down and it was to be glorious wall-to-wall sunshine for the entirety of our one-week stay, courtesy of Neil Warnock.

Also in holiday mode was Big Tony Winstanley, who consumed a large bottle of vodka accompanied by tonic and three lemons before our arrival in Torquay, Devon, which was to be our base for the trip. Tony missed out on our first night at the seaside opting instead to try out his comfortable hotel bed.

Our first venture from the hotel down to the seafront was via a very steep hill. I remember making a mental note that the climb back to the digs at the end of the evening wouldn't matter so much once we were assisted by a glass or two of the local brew.

We didn't get far down that hill before we called in at the first pub which we soon discovered was already under occupation by Billy Bonner and his lovely family – regulars on these Hewitt pre-season jaunts – engaged in a serious game of pool.

Much later that evening, my assumption proved correct on the trek back up the hill after a few pints, as Wub and I made our way to the hotel using the odd pub as respite.

First down for breakfast the next morning was Big Tony, bright-eyed and bushy-tailed after his vodka-induced coma. The hotel was fine, done out in a sort of 70s retro style, but the 'cardboard' breakfast tasted like it had been cooked in the 1970s, so the greasy spoon cafe not far from the hotel was the first port of call for most of us for the rest of the week. Besides, Boo Boo came in and sat opposite me all the time I was trying to eat my early morning cardboard, so I gave him it.

Conveniently, there are two Wetherspoons pubs in Torquay and many an hour was passed in these as more and more Leeds fans arrived each day, including Jim, who had travelled down from Scotland along with a few others. The Cider House, tucked away in a busy side street, also became a favourite watering hole as Tony, Bob Liddle and his son Andy and myself put the world to rights over a pint or two of the local scrumpy, with chunks of wood traditionally floating around the glass.

As we began climbing the hill back towards the hotel one sunny evening I pointed out a hotel to Wub. 'Our coach stayed there for the Exeter game a few years back,' I said. 'It was chucking it down.' We had arrived back at this hotel from the match absolutely drenched; it took over a week for my jacket to dry out properly. That night after the Exeter encounter, Basher and me decided against dodging the heavy rain outside and opted instead for the hotel's cabaret evening. What a hoot. It was a husband and wife duo with a comedy routine and they were pretty good, but they were about to be upstaged. I leant across to say something to Basher and he was now wearing his horse's head! This was quickly noticed by the male entertainer who didn't quite know what to say. 'Ah,' he said finally, 'we have a horse with us this evening.' The audience looked round at Basher and the place was in hysterics. After treading on thin ice with a comment about Leeds getting beat 2-0, the comedian announced an interval and within seconds, 'Harry the Horse' was up dancing with a frail old lady who was staying at the hotel with her 'turkey and tinsel' brigade. The image of her gazing lovingly up at this horse's head as they smooched will live with me forever.

Meanwhile, dozens of Devon and Cornwall holiday websites and holiday parks had seized on the opportunity of the arrival of Leeds United by offering package deals. Dolphin Holidays asked, 'Why not see if you can catch the mighty Leeds United play live in the county this summer whilst enjoying a stay at a nearby Cornwall holiday park – the perfect base for a British vacation and sport.'

Many local teams had written to Elland Road in the hope of playing Leeds United. Falmouth Town and Truro City were just two of the dozens of unlucky applicant clubs and the three teams eventually chosen, Tavistock, Bodmin Town and Torquay United, all reported sell-out crowds. Even a training camp set up for Leeds at Duchy College in Callington was opened to the public and was swamped by local and travelling Leeds fans alike. A regular at the training camp was our very own Jo Barrett, by far and away the most enthusiastic football groupie you will ever meet.

Leeds cruised through their first game against Tavistock 6-0, but it was to be the last game for Leeds favourite Robert Snodgrass – although it came as no great surprise to anyone connected to the club. A statement by Neil Warnock read, 'I've never tried harder to keep a player at a club; we offered him (Snodgrass) a much improved contract and even the club's captaincy.

'But he has always wanted to play in the Premier League and he's in the last year of his contract and players are in charge of the situation at that stage.' Warnock had invited all the players to his house for Sunday lunch where he had continued in vain to persuade Snodgrass to stay. Snodgrass was replaced by Luke Varney.

Just two seasons later, Snodgrass and his club Norwich City would be relegated, along with three other former Leeds players, Bradley Johnson, Jonny Howson and Luciano Becchio. Snodgrass soon moved up the east coast to join Hull City – where he was out injured for the entire season, before helping the Tigers climb back into the Premier League via the play-offs in 2016.

On the same day as the second game, in the lovely town of Bodmin, Yorkshire County Cricket Club were playing in their first ever T20 Finals Day against Worcestershire. It was televised live and every pub in the town was packed with Leeds fans, including an old mate of mine, John Rounding (brother of Frank) now an exile living in Cornwall. As we settled down to watch the cricket, I got a text from Billy Burton. 'Where are you?' he asked. I told him where we were to which he replied, 'Just had some fun in the bushes with Mafe, we're on our way!' Yorkshire won by 29 runs.

Leeds brushed aside Bodmin Town 4-0, but everyone, including the home fans were in high spirits, with a constant shuttle of beer being brought in from outside to counter the rapidly decreasing amount of beer in the pumps of the club's bar. It was a great atmosphere, which continued throughout the evening and the rest of the week.

On our regular strolls along the sun-drenched Torquay seafront, Wub and I had been intrigued by posters advertising 'Live Pig Racing' at a large pub just close by. To say we were curious was an understatement. So, on the evening before our final game against Torquay United, Wub and I duly arrived at the venue for the Live Pig Racing. Wub hesitated at the door. 'If they really are live pigs,' she said, 'I'm calling the police.'

There was hardly anyone around as I ordered our drinks at the bar. We both scanned the premises looking for pig cages, but there was nothing that would suggest that any illegal gambling was about to take place. But then, as we sat in a corner with our drinks, a very suspicious man entered, obviously casing the joint.

'He must be the organiser,' I whispered, as we watched his every move.

'Yeah, he's got to be,' agreed Wub, sounding uncannily like Miss Marple. We then watched him leave before returning with two large brief cases. These were obviously full of cash and betting slips, we both assumed. Just then a second man arrived and was asked, 'Have you got the pigs?' He nodded.

'Aha,' Wub said. 'Here we go.'

As Wub got out her camera phone in readiness, the second man returned with a box that was about the same size as a microwave oven and placed it on one of the tables near the first man.

'That must be one of them,' I nodded to Wub. 'They must be small pigs, I bet they're only babies.'

'Bastards!' said Wub. 'Look, there aren't even any air holes.'

I walked to the bar for more drinks, still eyeing the box.

'Same again?' asked the barmaid.

'Yes please,' I said. 'What time does the racing start?'

'Oh, not for another hour or so,' she replied, looking up at the clock.

When I returned with the drinks Wub said, 'I'm sure that box just moved – watch.' I stared at the box as I sipped my pint. Just then it definitely moved, and some kind of squeak emanated from within.

We both looked at each other. 'Shut that bleedin' pig up,' shouted the first man as the second man walked towards the box.

Wub gripped my arm.

The man then opened the box and took the pig out. And then another. Then another. The pigs were indeed small – about four or five inches tall and they were pink and fluffy. And they were clockwork.

There were six pigs in all and they would be wound up and placed at one end of a green beige table, then punters would place their bets before the clockwork pigs clicked, squeaked and whirred their way to the finishing line. Not dissimilar to the mechanical fluffy toys and the flipping over dogs on those famous Duracell battery adverts.

And then on top of all our distress and despite putting a quid on every race, we didn't have one single winner.

Thousands of Leeds fans attended the final game at Plainmoor, against Torquay United. The few pubs near the ground were packed with both sets of supporters and I had a pint with a lad who told me that he was originally from Leeds but had traded the blue and gold of Leeds for the blue and gold of Torquay. But tonight, he told me, he was 'on the fence'.

Two goals in the first ten minutes from Ross McCormack was sufficient to give Leeds a 2-1 victory thus bringing an end to a most enjoyable week.

This had been among the best of the pre-season tours, but the months ahead would bring an end to Warnock's reign, and towards the end of the season with Leeds sitting just five points above the relegation zone, he was sacked on April Fools' Day 2013. Warnock had appeared to be suffering from a mild case of deafness when, after claiming that he would only leave 'when the Leeds fans tell me to' he failed consistently to hear the Leeds fans telling him that it was time to go. However, there appeared to be nothing wrong with his speech as he blamed everyone but himself for Leeds' lowly position. After saying that there was a 'cancer in the club' he went on to accuse United's staff, individual players and even the local media of undermining and complicating his reign as boss.

The summer before Cornwall we had found ourselves in Scotland. Hewitt Tours had organised two one-day trips, the first one to the friendly match with Falkirk, and the second was against Motherwell the following Saturday. Seeing as both games weren't far from Glasgow, John 'Basher' Bates, Ash, Kjell and I decided to stay there for a few nights and sample the delights of the infamous Sauchiehall Street and Glasgow before returning on the coach back to Leeds after the Motherwell game.

The Falkirk match saw the debuts of Michael Brown and Paul Rachubka in goal. Our new keeper became affectionately known as 'Chewbacca' from *Star Wars* fame and uncannily the noise that the hairy monster makes, similar to that of a dying walrus, was the noise our keeper made quite often, especially when 12 goals flew past him in two consecutive matches against Forest and Blackpool later that season. Goals from Nunez and Snodgrass gave Leeds a 2-0 win over Falkirk and before the final ball had stopped rolling we were on our way back into Glasgow and a few late-night slurps.

Running through the centre of Glasgow, Sauchiehall Street stretches over a mile and a half and is full of shops, theatres, bars, pubs, clubs, restaurants and just about any takeaway food that takes your fancy. For over a hundred years, theatres along the 'Street' have been host to a wide number of world famous stars such as Bob Hope, Danny Kaye, Jack Benny, Judy Garland and Frank Sinatra. But one musical star in the form of a busker particularly took our eye as we strolled along in the afternoon sunshine. Complete with kilt, bonnet, sporran and bagpipes this busker was wowing the tourists when all of a sudden he was rudely interrupted by a rival 'street entertainer' carrying a paper cup with a few coins in it. 'This is my spot pal, fuck off!' he said to the bagpiper, who continued playing regardless. After a couple more tirades at him the beggar became agitated but unfortunately for him so did the bagpiper who was covered in tattoos and sporting sunglasses. After telling the beggar to 'go away' a few times he finally flipped and shouted, 'If ye dinnae fuck off, I'll ram these bagpipes right up ye wee arsehole!' With that our beggar slipped away shaking his cup at passers-by.

As night fell we found a couple of nice little bars including cheap student clubs and better still, some of the rowdier, atmospheric pubs. In one such pub there was a lad sat with his mate and a guitar. 'Bit of live music coming,' I said. After about 20 minutes, he took out his guitar and started strumming a few chords. It was then that I looked around for the stage, or where he was going to play. Basher had recently taken up the guitar himself and said, 'He's not bad at all.' Just then the woman behind the bar shouted to the guitarist, 'Hey, no!' We thought he'd started a bit early, but then when he started playing again, the same woman again shouted 'No!' She's a bit strict with the time schedule we thought, but then when he started playing a third time, she came from behind the bar and said, 'What part of "no" don't you understand? Now fuck off out of my pub!' This poor lad had been attempting to 'busk' *inside* a pub.

The drink was now kicking in, but surprisingly the four of us appeared remarkably sober compared to some of the locals who were shit-faced. Well it was Tuesday. We had arranged to meet Phil Hay, the award-winning chief sportswriter for the *Yorkshire Evening Post* and his trusty, also award-winning, photographer, Steve 'Fritz' Riding. I have known Fritz for around 40 years and we always manage a drink or two on pre-season tours once Phil and him have posted their match reports and pictures.

Scotsman Phil is a Hearts fan by trade and much like myself has an affection for the odd whisky. We soon found a proper whisky bar – a majestic oak-panelled hostelry boasting an incredible array of the finest scotch in the whole of Scotland. While the others stuck to the cider and Tennent's lager, Phil and I sampled one or two drams, savouring every sacred drop.

Later that evening we were stood in the queue for some late night chicken and something happened that started me laughing as much as I can remember for a long time. Kjell is Norwegian and moved to Leeds several years ago just so that he could follow United. He ordered chicken. 'What do you want with it?' asked the Scottish Cypriot behind the counter. 'Just chicken, please,' said Kjell. 'It comes with a side or any sauce you want,' said the helpful Cypriot. 'I just want chicken', said Kjell. 'You may as well have something sir, it's free, how about some chilli sauce?' By now, Basher, Ash and me were giggling like school kids. Kjell looked at him and through clenched teeth he said calmly, 'I just want chicken.'

'Are you sure?' said the persistent Cypriot. 'It's free.'

By now the three of us were laughing uncontrollably, and so were the rest of the late night customers in the queue. 'I just want CHICKEN!' said Kjell, who by now was getting angry. 'Just, fucking chicken!'

'So that's chicken with nothing on it then?' said the Scottish Cypriot.

By now, I couldn't see the menu for the tears in my eyes.

'YES!' shouted Kjell.

'Okay, you're sure I can't put anything on it? How about a mild sauce?'

With that, Kjell stormed out of the shop without anything, pushing aside people who were crying with laughter. The funniest thing about this delightful slice of comedy was that the Cypriot really wasn't winding Kjell up; he genuinely wanted Kjell to get his money's worth. We certainly got ours. It would have slotted seamlessly into any *Fast Show* sketch.

The following evening, we caught a train for the short journey to Stirling – the birthplace of officially Leeds United's Greatest Ever Player, Billy Bremner. We had tickets for the *Leeds on the Road* event in Stirling but first the lads wanted to go to Weir Street, the birthplace of Bremner. The taxi driver told us it wasn't there anymore but we decided we wanted to go to where it had been. I'd been to 42a Weir Street in this tough Raploch area of the city on a number of occasions and it was sad when we arrived to see nothing but an industrial estate and a few new office blocks – it was such a shame.

The *Leeds on the Road* event is a gathering that the club provide on the eve of an away game for local Leeds fans, for example when we are playing at say, Norwich, they put on a 'do' for the Norwich branch of the Leeds supporters' club and throw in a few guest players as well. This one in Stirling was a sell-out and a huge success, with Simon Grayson and Glynn Snodin, manager and assistant respectively, amongst the panellists. Our mate Alan from Aberdeen was with us in the audience and it wasn't long before he fired his question at the panel. Davide Somma was in trouble over a tweet he had posted on his Twitter page regarding an injury he had sustained. Alan asked Simon Grayson how long Somma would be out, although he and most of the people in the room already knew the answer. 'Hopefully, just a few weeks,' replied Simon.

Rumour was rife that the injury was far worse than that and indeed Somma would be out for much longer. Grayson had banned his players from using Twitter but not before Somma tweeted, 'Got scan back, torn my ACL (anterior cruciate ligament), am going to be out for five to six months.' Grayson, understandably, was furious. Alan mischievously persisted in keeping this particular debate going before 'Stix' Lockwood stepped in to change the subject. Stix is the players' liaison officer for the club and also a great compere at these *Leeds on the Road* events and he is an expert in moving things on from awkward situations such as this.

Although there has always been a Scottish branch of the Leeds supporters' club going back to the 1960s, the support for Leeds United in Scotland has increased significantly in the past few years and this was clearly in evidence when we rolled into Motherwell for Saturday's fixture at Fir Park. As we converged on Motherwell's Supporters' Club, Scottish Leeds fans, including Steve Cooke, were everywhere. Inside, the place was packed and as we made our way to the ground after a few pints, we chatted to dozens more Scottish fans. Even during the Don Revie era when Scottish names such as Bremner, Collins, Gray, Lorimer, Jordan and others were prominent, there wasn't what you would call a massive support for Leeds United north of the border – they were more like admirers. Although thousands of Scots admired Leeds, they were never classed as supporters, with only one recognised Scottish supporters' club. Even when we travelled to play Falkirk, St Johnstone, Hearts, Hibs, Motherwell and others in friendlies in the early 1980s, there wasn't much evidence of many Scottish Leeds fans, but now there are Leeds supporters' branches throughout Scotland, and they are still on the increase.

We beat Motherwell 2-1, with goals from Nunez and Alex the Bruce.

However, torrential rain and heavy mud throughout the match challenged the choice of Leeds keeper Chewbacca's choice of kit – all white.

At Falkirk, a third of the attendance had been from Leeds and for this final game at Motherwell, almost half of the 4,000-plus crowd were Whites fans. After a swift half in their supporters' club, it was back on board Hewitt Tours' coach for the return journey home with preparations already under way for a three-day trip to a match in Norway the following week.

Chapter 4

You Say Slovakia, I Say Slovenia

IN 2010, Leeds made a Slovakian army barracks their base for a couple of pre-season games against Ruzemberok and Kosice. The capital, Bratislava, can seem a bit intimidating on first impression. There are loads of bars literally underground (not dissimilar to The Cavern Club in Liverpool) and most have a dark and somewhat gloomy atmosphere. The favourite decor seemed to be dozens of glass tanks lit up in deep red or green and housing anything from tarantulas and black widows to scorpions and huge snakes. I felt at home and rather liked it I have to say.

One sunny afternoon though, it was someone a little closer to home that tried to appear intimidating. We had heard that there was a small group of Millwall fans in town hell-bent on causing trouble for the Leeds fans, and while we were drinking with some locals in a large beer garden, about a dozen Millwall fans charged in through the gate backed up by a hired mob of recruited locals shouting and screaming and generally running around. To be honest, the

Leeds fans – there were about 50 in this bar – didn't pay too much attention to this minor intrusion and most carried on drinking as though nothing had happened. I remember looking across the table at Dave 'Dr Doom' Green as he calmly lit a cigarette whilst shaking his head. The funniest thing about this incident was when one of the intruders snatched the Lancaster Whites flag that was tied up on the fence near a group of children playing on the slides and swings. Flag owner, Kev Morgan, was distraught as the mob disappeared with the flag, being chased off by other right-minded locals who had been drinking with us.

MFK Ruzemberok won the Slovakian league and cup double in 2006 and their away kit is all white. Leeds lost 1-0 to Ruzemberok, and we had to call debutant Billy Paynter over to us to point out that it is not the done thing for a Leeds player to wear red boots. Commendably, for the second game, Billy binned the red boots and scored the only goal against Kosice wearing yellow boots.

Later that evening, a group of us were sat outside a bar with some of the Bradford lads, Steve, Ian and others, when a shabby looking vagrant approached me. Despite his tatty appearance he seemed to know his music and before long we were doing an air duet to the tune of Deep Purple's 'Smoke on the Water' for which I tipped him a couple of Euros for his trouble. It was only later that I discovered that while we had been 'performing' the 1970s classic, the cheeky bastard had dipped his mucky hand in the side pocket of my shorts and lifted my passport. Luckily for me two police officers had been watching events unfold from across the street and soon apprehended him and returned my passport intact. Ladies of the night would hang around your table and just stare at you for sometimes up to 20 minutes before simply walking away, still staring – it could be quite unnerving.

Later, further on, a loud bang came from within a bar and all the lights went out. It transpired that *Yorkshire Evening*

Post chief sports reporter Phil Hay, covering the games, and other members of the media all had their laptops and other equipment plugged into the mains and the power surge was so great that it blew several fuses and shut everything down!

On our final night we went to say goodbye to the tarantulas and as we were leaving a bar, we spotted my Deep Purple vagrant. This time he was doing a duet with an unsuspecting tourist, blasting out the nauseating opening bars of Europe's 'Final Countdown'. And his favourite two police officers were once again in the audience.

And poor old Kev never saw his Lancaster Whites flag again. However, a very suitable replacement did arrive with him when we met up again when a Leeds X1 played an Isle of Man FA Representative XI in Douglas in 2015.

The peaceful dissolution of Czechoslovakia led to Slovakia becoming an independent state on New Year's Day 1993. Slovenia, however, found it much harder to break away from Yugoslavia. They had to fight for their independence, which duly came when the last of the Yugoslav army left Slovenia in 1991. I enjoyed a couple of holidays in Yugoslavia in the mid-1970s and I even stayed there for a European game against Craiova, Romania in 1979. And when Leeds rolled into Slovenia in 2013, I enjoyed that just as much.

Ljubljana, the capital of Slovenia, is one of Brian McDermott's favourite places in the world so consequently the Leeds manager at the time took his Leeds team there for the pre-season tour.

Murska Sobota is a pleasant and hospitable city in the north-east of the country and this is where we would stay for the first and third games of this tour. As usual, a healthy presence of Leeds fans was in evidence as we began to familiarise ourselves with our new surroundings. The bar at our hotel was the first port of call as unopened cases lay on the bed. Over the next four hours we managed to move 300 yards to the main square just around the corner from the hotel, where we settled in to some comfortable wicker chairs and basked in the sunshine with a cold pint of the local beer – Lasko. The alcohol prices were very reasonable and quickly resulted in a few renditions of the usual Leeds songs, while Big Tony treated us to some rare ditties from the 1960s which had the younger element of our troops mesmerised.

Our first game, against Pomurje (a select XI made up of teams from the lower Slovenian leagues), was to be played at the local stadium, which was about a mile away from the centre. Not far from the ground I spied a couple of umbrellas peering out above a high green hedge bearing the name of 'Lasko' – 'Pub stop!' I gleefully announced and into the beer garden we went. We sat at the table on the lush lawn and were quickly met by the barmaid.

'Four beers love please,' I said.

She looked somewhat perplexed. 'I'm sorry, who are you?' she asked.

'Never mind that love, have you got any menus?' Kev asked.

'Please, you are in my garden,' said the woman who we now realised was not a barmaid and this was not a bar, and we were in her garden.

There was a great little pub/bar inside the ground, which was situated in the stand right on the halfway line. This became our vantage point for the entire game. The Leeds fans were in good voice and a chant from the ones behind the goal produced a great comedy moment.

'It's your round Brian! It's your round!' they chanted at Brian McDermott, who responded by leaving the bench and walking round to hand a 50 Euro note to one of the fans. That fan was Dan Lambert, one of our White Rose branch members and although he bought a round of beers for those around him, he later got the 50 Euro note signed by McDermott and he still has it today.

Matt Smith and Noel Hunt were both making their debuts and both scored with a further goal from Dominic Poleon, making it a fine 3-1 victory. We then made our way back into town opting to leave the local lady to enjoy her 'beer garden' in peace.

'The beer has flowed here like the river through Ljubljana' was how the Leeds fans' presence in the capital was reported by the local media a few days later, adding: 'The owner of the Cutty Sark bar could retire on Wednesday morning with the proceeds of the last week'.

Flanked either side by an endless row of bars, restaurants and shops, the River Ljubljanica Kanal that runs through the capital was the perfect setting for the hundreds of Leeds fans arriving for the second game against Domzale. Some were diving into the river from the bridge, much to the amusement of other tourists. We began proceedings in a bar not far from the hotel where, after a couple of hours, we discussed our next move. It was unanimous, we would move on to another bar. So sticking rigidly to our strict policy of not putting too much strain on our legs, Rich, Tony, Bob, Andy and myself rose from our chairs and moved across a pathway and sat down in a bar barely two yards away from the first one. We were in the Cutty Sark and we would remain there for the next 11 hours until it closed. Part of the Bradford Whites contingent joined us as the crickets chirruped and big Steve, his son Lewis and big Ian became embroiled in, at times, a heated debate about rugby league, with a guest appearance from 'Hunslet Hawk'. Away from football, many of us support different rugby teams but the Hawk, who had commendably come by car to Slovenia, driven by his father, couldn't understand this, and despite being barely in his 20s he persisted in trying to wind up (in rugby terms) a 'Flat Capper' Rich, a Rhino, a Tiger, a Cougar, a Bull and even a Giant, so at the insistence of the committee he was removed from the conversation. Interestingly, his dad can still be seen at every Leeds United game home and away, but sadly the Hawk is seldom seen. What the Hawk couldn't understand was that the name Hunslet is embedded in every Leeds United fan's heart and is synonymous with our football club, despite which rugby team you support. Ljubljana is reputed to be the fifth safest city in the world, and by and large the locals appeared very friendly – except the bar staff at the Cutty Sark. They were downright miserable and seemed to resent receiving the many hundreds of Euros given to them by the fans over three days. But this seemed to appeal to the fans and in a way that can only befit our travelling hordes; we packed the place out, singing at the tops of our voices to the many recognisable tunes on the jukebox. It became a perverse pleasure antagonising the waiters with regular calls for, 'More beer over here please!' We became a sort of sideshow for the passers-by who clearly couldn't believe what they were witnessing. Even the local police kept drifting in and out of the scene, but were more than happy that there was no trouble, often posing for photographs with the fans. Our favourite game was ordering shitloads of beer when the bar called 'last orders'. There was not a hint of any major trouble and we were in full swing when we were joined by Phil Hay and his photographer for this trip, Jonathon Gawthorpe. Phil was looking for the fan who had received the 50 Euros from Brian McDermott to do a piece for the newspaper. I pointed out Dan who was in the middle of a crowd, with arms aloft and leading yet another Leeds anthem. There were so many fans crammed into the bar at one point that the overflow had to occupy the vacant seats in the bar across the pathway where we had started out that first day. The staff there in comparison seemed grateful for the business.

On matchday, we all headed for the home of NK Domzale. There weren't a lot of bars outside the stadium – two in fact – but aware that there was to be no alcohol on sale inside, we stayed in one of these until the very last minute. Once inside, Leeds fans massed down the tunnel side and were soon into the usual routine. Despite being a goal up courtesy of Poleon, Leeds were pegged back and eventually succumbed to a late winner for the home side. This was met by loud cheers from our fans, who celebrated so noisily that anyone outside the ground would have assumed that it was Leeds who had scored. This seemed to amuse the home fans, both sets of players, and even the armed police, many of whom roundly applauded the Leeds fans who by now had begun a large 'conga' up and down the steps of the stand. After the match the players from both sides, to a man, stood and clapped in admiration of the Whites fans that were now wallowing in the adulation. Our fans were still dancing after the final whistle and I risked life and limb by inviting one of the armed policemen to dance. I had one eye on him and the other on his machine gun as we linked arms and gaily spun around, surrounded by a circle of clapping supporters.

The following day we made our way back up to Sobota for the final game, which was to be against the Hungarian outfit, Ferencvaros. Rumours had been circulating all week that up to 1,000 Ferencvaros fans would be making the trip across Slovenia's north-east border for the game – and apparently, they weren't too friendly.

By now, many of our supporters had returned home after the weekend game with Domzale, leaving a depleted force of around 250 to 'man the fort'. On the morning of the game we were sat in the bar outside our hotel when our waitress Sienna who had become our favourite during our stay came running over to our table. 'You come with me please,' she said, grabbing my arm. Of course I left with her arm in arm amidst huge cheers from my fellow drinkers. But my joy was short-lived as I was taken to Big Tony, who had tripped on a step and had gone through a very thick glass panel in a door gashing his hand and wrist quite badly, and was now sitting on a chair near the rear entrance to the hotel. An ambulance quickly arrived and tended to Tony – it was only 11am and already we were a man down.

When he returned to our table all freshly bandaged up, Tony was greeted with the usual sympathy – 'Does your travel insurance cover you for just a single trip?' asked Rich Watson. 'Underdog!' another lad shouted. 'Have you been injured in an accident?' said another, and so it continued into the afternoon.

We made our way back to the main square where most of the bars were and rumours were gathering pace about the impending arrival of hundreds of Ferencvaros fans. What was very apparent was that the locals weren't particularly keen on Hungarians. It was a historic thing going back many decades, but it was something that still grated with the Slovenians. We eventually made our way back up to the same stadium where we had started off five days ago, keeping an eye out for the 'Hungarian Invasion'. But apart from a handful of Ferencvaros fans close to the ground it appeared to be all Leeds fans. I did notice though that the Lasko garden umbrellas had been taken down, I assume to avoid any further confusion.

We arrived near the ground and opted for the local tennis club for a final aperitif before kick-off. One or two Ferencvaros fans were in the club and were clearly surprised at the amount of Leeds fans present. When asked where the rest of the Ferencvaros fans were, one of them told us that they had all been taken directly into the ground under a heavy police escort that had been with them since eight coaches of their supporters crossed the north-east border into Slovenia. We left the tennis club shortly before kick-off, pausing briefly to watch two of our entourage, Coke and Macca looking splendid in pleated tennis skirts and engaged in a few sets on a nearby court.

Mayhem signalled our arrival inside the ground as Ferencvaros fans tried to the storm the bar on the halfway line. This was the bar that we had been in for the first game against Murska but tonight it had been closed on police advice. Armed police forced the Hungarians back into their designated end of the ground. The kick-off was delayed while the police restored order. Although only around 300 of an estimated 1,000 fans had turned up, they appeared very hostile.

The Slovenian police were severely tested as sporadic pitch invasions continued and torn-out seats were thrown at them. This was clearly a personal war between the two, and Leeds fans were merely interested onlookers. The owners of the bar that had been closed then decided that our fans (who had been called exemplary by the local press) should be allowed beer and began bringing endless trays of cold beer towards the Leeds end of the ground. And it was half price.

'This is the life,' said Billy Bonner as one of his lads, Matt, returned with a trayful of beer for the family. When Leeds became the first British team to win the Inter Cities Fairs Cup, later known as the UEFA Cup and now called the Europa League, they actually met Ferencvaros in the two-legged final in 1968. Ferencvaros were then one of the most feared teams in Europe, but when they came to Elland Road, they arrived with their second kit, which was all-white, and not their traditional all-green kit. Unbelievably, when you look at the game today, teams in those days would only travel with one kit, and this certainly posed a dilemma at Elland Road on that balmy summer evening.

Eventually, Leeds agreed to play in their unfamiliar blue shirts and then posted a 1-0 first leg win against an extremely good Ferencvaros side which included the prolific striker Florian Albert, who had been named the European Footballer of the Year in 1967. The great thing about this enforced change of strip was that when Leeds United went to the Nep Stadium in Budapest, Hungary, for the second leg and heroically defended their slender lead in front of a hostile 76,000 crowd to lift the cup, they did so in an all-white strip.

Meanwhile, back at the far less prestigious meeting between the two clubs here in Murska Sobota – and unbelievably, Ferencvaros had once again arrived with only white shirts. A compromise was agreed whereupon Ferencvaros would play in their colours in the first half and we would play in ours for the second half, with training tops replacing the first choice where necessary. Leeds lost a close battle by a goal to nil, but had two blatant penalty appeals turned down by the one man who seemed more afraid of the travelling Magyars than anyone else – the referee.

The normally placid Brian McDermott was seething over the non-penalty decisions, in particular the brutal attack on Rodolph Austin, which left him needing extensive treatment before resuming. Rudy was also the target for monkey chants from the Ferencvaros fans.

As the beer supply to the Leeds fans continued apace, a large bunch of unruly characters stormed into the Leeds end and began chanting foreign slogans – 'Madzarkis Barabe!' and 'Upijemo Madzari!'

At first we all thought they were Ferencvaros fans, as did the armed police who beat a hasty track down to the Leeds end. And as our supporters sent a chant of 'We are Leeds' across their bow, we were astonished when the 'foreigners' joined in with us. We found out later that they were Slovenian Ultras, a group of hooligans who were very opposed to the Hungarian element at the opposite end of the ground. We also discovered later that some of their chants translated into 'Hungarian bastards!' and 'We kill Hungarians!' Nice.

As the match ended, the police quickly rounded up the Ferencvaros fans who weren't allowed anywhere near the town centre, where it was business as usual with a few pints and a 'Kebap' for supper. As all the lights went out around us, Tony led a few choruses of a 60s Leeds song and the owner of the bar, realising he couldn't yet go home, began bringing more beers from his store and began reloading the fridge. In return, Tony, Bob, Andy, Steve, Ian, Rich, the Hawk's dad and myself duly obliged and drank them. Brian McDermott left the club after the following season, but I'm sure many Leeds fans will always be grateful to him for introducing us to the delights of Slovenia. We had been made so welcome that I don't think we could have caused any trouble if we had tried.

The next morning, I finished my final breakfast in the very pleasant city of Murska Sobota and after nicking the match poster from the hotel front door, I boarded our coach home.

Chapter 5

Call Us Legion, We Are Many

THERE are some things in life that have stayed with me forever; passing my driving test for instance; or buying my first Lambretta scooter – a 1969 SX 150. Even my first pet snake, Sid, I loved him. Or the first time your own *love snake* is set free to roam. But, the first time I saw Don Revie's white-shirted Leeds United under the floodlights is etched in my memory. The brown ball skimming across the early evening dew, does it get any better? And yes, before you ask – I do get out – quite a lot.

I vividly recall the scenes at Elland Road on 8 May 2010. It was 4.44pm and Leeds had finally escaped after three years in League One. Leeds United Football Club are not capable of doing things the easy way and despite leading the division for much of the season, we slipped down to second place, thus allowing Norwich to take over at the top and we then became in great danger of slipping into the play-off mix beneath us. It's okay reaching the play-offs from a position where you are looking up at the top six, but when you drop into the play-offs from first or second position, it is a huge disappointment as well as a great cause for concern. The maths was simple – beat Bristol Rovers in the final game of the season and we go up automatically – albeit in second place. Lose, and we could quite easily end up not going up at all. The capacity crowd of 38,234 raised the roof from the kick-off, but disaster struck early on when our winger, Max Gradel, lost his temper and got sent off after a tussle with his opposite number, Daniel Jones. The situation worsened when shortly after the dismissal, Rovers took the lead. As if to rub salt in to the wound, Jones played a major role in the build-up to the goal, scored by Darryl Duffy, and now the Leeds fans' nerves began to jangle. Thankfully, a stunning equaliser from Jonny Howson and a poached winner from Jermaine Beckford in the second half ensured promotion for Leeds, and sent the fans, manager Simon Grayson and his sidekick Glynn Snodin into raptures.

Almost everyone in football it seemed – opposition fans, players, the media and football authorities alike – had delighted in witnessing United's fall from grace in 2004 as we crashed through two divisions before finally coming to rest at places such as Cheltenham, Northampton and Hereford.

Rubbing shoulders with Europe's elite, United were, in 2001, within an hour of reaching their sixth European final. Yet nine years to the day of the Bristol Rovers game, a 3-0 defeat to Valencia in the Champions League semi-final brought the scythe of the grim reaper down on the club so hard and so fast that even now, the foundations at Elland Road are still trembling.

I was born two months before the end of the John Charles-led promotion season in 1956 and I saw Leeds win their first-ever major trophy, the League Cup, in a 1-0 win over Arsenal at Wembley in 1968. The following year, I had a day off school to witness the Whites win their first league championship with a 0-0 draw at Anfield. When I was 16, I saw Leeds triumph yet again over Arsenal at Wembley, this time winning the 1972 FA Cup. Add to that another league title, the Charity Shield and the Fairs Cup twice, and by the time I was legally old enough to drink, I had seen my team win six trophies. It's interesting to note how the media overlook Leeds with alarming regularity. Just recently, Sky Sports showed a table consisting of English club appearances in European finals. Out of four teams, Liverpool were top with 12 and in fourth place were Tottenham with four. Leeds, with appearances in five European finals (six if you include the play-off final with Barcelona in 1971), were not mentioned.

Along the way, I have seen in the flesh some of the finest footballers in the world and the vast majority of those have been in the colours of Leeds United. Bobby Collins was one of those players. I first saw Collins when I was a ten-year-old kid on the Lowfields Road terrace in 1966, and even though he was coming to the end of his career, I immediately saw what made Don Revie pay Everton, in 1962, £25,000 for this 31 year-old, 5ft 4in chunk of iron. Bobby was the main cog in Revie's revival of the struggling second division club who were tantalisingly close to dropping into the third division, to the dizzy heights of Europe in just four years. Despite his pocket-size appearance, Bobby took no prisoners on the park and I even witnessed this first hand. Bobby was still playing for the Leeds United ex-professionals team well into his sixties and it was then that I played against him. I was in goal for Bristol Street Motors of Leeds against Leeds United ex-pros in a charity match at Yorkshire Copperworks near Leeds. During the game, I ran out to pick up a harmless back pass when all of a sudden, out of nowhere, I spied from the corner of my eye a small object coming towards me with the speed of a train. The next thing, I had been launched into the air and came crashing down, still holding the ball, but with stars whistling around my head. Bobby Collins leant over me, ruffled my hair, grinned and disappeared back into the outfield as fast as he'd arrived. I came across Bobby again some years later one afternoon in Leeds city centre. I was decorating Digby's wine bar on York Place and was just putting the finishing touches to the front door when I saw this little man unloading a vanful of garments – it was Bobby Collins. I seized the chance to get his autograph and as he was doing so, an elderly traffic warden saw the van parked illegally and reached for his notepad. As he drew nearer he recognised Bobby and instead of a ticket he gave him a piece of paper to sign instead. He then winked, and with the traditional air of superiority that only wardens have, said, 'I'll give you 20 minutes Bobby, okay?' When the warden had gone, Bobby said to me, 'Fancy a drink? I've time for a pint now.' I can't remember who paid, but I'll never forget that ten minutes stood at the bar with a Leeds legend. That was in the days when a bottle of pils meant Holsten Pils.

Another diminutive Scot, Billy Bremner, joined Leeds United in 1960. But Bremner initially suffered from severe homesickness and it was only after meticulous coaching from Revie, first as his team-mate, player-manager and then as his manager, that Bremner developed into his captain and became a vital part of the Leeds machine for 16 years; eventually returning to the club in 1986 as manager. Bremner was the best player I ever saw. Leading by example, his never-say-die attitude, guts and determination were second to none, and he scored many vital goals including four semi-final winners. Eddie Gray, another Scot and certainly one of the most gifted of players I've ever seen, came to the club in 1966, the year we both made our debuts with Leeds United; me as a fan, him as a player. Regarded by many as having more skill than George Best, Eddie 'the last waltz' Gray tormented defenders for almost 20 years, winning the

Man of the Match award for the 1970 FA Cup Final against Chelsea. Don Revie once said, 'Eddie is so nimble and skilful that he leaves no footprints in the snow.' I was once doing some work at Eddie's home in North Yorkshire during the 2010 World Cup, and as it was a very hot day, I was grateful when Eddie brought me out a cold bottle of lager. As it was the World Cup I was proudly flying two England flags from the windows of my van parked in the front drive. A little later, I needed something from the van, but I was met by the sight of both flags covered over with something; I couldn't quite make out exactly what. Closer inspection revealed that the 'something' was Eddie's Scottish shirt and cap from the game against England at Wembley in 1969.

Wub and I regularly holiday in Oban on the west coast of Scotland. It's a great seaside town, with stunning views all around. On this particular occasion I was, once again, rather cheekily flying my England flags from the car. I parked up one afternoon and went into the local supermarket to re-stock with beer and meat for that evening's barbecue. When I came out, two Tesco carrier bags had been tied over my flags. Many of the pubs in Oban are similar to the pubs we used to have in Leeds: The Madhouse Market Tavern, The Scotsman, Nags Head and many more. One in Oban is called the Tartan Tavern and I chat regularly with the locals in there.

They know by now that I'm from Leeds, and they talk affectionately of the likes of Bobby Collins, Billy Bremner and Eddie Gray, and even Jack Charlton. One night, we had a rather heated debate on how hard Peter Lorimer's shot was. I think the last count was around 200mph. I've spent many happy hours in the Lochavullin too. I watched the England games of Euro 2016 in Oban and I had the odd dig at my Scottish rivals about them not being in the competition at all. Was I glad I was back home when we were humiliated by Iceland in the last 16!

Lorimer was in the Leeds line-up for those ex-professionals that afternoon at Yorkshire Copperworks. After 23 years as a professional, 'Hotshot' Lorimer retired from the game but continued to play for the ex-pros. Even though he was now carrying a few extra pounds, he had the crowd gasping with his blistering shots at goal and during his pomp, Lorimer's shot was timed at over 20mph faster than the national speed limit (not quite 200mph) – and his superb cross-field passes were something to behold.

Johnny Giles was an even better passer of the ball than Lorimer. Pure genius in fact. I don't think I've ever seen a more technically gifted player than Giles, and as with all Revie's team, he could more than handle himself. But for skill, Giles had very few equals. I once saw Giles score three penalties against a very large bloke in a five-a-side goal. But the really impressive thing about this is that it was at a black tie evening attended by many of the ex-players (Jack Charlton was dressed as a fairy, but that's another story), and the fact that the goal was on a small raised platform made it all the more impressive, as Giles, in his dinner suit and wearing shiny black leather shoes, effortlessly tucked away a plastic 50p football three times – it was truly mind-blowing.

Lump all these Revie players together with Allan Clarke, Paul Reaney, Jack Charlton, Norman Hunter, Paul Madeley, Terry Cooper and Mick Jones, not to mention Mike O'Grady, Terry Yorath, Mick Bates, Albert Johanneson, and a reserve squad containing such high calibre players as Nigel Davey, Rod Johnson and Rod Belfitt, all of whom could have walked into any other first division side of their choosing, and you get some idea of the talent that was on offer during those glory years of the 1960s and 70s. In May 1972, I left school on a Friday, was at Wembley the next day for the FA Cup Final against Arsenal and on Monday started work – that was my gap weekend.

One man I never saw play was the legendary John Charles. Of course I have read about the Gentle Giant and seen footage of a really brilliant footballer. I met Charles on a number of occasions and his presence always amazed me. He cut a very impressive figure with an air of sheer class as he towered head and shoulders above everyone else in the room. It was a shame to see John become ill later in life and I recall a story my mate told me about King John's latter years. I was sat on a plane next to Dick Fenwick as we were flying to a pre-season Leeds tour of Australia, China and Thailand, so we had plenty of time to have a few beers and chew the fat on what would be a 30,000-mile round trip. Dick was a really good friend of John Charles who gave Dick the original manuscript for his autobiography. Dick recalled an afternoon he spent at John's house with Mrs Glenda Charles. John told Dick as they sat having a beer in his living room that he had been invited to a European match involving Juventus, one of his former clubs in Italy, and Newcastle United at St James' Park.

The Italian club held John in such high esteem (as did millions in Italy) that they sent a car down from Tyneside for John and Glenda to take them to two VIP seats in the ground where they were wined and dined before being chauffeured home after the match. Dick was impressed, saying that it must have been brilliant. But John replied with something along the lines of, 'It was very good of them, but I really couldn't be bothered with all the fuss, so we didn't go.' Glenda later told Dick that they had indeed been to Newcastle as arranged, but he simply couldn't remember it and that John was suffering from an early form of Alzheimer's. John died in 2004 and after a real heros send-off and ceremony at the Leeds Parish Church, the hearse took him on his last trip around the Elland Road pitch applauded by the crowd all the way, and accompanied by the powerful voices of the Welsh Male Choir.

Recently, Terry Venables revealed his top ten all-time British players and one of those was indeed John Charles, with Venables saying, 'Charles never received the recognition he deserved.' Simple reason for that Tel: he played for Leeds United! Charles did recently top a list of *Sportsmail*'s all-time British exports though. Charles, who was never booked in his entire career, scored 108 goals in 155 games for Juventus after his British record signing of £65,000 in 1957.

More of a shock to me came in 2012 when Dick Fenwick died suddenly. Dick was the original 'Del Boy', entrepreneur, market trader and all-round good bloke. I have many special memories of Dick – one is of him chasing Shane Warne up the players' tunnel at Headingley for his final Australian squad autograph. Warne had nipped out for a quiet smoke and eagle-eyed Dick had spotted him and within seconds he was in hot pursuit, but Warne spied him and ran off. Undeterred, Dick was lurking outside the Australian players' hotel, the Crowne Plaza on Wellington Street in Leeds the very next day, and the minute Warne lit up outside the hotel foyer Dick leapt from behind a bush like David Bellamy and finally got his final Aussie autograph.

Another endearing memory I have of Dick is one of him getting Tony Yeboah to sign an old pair of football boots at Elland Road. Yeboah had returned to the club to attend a function marking the best ever goal scored by a Leeds United player. Yeboah's blistering strike against Liverpool was the eventual winner and as soon as he spied Yeboah waiting in the adjoining room, Dick did everything but wrestle him to the ground and asked him to sign the boots. Dick then returned to the table with the signed boots proudly encased in a Woolworth's carrier bag and before the end of the evening had sold them off as 'match worn' for a handsome profit. Dick certainly left an indelible impression amongst the Leeds faithful and his presence and character will live forever.

On the subject of the greatest ever goals, the debate continues whether Yeboah's strike against Liverpool in 1995 was indeed the best. I preferred the one at Wimbledon a few weeks later, but a very strong contender is Eddie Gray's peach of a goal when he famously beat six or seven men before slotting the ball past Burnley keeper Peter Mellor back in 1970. Arguably, his first goal in that game when he lobbed Mellor from easily 40 yards out – was even better. Then there were goals from John Charles, Peter Lorimer, Billy Bremner and too many more to mention as strong contenders. With all these world-class stars passing through Leeds United's ranks all those years ago, is it no surprise that the support is as loyal as it is. But there is evidence that their terrace predecessors were just as passionate.

In 1950, when Leeds were a second division side and fifth in the table, 50,476 fans filed into Elland Road to watch United beat Tottenham Hotspur 3-0. This was a superb achievement considering Spurs went on to win the league and the division one title the following year. Leeds were also on a good run in the FA Cup and well over 51,000 saw Leeds draw 1-1 with Nat Lofthouse's Bolton Wanderers. Around 10,000 Leeds fans made the trip across the Pennines to witness United beat first division Bolton 3-2 in the replay in front of 30,000. And over 53,000 fans were at Elland Road for the fifth-round 3-1 victory over Cardiff City which gave Leeds a plum tie against the mighty Arsenal at Highbury. In the early hours of 4 March 1950, 150 coaches full of our fans set off to London and saw Leeds almost topple the high-flying Gunners before succumbing to a narrow 1-0 defeat. Six years later, 15,000 United fans made up the 30,000 crowd at Hull City as United swept to a 4-1 victory and promotion on the final day of the season.

The fans of today have continued that proud tradition and Leeds United sell out every away ticket allocation within hours and in the depths of League One in 2007 to

2010, broke all other clubs' records as United fans packed into their grounds, often quadrupling the home clubs' average attendance. This routine has continued in the Championship and will certainly continue when the club finally arrives back in the Premier League. Leeds United are supposedly one of the most hated clubs in England, but while on my summer jobs – following Yorkshire County Cricket Club, Castleford Tigers Rugby League Club, horse racing whenever I can, and my holidays – I often chat with supporters of Premier League clubs and they tell me how much they miss the appearance of Leeds United and its fans at Goodison, Anfield and the like.

Liverpool fans, of course, are noted for their sense of humour, but I feel that this pales into insignificance compared to the sharp wit and unique spontaneity that has been prevalent at Elland Road for as long as I can remember and as you'd expect, our Leeds-supporting forefathers set the bar in this department too.

In 1962, John Charles returned to the club from Italy and chairman Harry Reynolds immediately put the price of season tickets up. Reynolds had pre-warned the fans with a pre-season note saying, 'There may be the possibility of John Charles returning to the club, in which case there may be an increase in price.' Even so, the rather large increase did not deter United fans and many letters appeared in the *Yorkshire Evening Post*. One fan wrote: 'Come four divisions of the league in arms. We shall shock them, naught shall make us rue. If Leeds United to John Charles be true.' Another aimed at Charles himself, said wryly, 'Tha'rt costing us varry dear. Aye, US – WE'RE carrying t'load. But if tha shoves us up next year, tha'rt more na welcome at Elland Road.' Unfortunately, King John returned to Italy after just 11 games.

Of course, the originality and uniqueness of Leeds fans seems to have gone unnoticed by the majority of the media, as their notepads and laptops appear to be programmed only to report on the negative aspect of Leeds fans, an aspect that even the staunchest of anti-Leeds press would admit is thin on the ground these days.

An unofficial Hooligan League of Shame for the 2011/12 season placed Leeds fans in third place in an overall table of arrests for the top four tiers of English football. Considering that the average home attendance is higher than the entire Football League as well as a sizable chunk of the Premier League and that the club, as I mentioned, sell out every away allocation, 101 arrests for all of that season (an increase of 39 from the previous season), although not ideal, isn't drastic in the overall picture. Steve Clay of the Leeds United Supporters' Trust said, 'We are saddened to see the rise in arrests and are working with West Yorkshire Police and other forces up and down the country to try to reduce the figures. However, I do think we are often policed on reputation rather than reality.'

Yes, there are times when Leeds fans have let the club down in the past, which goes without saying, but nowadays these occurrences are very rare. The incident at Hillsborough in 2012 when the home keeper was attacked by a Leeds fan was unfortunate, only a fool would deny this.

As manager at the time, Neil Warnock, said of the incident, 'But he (the Wednesday keeper Kirkland) did go down a bit easy didn't he?' But you have to put these things in perspective. Leeds fans were subject that evening to sickening chants referring to the murder of two of our supporters in Istanbul in 2000 from the Sheffield crowd and Wednesday manager Dave Jones chose to ignore this by branding ALL Leeds fans 'vile animals'. This was the same manager incidentally, who was the boss at Cardiff City when his fans invaded the pitch after his side's 2-1 FA Cup victory in order to attack the Leeds fans at the other end. During the same game, he chose to condone his own chairman Sam

Hammam, who continuously taunted the Leeds fans with his head patting routine 'Do the Ayatollah' despite several warnings from the police. The FA fined the club a paltry £20,000, but Dave Jones never condemned his fans or his chairman. Hammam was an utter fruitcake – he once made a player eat a sheep's testicles before he could sign for Cardiff City. And while he was at Wimbledon, he often put salt in the opponents' half-time tea. And he would remove all toilet rolls from the visitors' dressing room. He even tried, without success, to move Wimbledon FC to Dublin.

But there have undoubtedly been countless occasions where the powers that be have tested the resolve of the Leeds faithful. Midweek games at the far end of the country are commonplace with regular 400-mile-plus round trips on a Monday night. Granted, other fans have had to travel long distances at awkward times, but I'm convinced none to the degree that Whites fans have had to endure. Leeds have certainly appeared on Sky TV more than anyone else, disrupting the plans of those who had arranged travel for the original date. Irish and Scandinavian fans have been the hardest hit in recent years. Massimo Cellino crossed swords with Sky TV many times, even denying them access to Elland Road for a game against Derby. The huge Sky trucks remained parked outside all day and were only allowed in at the last minute when the Football League intervened with the threat of a possible points deduction. The league is firmly in the pocket of the Sky giants and bow to their every whim while pocketing large dollops of revenue. But despite games being rearranged more times than Michael Jackson's face, Leeds fans continue to snap up the entire allocation at every away game. *Yorkshire Evening Post* chief sports reporter Phil Hay wrote at the start of the 2015/16 season: 'An away crowd of 4,000 at Reading for a Sunday dinner time fixture does not make Leeds United unique. There are other clubs in the Championship that can muster those numbers when the wind blows in a fair direction. But United's following is a precious rarity because of its ability to repeat in any circumstances: 4,000 at Reading three days after 3,400 at Doncaster and three days before a full allocation of 2,000 at Bristol City. Uwe Rosler (manager at the time) is worried about his players undervaluing that support, but his players aren't the problem. The Football League's fixture list is where liberties are being taken. One look at the club's schedule in August – three away games in six days, rearranged kick-offs on all four weekends and a Thursday cup tie – is enough to query why clubs tolerate so much tinkering. Then you remember that money talks and English football takes more money from Sky than anyone else. Was Rosler happy to play at Doncaster last Thursday? 'I wasn't asked,' he said.

'Away from the influence of television scheduling, there is a separate trend developing by the year: the uncanny way in which midweek games seem to throw up the longest away trips. Leeds were lumbered with five 400-mile round trips on Tuesdays and Wednesdays last season. But although clearly tested more than most, the club are not being victimised. Brighton were at Huddersfield Town on Tuesday.

'A former Leeds director once told me that the arrangement of long, midweek journeys has tacit support among Football League clubs. Those clubs would never admit to that for fear of being seen as complicit in the late finishes and regular road closures their supporters have to put up with, but financially it makes sense. Leeds are an anomaly because their away following is so large and consistent but clubs have come to realise that teams travelling 200-odd miles will typically bring a reduced crowd with them, regardless of when the game is staged. And so the thinking goes – take a marginally bigger hit on midweek attendances and maximise income from away supporters with more local opposition at the weekend.'

The tenacity of Leeds fans was never more evident than during a period in the mid-80s, when, following a serious street fight with Millwall supporters, United fans were banned from travelling to games at Carlisle United and Wimbledon.

In a *Daily Express* exclusive, Frank Malley wrote, 'Leeds United fans are set to blow open the FA's ban on their travelling supporters. Almost 2,000 of them were at Saturday's all-ticket match at Carlisle. Now the Elland Road Army plan to gatecrash Leeds' away game at Wimbledon in a fortnight in even greater numbers by using a highly-organised plan to obtain tickets.'

On Saturday 23 November 1985, the usual express service train left Euston bound for Carlisle. On board one of the London branches of the supporters' club had block booked F carriage under the name of Mr Danger. The Derbyshire branch parked their coach five miles from Brunton Park and caught taxis to the ground to evade police who would be waiting to turn them around. A 'fishing trip' travelled to Carlisle from Knaresborough and a shopping trip with 'wives' on board left Hull bound for Carlisle. One girl made two 300-mile round trips to Carlisle in a week to buy fistfuls of tickets from the Cumbrian club and other Leeds fans travelled up the week before buying 20 tickets each.

The FA ban which cost Carlisle United an estimated £6,000 was thrown into a farce and after seeing every part of Brunton Park infiltrated by our supporters making it a police nightmare, match secretary Neil Irving said, 'We took precautions to make sure as few Leeds fans as possible got into the game. We returned letters requesting tickets from Yorkshire, but there is a limit to the measures you can take.' Leeds chairman Leslie Silver said, 'I don't think the ban is unenforceable but there are obvious loopholes. Certainly, no official coaches or trains ran from Leeds and we strongly encouraged our people not to go to Carlisle.

05/05/

Leabharlann Chontae Liatroma

item(s) checked out to :
Kenny, Michael

Fifty shades of white - half a century of
pain and glory with Leeds United / Gary
Edwards

Date Due: 26 Jun 2018

To renew your items:
Go online to www.leitrimlibrary.ie
Phone Manorhamilton Library on (071) 98

Opening hours
Mon, Wed, & Thur 10am - 2pm and 3pm - 8
Tue & Fri 10am - 2pm and 3pm - 6pm
Sat 9.45am - 1pm and 12.30pm - 3.15

Leitrim County Library

We are not selling tickets for these away games. They are all coming from the host club and it is not under our jurisdiction.'

The Kippax Branch took a similar route to the Derbyshire Branch and parked up at Longtown, a few miles outside Carlisle. As we arrived at the turnstiles by the Carlisle end of the ground, the police immediately told us to go away. We protested, claiming that we came from Longtown to which we were told that there was now a turnstile open at the other end for Leeds fans. Our master plan had failed to include the fact that Longtown is pronounced *Long-toon* locally.

Similar plans were put into place for the away match at Wimbledon. Tim Maitland, an official of the Leeds University branch of the supporters' club said, 'I have organised several tickets for the Wimbledon game. Leeds fans feel that this ban is unjust... that's why so many were at Carlisle and why there will be even more at Wimbledon.' Meanwhile, several Leeds fans turned up at Plough Lane a few days ahead of the game to buy hundreds of tickets. After the game, a 3-0 victory to Leeds, Wimbledon manager Dave Bassett said, 'Leeds fans behaved impeccably and they are welcome here any time.'

During the 1960s the Scratching Shed was home to the hardcore of Leeds fans at Elland Road. The 'Mighty Shed' as it was nicknamed, originated from the 1920s and was a quaint, wooden barrel shape, not dissimilar to many of its occupants. Fans would sing their anthems, accompanied by guitars, woodwind instruments and tambourines. One favourite of mine at the time was: 'We're only warming up!' as Leeds raced into a 3-0 lead in the first 15 minutes. Sadly, when the hardcore switched ends and moved into the newly constructed Spion Kop in 1968, the instruments seemed to disappear with the exception of a flute, which can still occasionally be heard today, along with Ray Johnson's drum. The attention seemed to switch more to the chanting and songs. In the Shed in the early 60s, a policy of no swearing had been laid down by two of its leaders, Neil and Keith Peniket from Horsforth. Neil: 'When I get up in front of the crowd, I tell them straight away that I don't want any swearing. But you can always hear swearing at any football match.' When asked how the swearing started Keith said, 'I think it was started by people who had drunk too much before they go into the match.' The two brothers say they made up several songs for the fans to sing but other fans in the crowd add filthy words to the lines. 'We will continue to campaign against bad language, but with around 5,000 people in the Shed it is difficult, but we will certainly keep trying to get our message across.' Even when the majority had moved to the Kop the 'no swearing' policy was adhered to. With a hint of mischief, the chant of, 'He's here, he's there, he's every fuckin' where, Eddie Gray!' was replaced with, 'He's here, he's there, we're not allowed to swear, Eddie Gray!'

And even the Liverpool fans must have smiled when their team visited in 1973. It was student rag week, and during a lull in proceedings on the pitch, a pantomime horse vaulted over the wall in the Lowfields Road stand and galloped on to the pitch whereupon a lone policeman gave pursuit. Eventually, with the help of a second bobby, the horse was caught and escorted away. As the entourage disappeared down the tunnel, with the horse waving a hand from beneath his belly, the Kop responded with an impromptu chant of, 'Goodbye horse, goodbye horse, I was saying goodbye to my horse, and as I was saying goodbye to my horse, I was saying goodbye to my horse.' This was repeated several times while everyone twirled their woollen scarves above their heads. This practice still continues today, but the equine words have been replaced with, 'We are the Champions, Champions of Europe'. Interestingly, this chant is often the topic on rival fans' website forums, stating that: 'Leeds fans arrogantly chant: "We are the Champions of Europe," when they've never won the European Cup.' What these contributors fail to recognise is the irony in the chant. Our fans sing this song with reference to the 1975 European Cup Final in Paris when Leeds were subject to some diabolical refereeing by Michel Kitabdjian. After refusing a seemingly perfect goal for us, and also a couple of clear-cut penalties, Bayern Munich went on to win the match. Kitabdjian was later given a life ban by UEFA. Meanwhile, the twirling of the scarves has spread amongst fans worldwide, each adopting it as their own.

It was during the 1960s and 70s that the famous Wallace Arnold coach company ruled the road, bussing thousands of United fans up and down the country. They didn't have a complete monopoly on coach travel however, as Heap's was a noted 'fan carrier' as too was Fallas Coaches, situated near the Peacock pub on Elland Road. I always felt that they should have re-spelt the name 'Fallas' and replace it with the much more adventurous name of 'Phallus' with the appropriate signage and artwork on the side.

It is the spontaneity of the Leeds crowd that stands them head and shoulders above the rest. During the winter of 2011, the Whites travelled down to Portsmouth, who were deep in the throes of serious financial difficulty. Late in the first half the floodlights were necessary. However, during the closing stages, the lights began to flicker and after going on half power, they went off completely, leaving the whole ground in total darkness. This happened three times. Portsmouth's famous anthem is 'Play up Pompey'. But instantaneously, Leeds fans altered that to chants of, 'Pay up Pompey!' with obvious reference to them maybe not paying their electric bill. Leeds defender Paul Connolly said, 'It was totally bizarre – the maddest game ever. To be honest, I was half glad when the referee blew the whistle at the end because I didn't want the floodlights to go out again.'

During the same season Leeds played the Turfites at Turf Moor. We had a bit of a hold on Burnley for a few seasons – Leeds would regularly come from behind to win the game, 2-1 or 3-2. It was Christmas and as usual we were behind – 2-0. United mounted a comeback and won the game but our fans were also brilliant. 'You should have gone Christmas shopping!' was the chant from the away end as the home fans, heads down, shuffled out of the ground.

Jermaine Beckford was a popular player during his four years with us, but understandably, was itching to play in the Premier League. Leeds reluctantly let him go to Everton at the end of his contract – but not before manager, Simon Grayson, pulled off a masterstroke by making him captain for the remainder of the season as, during this period, Beckford scored vital goals including the one that beat Bristol Rovers to ensure promotion to the Championship in 2010.

Many of that euphoric crowd were present when a couple of years later, Beckford returned to Elland Road in the colours of Leicester City. Not long before half-time, Leicester won a corner in front of the Kop, which was delayed while an injured player received treatment. It was this delay that gave the Leeds fans their opportunity. 'You're Leeds, and you know you are, you're Leeds, and you know you are', they chanted at Beckford who stood in the penalty area and responded with the Leeds Salute that was met with loud cheers. Leeds defender Alex Bruce then walked towards Beckford with a gesture to swap shirts to which he played along without of course going through with it. Everyone had a laugh and play resumed. But in fact, not everyone was laughing, and when the two teams turned out for the second half, Beckford had been substituted by Leicester's manager at the time, Nigel Pearson. 'You're Leeds' was sung to Grayson in 2016 when he was manager at Preston, resulting in a courteous wave back to the Leeds fans.

In 2014, Bolton came to Elland Road and beat us 5-1. Leeds were 5-0 down and as you would expect the Wanderers fans were enjoying themselves; then Leeds scored a consolation goal to make it 5-1 in the closing minutes. 'You're not singing anymore,' cried the Leeds fans at the bemused travelling support – priceless.

Another absolute gem that Leeds fans invented is the 'Phantom Goal'.

Used to getting hammered every week, they invented their own entertainment. It all began during a routine 4-0 hiding by Man City at the Etihad in 2013 when the 6,000 plus Leeds following began cheering a goal. The only thing wrong here was that Leeds hadn't scored. 'Let's pretend we've scored a goal,' the Leeds fans will sing. The home fans up and down the country have been left baffled, when after an orchestrated countdown Leeds fans leap up and down, hug each other, kiss a complete stranger, throw their shirts off and then stand there, hands folded or in their pockets looking like nothing has happened. The best thing about this jape is watching the reaction, not only on the faces of the home fans, but those of the stewards and police – it really is worth a goal.

I have often said that the only way Leeds can stop someone scoring against them is to buy them. Brian Deane used to score against us for fun when he played for Sheffield United, but when we bought him, his scoring boots stayed at Bramall Lane. Billy Paynter was another. He scored against us virtually every time he kicked the ball for Swindon Town, so we signed him and that put paid to that. In fairness I liked Billy; he is a really funny scouser, and I got to know him fairly well, exchanging phone numbers. But sadly he didn't score many goals. I was once a guest alongside him for a Darlington Whites On the Road event, and someone asked Billy about Facebook and Twitter to which he replied, 'I don't do that shit.' And the questioning moved on.

Billy Paynter would be the first to admit that his time at Leeds wasn't brilliant. Leeds fans would often sing, 'If Billy scores, we're on the pitch!' Once, during a match at Blackpool, the Leeds fans sang, 'If Billy scores, we're in the sea.' Suffice to say, everyone went home with dry feet.

When Billy scored twice against Peterborough in 2012 in what would be his last game for Leeds I couldn't resist texting him to congratulate him and I honestly was watching to see if he pulled his phone out of his shorts. I'm happy to report that it wasn't until shortly after five o'clock that I received a text back saying, 'Cheers pal.'

On the subject of Twitter, in July 2015 Leeds fans were named as the most vocal on Twitter out of all 92 English professional clubs. Our supporters came out top in the study, averaging 7.7 tweets per fan over six months. Middlesbrough came second with 6.6 tweets per fan. Everton were the leading Premier League club with 6.3, ahead of Arsenal on 4.7. The study was conducted by social scores network Crowd Scores and looked at fans' interaction with their club's official Twitter accounts.

They compared how many followers each club's official account had against the number of mentions of the Twitter handle. It also analysed the sentiment of each tweet, marking each as positive or negative. David Walker, CEO of Crowd Scores, said, 'When you combine Leeds United's rich heritage with the various goings-on during the last season, it's not too surprising that their fans are vocal on Twitter. But to see them top all 92 teams demonstrates just how passionate they are.'

Considering the contempt that the Football League so obviously holds against Leeds United it was a surprise, a pleasant one nonetheless, when the league awarded the Football League fan of the year to a Leeds United fan in 2014. Phil Beeton is a fan of the highest order and blew every other fan out of the water – top bloke.

One thing that has worried me is the generation gap created by some Leeds hierarchy such as Ken Bates (and others) where young fans were definitely priced out of watching the Whites, and fans of recent decades have been forced elsewhere because of cheaper turnstile prices. For me, watching Leeds United is the most natural thing in the world; it's not like you're forcing the young kids to listen to country music – that will happen in time, trust me, but they need to have reasonable access to follow their team when they choose to.

ET LEGIO ET MULTI was the logo on the shirt badge of the Kippax Branch – loosely translated it means Call us Legion We are Many. I was immensely proud to be part of the Kippax and yes we did end up in a few scrapes over the years, it was inevitable. And our somewhat rebellious reputation was not just confined to the rank and file of Leeds fans nationwide, but indeed by fans of other clubs too. But I can say, hand on heart, that the vast majority of our scuffles were because we were in the wrong place at the wrong time. Nowadays going into pubs for an away match is relatively easy but back in the day, you had to book in advance before they would let a coachful of 50 Leeds fans into their local – or sometimes we just took a chance and often ended up on the dark side. The Flowerpot en route to West Brom was so full of West Indians that we literally thought we'd taken a wrong turning and ended up in Jamaica. Another pub on the way to Birmingham was just the same. Some of our lads took on some of the locals at pool, but things almost took a turn for the worse when one of our lads shouted, 'Come on you Whites!' You could have heard a pin drop until normal service was resumed with a few knowing white teeth smiles from our hosts. With our constantly evolving history of black Leeds players going back to the 1950s, it's virtually impossible for a Leeds fan to be racist, but our hosts at the Flowerpot that day took a bit of convincing.

We once got holed up in a pub very close to Villa Park on a Boxing Day in the early 1980s. A lad stood at the bar said, 'Either you lot are really stupid or really hard – this is Villa's main pub.' Fifty of us remained inside as Villa fans began to gather both inside and outside of the pub, with the on looking police seemingly unwilling to intervene. Half an hour or so afterwards we all left the pub to head for the ground, and were immediately surrounded by well over 100 Villa fans. All of a sudden Collar started singing, 'If you're sick of fucking turkey clap your hands!' To which we all joined in. The Villa fans didn't know whether to attack us or applaud us, instead they just parted and allowed us to pass and we carried on our way. Despite trying to maintain a high level of decorum, many of us did see the inside of quite a number of police cells – but that's for another tome and quite possibly for another author. But even then, there are certain exploits and occurrences that will almost certainly remain within the ranks.

When the LUSC Kippax Branch ceased to be in the summer of 1995, it brought to an end 17 glorious years of unforgettable exploits and adventures. From plucking a well-known street tramp from his usual begging spot and taking him on a day out to Middlesbrough, were we wined and dined him and then took him to the game before returning him to the streets of Leeds. Again on a trip north, we had a professor from York University on board our coach who was carrying out a survey on football fans. After sampling the on-board 'Fayre Menu' he was so drunk and stoned that when he arrived at the visitors' turnstiles of Roker Park, he was arrested and not released from a police station in Sunderland until the following afternoon. We never saw him again. Then there was the time when a fully functional mechanical vagina from a sex shop in Leeds did the rounds on the coach to an away trip to Brighton. On our return to the coach after the match, the vagina was nowhere to be seen. Although he had a permanent grin on his face all the way home, the driver denied all knowledge of ever having seen it. Just like the professor, the vagina was never seen again. We even had Leeds players travelling home with us including none other than David Batty who blended in seamlessly. The Kippax Branch was a marriage with several other parts of Leeds including Bramley, Gipton, Seacroft, Guisley, Sherburn, Garforth (GYL) and of course the Castleford contingent. We also regularly carried our friends from Holland, Norway, Sweden and Belgium.

Sadly, things without the Kippax were never the same again after we were disbanded, and for the 1995/96 season Kippax members seeped into various other branches and many of us adopted the Holbeck Branch as our mother ship, installing a portly chap by the name of Ralph as our leader. Ralph is not that dissimilar in appearance to that well-known Hollywood legend – Fred Flintstone. Although it never replicated anything close to the Kippax days, we had some very memorable jaunts over the years. With Ralph at the helm, things were never dull; fights on the coach became a regular feature, and a number of these involved Ralph himself. In fact, as the coaches were waiting in the coach park after a game at Peterborough, someone shouted 'Look at them!' Looking out of the window we saw the minibus that was carrying our overspill of members. Ralph was trading punches with the driver that carried on down the steps of the coach and on to the concrete as the police watched on in bewilderment. Ralph is a determined man, and likes things done his own way, this was one of his endearing qualities, but this was also to be the reason for our parting of the ways a couple of years down the line. Ralph was with us one afternoon in the Viaduct pub in Leeds for an unusual function. Within the Leeds support is a large group infamously known as one of the most notorious hooligan gangs of the past 30-odd years and 300 of them were here this afternoon to pay their respects to one of their own who was tragically killed in a road accident whilst returning from the Liverpool v York City FA Cup tie in 1986. It was 20 years to the day when the accident happened and to commemorate the sad occasion, the lad's mother was in attendance to watch a plaque being unveiled in her son's honour. Leeds United's captain at the time Paul Butler was present as were the local media, including the popular Paul Dews, Leeds United's press officer who has since defected to Middlesbrough Football Club. After a few hours in the pub reminiscing, things were taken outside into the street to witness the unveiling.

It was an unreal atmosphere as hundreds of burly, menacing-looking men, ranging from their early 20s and into their 60s filed out into the street, stopping the cars from proceeding up Lower Briggate. Just one driver got out to object, but then thought better of it and returned to his car and promptly turned it around. The few police officers who were clearly observing the occasion kept a very discreet distance away from the ceremony. Butler had been given the honour of the unveiling and after a few carefully chosen words prepared to pull the cord. Just then, one of the crowd interrupted, 'Just a minute Butts!' Everyone turned around and this lad was walking down towards a parked car about 25 yards down the road.

Two traffic wardens were just about to put a parking ticket on the car when the lad, after putting his bottle of lager on top of a nearby electric box mounted on a wall, said to the by now trembling wardens, 'Put that ticket on that windscreen and I'll smash both your heads together and shove them through it!' After thrusting the ticket into each other's hands like a hot potato, both turned around and disappeared round the corner, one of them still with the ticket. Picking his bottle up and returning to the congregation, the lad then said calmly, 'Sorry Butts, carry on mate.' I heard one lad say to another, 'I didn't know that was his car,' to which the other lad replied, 'It isn't.'

Without wishing to glorify this gang of outlaws, and quite frankly, that is the last thing they would want anyway, it has to be said that they have done a tremendous amount of charity work.

I know what you're thinking; 'my client, your honour, is a reformed character and as well as finding God he has donated time and effort into raising funds for charities such as the homeless kittens' organisation and the endangered lesser spotted blue beaked turtle neck warbling three legged tit from the African rainforest. But in memory of the two Leeds fans murdered in Istanbul in 2000, these so-called thugs were the main instigation behind fundraising events such as coast to coast bike rides, the gruelling Tough Guy challenge, the Three Peaks climb and many more events that raised over £100,000 for the Candlelighters, a charity for children with cancer.

That afternoon at the Viaduct was just a small glimpse into the other side of these men, whose calling card could well read, 'See you tomorrow Lynch Time'.

Unfortunately Ralph has been very ill recently and of course I send him my best wishes. I like Ralph and have even roomed with him on the odd European trip, most notably one foray deep into France during an absolutely freezing November in 2006. As to why Leeds chose to play here I have absolutely no idea, but I do know that Ralph and me stood in the freezing cold at a bar behind the goal for the entire friendly game against Rodez, which for the record, Leeds won with a solitary goal from Danny Pugh.

I have to admit that I'm no great lover of the French; I find them arrogant, ignorant and extremely pompous. And their food is crap too. My feelings towards our Gallic cousins can be found elsewhere in this book, but on this particular trip I have to say I found a couple of decent Frenchmen in a little bar just across from our hotel. Here we drank and even played cards with the locals, although I have to say, we were a few Euros light on our departure.

Towards the end of the 2005/06 season many of us had decided to leave the Holbeck Branch and look towards starting our own branch once again. So, during a holiday in Australia in 2007, I thought about the idea of having three girls in charge of a new branch, so I made an expensive phone call to one of the girls, Annette, who had been travelling with us now for a number of years and I asked her how she felt about forming a new branch with her and two of the other girls, Jo Barrett and Vicky Ward, in charge. Luckily they all agreed and the LUSC White Rose Branch was formed with 'Charlie's Angels' in the driving seat and we parted company with Ralph. There'll be much more on the White Rose a little further on.

There's been many a time when I've been mistaken for a Leeds player; in Germany in 1996 one of the lads told the waiter in an Indian restaurant that I was Carlton Palmer, so after a free king prawn vindaloo and a bottle of wine, I signed the visitors' book and left to supposedly get changed for the match. Before that, in 1994, we were in a bar in Kuala Lumpur and I was Chris Fairclough that night, but after a free beer we were rumbled by the football-loving owner and after having a forefinger wagged in front of my face we had to buy our own beer from then on in. In Johannesburg a year later, it was a team effort as once again I was Carlton Palmer; Whitby John was Gordon Strachan and Ralph from Thornton le Dale near Scarborough was Brian Deane. By now I was getting pretty good at being Carlton Palmer, cocky, obnoxious and a real pain in the arse; John resembled Strachan, well he had ginger hair, but Ralph's pretence was much more daring. He was barely five feet tall, white and had a hairstyle like Rowan Atkinson's first Blackadder. A couple of months later, Leeds played AS Monaco in the UEFA Cup and we walked into a bar in Nice. This time it wasn't our intention to gain free beer by deception – but, the landlord greeted us warmly saying, 'Ah, Leeds, welcome, welcome. Please sit, sit.' He hurriedly waved over a waiter and it was obvious by their conversation and actions that they genuinely thought we were some of the players. He shook hands with Ray, who instinctively responded by saying, 'Brian Deane, hello there.' Steve became Tony Dorigo and I instantly upgraded myself to Tony Yeboah. After a complimentary dish of garlic prawns and mussels washed down by a couple of small beers, we said that we'd better be going off to the stadium, which in itself was true. But I would love to have seen the landlord's face when he watched the game on TV later and watched 'me' get a hat-trick.

Despite Don Revie putting the name of Leeds United on to the world map, and making players such as Bremner, Charlton, Lorimer etc., household names in the early 1960s, the city of Leeds is widely overlooked too (try looking for us on the weather map on morning TV) and the many achievements are only generally known by the people of Leeds, a city hoping to become the City of Culture for 2023. Broadcasting Place in Leeds has been voted as the world's best tall building, fending off such prestigious competition as the Burj Khalifa in Dubai, the world's tallest building. Leeds market is the largest indoor market in Europe and the birthplace of Marks & Spencer in 1884. And the world's first moving pictures were filmed in the city in 1888. The achievements of Leeds Rhinos have been phenomenal and they have been domestic and world champions on countless occasions, even though their fans do constantly steal terrace songs from their football neighbours. Celebrity Rhinos fans include Sue Barker, Russell Crowe, Sean Bean, Tim Henman, Boris Becker and Wayne Rooney.

Peter O'Toole was born in Leeds as was Ernie Wise. Malcolm McDowell was superb as the lead actor in *A*

Clockwork Orange and he too is a son of Leeds. Hundreds of thousands of folk are delighted that Joshua Tetley was born in our great city and even happier that he chose to brew the world's most famous beer, Tetley Bitter, right on our doorstep. Alan Bennett, Billy Pearce, Gabby Logan, Jeremy Paxman, Mel B, Keith Waterhouse, John Craven, Barry Cryer, Leigh Francis, aka Bo' Selecta, Avid Merrion and Keith Lemon, and renowned chef, Marco Pierre White all hail from the city. The man famous for thwarting a hijack attempt by a suicide bomber in Cyprus came from Leeds. Ben Innes was on board an Egypt Air flight bound for Cairo in March 2016 when it was hijacked by Seif Eldin Mustafa wearing a suicide belt. Ben approached him and had a selfie with the potential bomber who, having been thrown off his stride, gave himself up to airport security forces. The bomb turned out to be made of empty toilet rolls and empty plastic bottles, but Mr Innes had clearly defused the situation. Amongst other famous Leeds landmarks were the Quarry Hill flats in the centre of town, sadly demolished in 1978 and exactly 40 years after they were built. The flats were the largest housing complex in the United Kingdom, but more importantly they caught the watchful eye of none other than Adolf Hitler.

In his quest for world domination during the Second World War, Hitler, should he succeed in conquering Britain, planned to transform Leeds into the capital of England and build a network of motorways from the city to all corners of the country while using Quarry Hill flats as the base for his SS troops. Barnbow Munitions Factory in Leeds was famous for the war effort – and my Grandma was a crane driver there.

The world's most famous bear was also the product of Leeds; Harry Corbett, Sooty's creator, was born in Guiseley as was his son and Harry's Sooty successor Matthew. They were part of the family of Harry Ramsden, also from Leeds, whose fish and chip restaurant was the world's first fish and chip shop, and now has shops all over the world. And the brilliant soul singer-songwriter Corinne Bailey Rae was born and bred in Leeds.

It wasn't long before sports promoter Barry Hearn saw the potential of the new Leeds Arena. In the mid-1970s Leeds was the location for the first ever televised darts competition. He took Premier League darts to Leeds in 2014 and was blown away by the response. 'I was amazed at the record attendance for world darts turning out at the Leeds Arena,' he said after 11,000 fans turned up. 'I was super-impressed with the arena and the fans. I heard some good things about it, but until you actually see it, you don't know. This was the biggest ever event held for professional darts in the modern era. That's what Leeds has given us. The man in the street of Leeds has turned out in great numbers to give their support. This is now a nailed-on Premier League darts venue.'

Darts world champion Adrian Lewis said of the Leeds Arena atmosphere, 'It was quite daunting at first. I was gobsmacked. It was fantastic, unbelievable.' Robert Thornton added, 'The fans were brilliant, it was a great atmosphere, absolutely awesome.' Phil 'The Power' Taylor simply said, 'I was in awe of the fans – incredible.' And 'Mighty' Michael van Gerwen said, 'I have never seen anything like that before in my life!'

Even the Master of Ceremonies, John McDonald, was impressed: 'I have seen some atmospheres in my time, but this will take some beating. Well done to the people of Leeds, it's magnificent.'

The success of the darts was quickly followed by boxing, when Barry Hearn's boxing promoter son, Eddie, saw the potential of preparing a home-grown fighter to box at the Leeds Arena. Albert Johanneson played for Leeds United in the 1960s and became the first black player to ever play in an FA Cup Final when he played on the left wing for Leeds against Liverpool at Wembley in 1965. Albert's nephew, Carl, became a very successful boxer and won the British featherweight title in 2006 and with the Leeds public firmly behind him, he enjoyed much success and would walk out into the ring to the tune of 'Marching on Together' draped in the Leeds flag and wearing a Leeds headband. He would then fight in Leeds United shorts. So Eddie Hearn wanted another Leeds fighter to capture the hearts of the public and found one in Josh Warrington. The atmosphere has been absolutely electric as Josh fights there on a fairly regular basis, and already he has won the English, British, European and Commonwealth featherweight titles. Josh, too, enters the ring to 'Marching on Together' and 'I Predict a Riot!' while Vinnie Jones escorts him carrying Josh's latest belt. Eddie Hearn first saw the potential of the Leeds crowd in relation to Warrington when Josh fought and beat Samir Mouneimne in 2013 for the Commonwealth title at the Hull Arena. Hours before the fight, Josh had been supporting Leeds United at Elland Road as they beat Yeovil Town 2-0. The Leeds fans then returned the loyalty by heading to Hull in their thousands. Hearn said, 'I was mesmerised by Josh's vociferous and passionate fan base that for me has been totally infectious.'

Hearn first visited Leeds when he attended the FA Cup semi-final between Tottenham and Everton back in 1995 as a Spurs fan, but when asked in 2014 if the legion of Warrington's fans could make him into a Leeds fan he replied, 'I think I already am. The atmosphere in the Arena tonight was breathtaking. It's an atmosphere that leaves you very warm when you leave the venue. It's not hostile, but it is very, very passionate, and for an away fighter it's not the greatest place to be. That's what you try to make it for a football match. You want a cauldron of passion rather than a cauldron of hate. It's not like that – it's not that kind of environment and for me as a promoter every time we go to

Leeds we are showcasing Leeds. It's by far one of the best atmospheres in British sport.'

Hearn also witnessed the Leeds fans' passion for Warrington when he fought Edwin Tellez in Berlin in 2015. Five hundred supporters from Leeds roared Warrington on to yet another victory. 'Berlin was absolutely nuts,' said Hearn. 'This is passion for Josh Warrington and this is passion for someone who is putting Leeds back on the map and someone who can win world titles for Leeds.' Josh himself concurs with this: 'I watched Ricky Hatton when I was growing up and I used to see those atmospheres and think, "Why isn't this happening in Leeds?"'

Another boxing favourite from Leeds is the bubbly Nicola Adams, who is Britain's most successful female boxer and became the first female to win a gold medal when she triumphed at the London Olympics in 2012. And more recently, her ultimate goal, the world title.

Amongst the world of showbiz entertainment we have many supporters. The tennis player Stefan Edberg is a long-time fan. Other sports stars include Nick Faldo, rugby league legend Karl Harrison (who follows United home and away), Stuart McCall, Howard Clark and Norwegian cross-country skier Frude Estil. Just for good measure, BBC sports presenter Mike Bushell is a Leeds fan too. Entrepreneur James Brown is a lifelong supporter and a most unlikely fan comes in the form of porn star, the delicious Poppy Morgan.

International singing star Michael Bolton is a fan, so too is Tony Christie as is Gareth Gates and Chris Moyles. Chef Ken Hom declares his love for Leeds and actor Ralph Ineson (Finchy) from *The Office* and star of several other TV shows has been a Leeds United fan all his life and outstanding comedian Jon Richardson is a fan too. Who could forget the hilarious comedian and compere, Jed Stone, who hails from Liverpool but is a season ticket holder at Elland Road? Russell

Crowe became a fan in the 1970s saying that 'Don Revie's Leeds United were hard, but fair.' Crowe was linked with buying Leeds United in 2015, but as with many potential buyers in the past the poisoned chalice that is Leeds United proved far too complicated for him to proceed any further. He did however say at the time, 'It would give me nothing but pleasure to see the White Army marching on together back into the Premier League and being where we should be. I stand by my belief that LUFC is a massive opportunity. When my trusted associates tested the idea we found multiple potential. But without my hands on the wheel in Leeds, I can't guarantee investors a return. I've loved Leeds all my life, I always will. I love the club, I want nothing but success for the club, like most Leeds fans, probably 99.9 per cent, I'm getting a little impatient.'

Top comedian Ardal O'Hanlon was the star of *Father Ted* as Father Dougal, and is another famous supporter. 'I've been a Leeds fan for as long as I can remember,' he says. 'When you're five or six years old you adopt a team. I chose Leeds United.

'Johnny Giles is my favourite player without doubt. Tony Currie was another favourite of mine. In some ways we have lost the plot in recent years. The Woodgate/Bowyer incident which of course should never have happened, had a huge impact on the club and the victims. These things go much deeper than superficial football matters. I think it's fair to say that David O'Leary lost a sense of proportion and he should never have published that book, *Leeds United On Trial*. He just couldn't shut up.

He and Peter Ridsdale were swept away by ambition; they had a vision for the club that forced them to start buying players that they didn't even need. We had the nucleus of a great squad, a youthful and inexpensive squad, and they didn't really need to keep adding to it with expensive signings. Ridsdale, I guess, was your characteristic smooth-talking egotistical charmer. David O'Leary had a keen eye for self-publicity.' Many of the cast of *The League of Gentlemen* are fans including Jeremy Dyson.

As well as on the pitch, Leeds United songs were also riding high in the charts in the 1970s, so it's no surprise that the music industry has more than its fair share of Leeds fans even today. As well as the obvious Leeds-based bands; Kaiser Chiefs, Pigeon Detectives, Chumbawumba, 60s stars Paul and Barry Ryan, Grumbleweeds, The Wedding Present, Embrace, Terrorvision, Po Boys and The Strikes, Leeds loyalties can be found all over the country. And let's not forget Nicky Byrne, who played in goal for Leeds United as a youngster before bizarrely packing it all in to play in a band called Westlife, or something or other.

One leading celebrity following the club's fortunes is Ray Johnson, who starred in the TV series *The Undateables* in 2014. Now in his mid-50s, Ray from North London took his girlfriend Janette to Elland Road to watch Leeds play Barnsley, but things didn't go quite according to plan. The couple both suffer from slight learning difficulties and Ray works at People First, a campaigning organisation for people with learning difficulties, but it was difficulties of a different kind that prevailed at Elland Road that afternoon. As the cameras filmed them walking to the turnstile, Janette told Ray, 'I think it's going to be 3-0 to the other side.' Ray looked down at the ground in silence. But once inside the ground, Janette began shouting for the wrong team! Sitting at the front of the Kop surrounded by Leeds fans, she constantly shouted, 'Come on Barnsley! Come on!' Poor old Ray tried to tell her, but she seemed oblivious to his words of wisdom. 'Come on Barnsley,' Janette shouted again, 'score a goal!' Just then a chap sat behind Janette gently tapped her on the shoulder and quietly told her of her mistake. Janette, wearing a pink Leeds hat and scarf, then, said, 'Oh, no,' and put her head in her hands.

This particular episode however was a huge success attracting an audience of over three million and was hailed for its 'warm and inclusive tone'. Ray, famous amongst Leeds fans for playing his little drum at matches said, 'The show was quite impressive.'

Member of Swedish band Roxette, Per Gessle, also has our colours firmly nailed to his mast, as does Chris Edwards of Kasabian. Poor old Chris has had his loyalty challenged recently following the Foxes' unlikely lifting of the Premier League title – hang in there, mate, our time will come again; you may be sitting down to perform by then, but it will come again. Def Leppard's Vivian Campbell once said, 'Leeds was a sound venue tonight. Don't know if I've ever mentioned it, but I am actually a Leeds fan.' and Stereophonics front man, Kelly Jones, told Mark Lawrenson that his favourite moment as a Leeds fan came with the 1-0 FA Cup triumph at Old Trafford in 2010. Another front man, Tim Booth of the band James said, 'I was taken to see Leeds play when I was seven by my Dad and saw Don Revie's amazing team. That's all you need. At that age, that imprint comes in. Later when I was 11, my Mum let me go on to the Kop on my own and it gave me a great sense of freedom. It seemed really exciting to me – a different world. How often do men sing together, apart from in church? Cellino is an autocratic millionaire; like a dictator of a small nation. You know with him, it's not gonna be about the manager! No real manager is going to come to Leeds. We were deceived in the Ken Bates period with the slow sell-off of our best players. Anybody with any ounce of talent disappeared – mainly to Norwich – and that was really depressing. But we've got a wild ride ahead of us with Cellino at the helm.' Colin Montgomery and Nasser Hussain were once Leeds fans, but the emergence of Chelsea a few years back turned their fickle heads.

BBC sports presenter Mike Bushell is a Leeds fan and Jeremy Paxman, journalist, author and lifelong Leeds fan was once described by *The Independent* as an extraordinary combination of intellect with the brutish approach of the Leeds United teams in the 1960s and 1970s, and in particular their stalwart defender Norman 'Bites yer Legs' Hunter. One celebrated victim of Paxman, recalling one of their many confrontations said of Jeremy, 'But he doesn't stop at your legs!' And even Noel Gallagher recognises that Yorkshire Tea is the best. 'We always take it on tour with us – I can drink up to 20 cups a day – easy. Tea must be Yorkshire.'

One of the most important exports out of Leeds has to be the HESCO Bastion. Basically, a blast wall used by the military to counter explosions and gun fire. Jimi Heselden from Halton Moor, Leeds, was the man behind the operation which was used in Iraq and Afghanistan and is still used all around the world today. Jimi, who died as a result of an accident in 2010, was a self-made multi-millionaire with an estimated fortune of £340m who put millions of pounds into Leeds United and countless charities: 'There are people out there who are making money and when times are good I honestly believe that people have a moral obligation to use their wealth to help others.'

Jimi Heselden, September 2010.

Chapter 6

Viking Inflation

THE Vikings first began chomping away at our shores in AD 793 and they liked it so much that they hung around for over 200 years, building their own towns and cities. One of the early Viking kings of England was called Cnut – now there's something to think about. But the axes, longboats and horns were long gone by the time of the Second World War when Nazi Germany occupied neutral Norway. The British 1st Airborne Division played a major part in the liberation of Norway and the Division maintained law and order in Norway until the arrival of the rest of the Allied troops. It had been a difficult, and at times tragic operation, which finally resulted in the Division being tasked with the supervision and eventual surrender of the German forces in May 1945 when 30,000 Allied troops oversaw the disarmament of over 350,000 German soldiers.

Six years previous to the liberation, almost to the day, Leeds United had recorded their first visit to Scandinavia while embarking on an end of season tour of Norway and Denmark which involved five matches – two against an Oslo

XI, a game against Aalborg in Norway and then two against a Jutland XI in Denmark. Leeds won all five games.

During the Revie era of the early to mid-1970s, Leeds visited Scandinavia several times; SK Brann, Lillestrom SK and Viking Stavanger in Norway and Odense BK in Denmark. And it is almost certainly this era that is responsible for the ongoing support for Leeds from Scandinavia, and in particular Norway. The passion for Leeds United in Scandinavia has been handed down through generations and is nothing short of amazing and although frighteningly expensive, Norway, as with the rest of Scandinavia, is a fantastic place to visit for a holiday, or more precisely, a pre-season tour.

One particular trip to the seaside town of Stavanger on the south-west coast of Norway in 2005 was memorable to say the least. As usual we were travelling with Big Mick Tours. On board we had 'Our Stu'. Stuart Hayward was the victim of a horrific car crash in the mid-80s, which confined him to a wheelchair and crutches for life, but a more determined Leeds United fan you will not find anywhere. With a sense of humour that could slice you in two, Stu, who is affectionately referred to as 'Sticks', has overcome every obstacle in front of him. That was until he was entrusted into the care of Richard Watson and me for this particular trip to Norway. In many ways, Stavanger is a smaller version of Whitby, on the north Yorkshire coast. It has very steep hills sloping down towards the sea and as fate would have it, our hotel in Stavanger was perched right at the very top of one of those hills. More importantly though, both Whitby and Stavanger have bars and pubs dotted along the seafront and little harbour bays. There are also small, secluded marinas, and one evening at around 1am, we were just chilling outside a bar on one of those marinas. Dozens of little boats were all moored up for the night all around the marina as we chatted away and had another nightcap. A group of Norwegian

Leeds fans turned up in a camper van and joined us at our table and they had a ghetto blaster that was the size of an average family car. Our hosts at the bar clearly wanted to close, but to their utmost credit they kept giving us more beer. The ghetto blaster was belting out Leeds United songs, which we were happily singing along to, oblivious of the need to quieten things down, so we agreed to try and wrap things up. 'Shall we just have another?' Ralph said. 'No! Go home please!' a voice said through the closed curtains of a nearby boat. So we went home.

In Stavanger at the same time as us were Birmingham City. Both clubs were playing the same team, IF Stavanger. Birmingham at that time were in the Premier League, while Leeds were in the Championship. A couple of years later, we would widen the gap between our clubs even further by dropping into League One. Birmingham had around 50 fans in Stavanger; Leeds had in the region of 600. One afternoon, our fans were basking in the glorious sunshine sampling a couple of expensive beers. As I've mentioned in previous volumes, we always try to strike a deal with the bar owners in Norway. It's a simple proposal really: not many people turn out in Norway during the week; we're usually here for the week, so we ask the owner to drop the price of a pint and in return we promise to come in every night for a week – at least upwards of 50 of us at any given time. Every bar we have ever asked to do this has agreed – except one. And that was in Stavanger. This particular landlord said he couldn't conform to our proposal of a discount, so we wished him well before going to the next bar a few yards up the road. And after agreeing 'terms and conditions' this became our 'local' for the duration of our stay. We had only been in our local no more than a couple of hours when a blackboard appeared outside the bar who had refused our discount announcing, 'Leeds fans welcome here for cheaper beer!'

As aforementioned, Sticks was basically in the care of Rich and me and, normally of course, that wouldn't be a problem. After our hotel breakfast of rolled herrings, boiled ham and eggs, brown cheese and other slices of rubber-like cheese with big holes in it, we would descend on the seafront bars and go about our usual business of wrapping ourselves around one or two cold Norwegian beers. We were watching some cricket from back home in a bar when it was reported that Stu had become involved in a fracas with a Wolves fan – a Norwegian Wolves fan. Although this Wolves fan was able-bodied he wanted to have a go at Stu, who had been winding him up – which is what he does best. Not that this stopped Stu from confronting the fan, driving into him in his wheelchair and trying to take a swing at him, before the fan was ushered away by a couple of friends. On the domestic front, Stuart has often clashed with opposition fans in wheelchairs, conjuring up a scene like something from TV's *Robot Wars*.

As the Wolves fan went off in one direction, Rich and I shoved Stu off the opposite way, to another bar across some railway tracks. But, just as we were taking him across the track, one of his wheels got stuck. A couple of attempts to free Stu and the chair proved futile and with a train coming from not too far away we had to act fast. The train wasn't moving at any great speed, but it was a bloody big train. After a couple of attempts, I said, 'Right Stu, we'll have another go to free the chair up and then we'll have to get you out of there pretty quick.' Luckily, we freed the chair, and Stu, just in time for the large cargo train to trundle past at about 3mph and honking his horn. We retired to a bar and ordered three large whiskies – which came to about 50 quid!

Later that afternoon, a large number of Leeds fans were sunning themselves outside a seafront bar and with the beer flowing nicely, someone spotted the Birmingham City manager inside the bar. Steve Bruce had sampled a few beers, naturally, and was happily chatting away to the Leeds fans when a few of the Birmingham team strolled by outside. 'Fuckin' 'ell it's not often we see you stood up!' shouted one Leeds fan to Darren Anderton, and just as Emile Heskey was laughing, another fan shouted to him, 'You neither mate – you diving bastard!' By now, everyone, fans and players alike were laughing and the atmosphere was good.

Meanwhile, Steve Bruce had told one of our lads, 'We're a big team, but Leeds are a much bigger club, and I'd willingly walk to Leeds tomorrow to be the manager there.' Okay, that's easy to say when you're surrounded by maybe 200 Leeds fans having loads of beers – but many around him felt that he meant what he said. The atmosphere was really rocking with loud music pounding out of the bars and sunset came and went with no sign of a let-up in proceedings. We spent the final hours of the evening in our local, dancing to loud ska music with a mob of Birmingham fans, who, we were informed by Mick Garner, were the main hooligan element from St Andrew's. Mick had seen them at many of the England games. But for tonight at least, hostilities were put aside as we lapped up everything that the DJ threw at us.

The price for a pint with our negotiations was around £3 which was about half of the normal price, but the place was always busy with Leeds fans, so everybody wins as they say. It was soon time to make our way back up the steepest hill in the world and Rich and myself panted and wheezed as we slowly pushed Stu, puffing away on his cigarette without a care in the world, back up the hill with our arms outstretched and our bellies a mere four or five inches from the ground. 'Are you comfy there Stu?' Rich enquired sarcastically. Seriously out of breath at one point, we had to stop and refill our lungs. We were about halfway up the hill and reckoned that after a ten-minute break we'd have Stu up to the top in no time. What we didn't reckon with, however, was forgetting to put the brakes on the chair. The next moment, Stu was whizzing back down the hill with Rich and I in hot pursuit. Stu was like some sort of 'Turbo Ironside' – his trusty Leeds scarf was sticking out at a right angle and his baseball cap askew. Stu somehow managed to keep his cig in his mouth, which was now roaring away like a furnace. Then by pure luck, the chair turned itself into a drive and came to a halt. Although clearly trying to remain brave, Stu was trembling slightly when we arrived at the now stationary wheelchair. I can't remember a word being spoken between the three of us as we resumed our uphill marathon back to the hotel. I don't know if it was just my imagination or maybe I was reading too much into it, but Stu did appear to stay clear of both Rich and me for much of the rest of the trip. In fact, he physically jumped when I greeted him from behind with a tap on the shoulder one afternoon in town.

The day after our wheelchair calamity was a free day, so we did what every normal tourist does, we sampled the local brew. We watched a live cricket match between England and Australia in a sports bar and after a beer or two I entertained Andy and Annette with my dance version to 'People are Strange' by The Doors which emanated from the jukebox. Later, about a dozen of us wound up in our local and the landlord greeted us happily. We had been sat in there for about an hour when six or seven Birmingham fans walked in. They ordered their beer but were aghast when the landlord asked for the full price, which was over £6 a pint. 'No mate,' one of them said in a broad Brummie accent, 'we want Leeds prices?' he asked. 'Oh, I'm sorry,' said the landlord, 'I didn't know you were Leeds United fans.' To which another of the Brummie lads exclaimed, 'We are today mate!'

Leeds beat IF Stavanger 2-0 with goals from one of our own Norwegians – Eirik Bakke – and a second by Matthew

Spring. The other game on this tour saw Leeds go down to a 1-0 defeat at Haugesund on the west coast of Norway – a seven-hour coach trip inland takes you to Oslo and it was near here that we hooked up with a good friend and Leeds fan, Eirik Sveen. Eirik has also known Stu for a number of years and he took us to see the iconic Holmenkollen ski resort which with a capacity of 70,000 hosted the 1952 Olympics as well as several World Championships and World Cups.

Eirik, Rich and I were soon scaling the long ladder inside of the huge ski jump tower from which all those Olympians took flight in those Games. Stu, perhaps quite understandably, chose to remain on the ground and kept a good distance from Rich and myself.

Probably just as well, because it wasn't long before Rich and me were larking about at the very top of the tower. It truly was a daunting sight looking down the long slope, which descended into the large arena below. It wasn't hard to imagine the adrenalin pumping through the thousands of skiers that have passed this way before us. Although it was summer and there was no snow, we asked the attendant if we could go down the slope on a bin liner to which he replied, not surprisingly, 'No'.

This trip came to an end far too quickly for me, although not perhaps for our Sticks. Stu had begun to come around a bit and we chatted over a few cans on the coach trip back to Leeds and phoned a taxi to be waiting for us when we arrived. As Jeff and Rich got off to go get the taxi, Stu allowed himself into my care once again. As we came to the kerb, I completely misjudged the height of the step and within seconds, Stu was lying helplessly in the middle of the road looking like a Guy Fawkes dummy. A bewildered driver in his little Nissan peered over his bonnet as I scooped Sticks back into his chair. It has taken many years for me to get Stu's trust back.

Aside from the fact that it is hellishly expensive, I enjoy our trips to Scandinavia. It's always clean and you can guarantee that there is always a Leeds fan close by. Norwegian folk, in general, seem to enjoy killing whales and other sea creatures. Almost without exception every hotel I have ever stayed in has had some reference to the savagery and the brutal killing. Some more gory than others, the more refined modern-day hotels tend to have discreet framed prints placed strategically around the reception and mezzanine areas whereas the older, more traditional, wooden type hotels, go for the more 'in your face' look and openly display huge delightful whaling weapons such as harpoons, guns, lances, ropes and crossbows. One hotel we stayed in high up in the mountains had an enormous one-ton harpoon shooter on a swivel. The 'authentic blood' on the end of the huge harpoon had to be touched up every so often by the maintenance man with red paint. I suppose worse things happen at sea...or maybe not.

Luckily, many whales do survive the savagery. On one tour sometime in the late 90s we found ourselves in the very far north of Norway where it never gets dark in mid-summer and the sun and moon fight for superiority throughout the clear night. Wub and I sat peacefully on our wooden veranda gazing up at the simultaneous sunset and moonrise. I sat on my chair tilted back to take in the full spectacle as I sipped on several cool Jager-tonics for what seemed endless hours. With the waves crashing majestically over the rocks and whales breeching the sea I gazed across at Wub, who was so happy and content reading her book, and smiled. It was about then that I slowly closed my eyes and suddenly saw my flip-flops fly over my head as my chair fell backwards and with legs and arms akimbo, I was catapulted into the cabin wall before falling fast asleep in a drunken heap.

It was a game against SK Brann in 2010 that threw up a bit of a challenge for the travelling fans when Leeds played there. We had initially flown to the capital of Norway for a game against Lyn Oslo, who were managed by former Leeds player Gunnar Halle. But that game was cancelled at the last minute because of financial difficulties that were threatening Lyn with bankruptcy. A hastily arranged game against SK Brann in Bergen was scheduled for the following night. This created a major problem for our organiser Big Mick; Bergen is over 300 miles from Oslo and the hotel in Oslo was refusing to refund our money. We had a hotel for two nights in Oslo, but we now had to stay in a hotel in Bergen, as it would be impossible to return to Oslo after the game in Bergen. In effect, we had to pay for three nights but only stayed for two. Under other circumstances, we could have understood the difficulties of having booked two nights, but we were using the same hotel chain in Bergen as in Oslo – Radisson Blu. We couldn't understand why they couldn't just transfer the rooms. Add the cost of travel getting to Bergen and it incurs extra expense on top of an already expensive trip. But we had no choice and duly arrived in Bergen mid-afternoon, a good five hours before kick-off. The sports bar that we were in was full of around 500 supporters, the vast majority in Leeds colours, and most of them Norwegian.

A very special guest dropped in as we enjoyed a glass or two of very expensive lager. It was Eirik Bakke, a massive favourite with the fans during his seven years at Elland Road; he now played for SK Brann but would not be turning out tonight. One former Leeds player who would be playing for Brann was our former Icelandic star, Gylfi Einarsson. Before he left, Bakke paid for everyone in the club to have a beer – it would have cost him an absolute fortune, but it was a terrific gesture all the same.

We were disappointed to discover that there were no bars around the ground, so we promptly put 'Plan B' into operation. Basher and me headed for a local house in search of beer. We arrived at one such house where a man was standing on his veranda. 'Hello,' I shouted up, 'can we buy some beer from you?' Our friend from Oslo, Eirik Sveen was with us, and him and his mate Hakon Sarnblom took over the dialogue and we left with a large carrier bag full of beers, at no charge. I love these Norwegians.

We returned to our group with the booty and I, along with Tel, Jonathon, Bob, Andy, Ian, Rich and Basher, who by now was wearing his horse's head, sat in the nearby playground for kids, sitting on swings and slides drinking bottles of beer. Leeds won the game fairly easily 3-1, with two goals from Luciano Becchio and one from Lloyd Sam, but it was a horrific challenge on Robert Snodgrass that grabbed the headlines. Snodgrass had to be stretchered off after David Nielsen launched what could only be described as a savage attack.

We had to leave fairly early next morning to catch a late afternoon flight from Oslo back to Leeds, but I'd had a word with Basher on how we could exact some sort of revenge for the way we had been treated by the Radisson – it was still rankling with our party. When we arrived in Oslo, we all went back into the hotel and asked for our room key card. The receptionist was stunned. 'I'm sorry,' she explained, 'they've all been cleaned ready for the next guest.' I walked to the counter, 'We still have our rooms that we paid for until 1pm, could I have the card for 578 please?' She had to reluctantly hand back about a dozen cards. We all then enjoyed a shower and an hour's chill, before handing back our keys. It seems a petty thing to do I know, but if they had been right with us, then we would have been right with them and they wouldn't now have over two dozen wet bath towels to wash all over again, to clean all the steamed-up mirrors and make all the beds again that we had been lying on for an hour.

Our next visit to Norway was an extremely sad time.

On 22 July 2011, Oslo was devastated by two horrific attacks. First a car bomb was detonated in the business centre killing eight people and injuring over 200. The perpetrator was a 32-year-old right-wing extremist called Anders Behring Breivik. Just over an hour after the car bomb, Breivik boarded a ferry to the island of Uteya, 40 miles north-west of Oslo where a gathering of over 500 people, mainly in their teens and early 20s, were attending a camp organised by the youth division of the Norwegian Labour party. Breivik was dressed in a homemade police uniform and was carrying fake ID and an illegal police badge that he had purchased on the internet. He had assumed the name Martin Nilsen from the Oslo Police Department. Breivik told the camp leader Monica Bosel that he was investigating the car bombing, to which she became suspicious and summoned the security officer for the island, Trond Bernsten.

Within minutes they had both been gunned down and killed by Breivik who then began indiscriminately opening fire. A little over an hour later, 69 people were dead and 66 had been wounded. The police operation was slow and drew much criticism, but Breivik was eventually overpowered and forced to surrender. He was eventually sentenced to 21 years in prison, with allowance to increase the sentence if necessary.

Four days after the massacre, we arrived in Sandefjord for a Leeds game.

Understandably, there had been calls for the Leeds game to be cancelled, but overall the general consensus was to get on with normal life as soon as possible. The whole country was still in mourning and congregations and marches were organised all across Norway. One such march, 'Rose March' as it became known, came past our hotel the first evening we were there. We watched in complete silence as hundreds of men, women, children and their dogs filed past carrying flowers and candles in the pouring rain.

As our coach arrived at the ground the following day, I noticed Tore Pedersen doing a TV interview. When he'd finished he came over to have a chat and told me that he was to deliver a speech in memory of those who had lost their lives on Uteya after the minute's silence before the game. These were the words that he addressed the crowd with:

'The last few days have been the most unreal, bizarre and shocking nightmare for me as it has for you. But mostly for the victims and their families. Our deepest and warmest thoughts are with **them.** The news of Friday's attack on Oslo and the Labour summer camp massacre has now reached all corners of the world. The eyes of the world are upon us for reasons that never should have existed. Acts of pure evil. It didn't take long before messages arrived from Britain, America, Africa and Australia full of warm thoughts, sympathy and compassion.

'Everyone who lives in a democracy felt that this was an attack on them. And it was.

'I attended the mass assembly in Oslo last night along with about 200,000 others, to tell the world that terror shall never prevail. Therefore, I am massively impressed and proud of the club I love and am here to support. Despite the horrible events four days ago, Leeds United and their fans chose to carry on with their trip to Norway. To me they have thus told the whole world with their presence here one thing: "If we lay down our lives and let the fear and horror reign, terrorism wins. **We will not allow this to happen.**" We are proud and lucky to be Norwegian. You are proud and lucky to be British. Today we are all proud to be fellow human beings. But mostly we should be proud and lucky to be part of a democracy that provides freedom so that we can all walk freely, have freedom of speech, a right to vote and support the team of choice.

'Do not forget that we are fragile individuals, but together we are strong as long as we look out for each other.

No matter what colours we wear or are – the last few days have told us that. This is also why the official anthem of Leeds United has taken on a whole new meaning:

'We are *MARCHING ON TOGETHER* stronger than ever. Let us appreciate and use this freedom we are blessed with, and enjoy this friendly game. The recent reminder of what's important in life puts football in another perspective. But it is still such a big part of our lives, so let us make an effort and put it to even better use. Thank you, Leeds United, for doing the right thing in such hard and demanding times.'

Our friend and regular troops' entertainer, Øyvind Bratlie Skaare had also composed a moving tribute. These were his poignant words that he delivered to Leeds fans in a large square in the town during the early evening after the game.

'Leeds United and the considerable amount of supporters from overseas must have arrived here in Norway with a certain amount of tension for this pre-season game against Sandefjord, due to the recent attacks so close to where it was to be played the very next day. When finally here, I believe you all met an emotionally stunned and unusually calm and reserved Norwegian group of the Leeds United Family. I can tell you there were none of us attending the game that was unmarked by the incident. In order to try and give you all an insight of our emotional state at the time, we strongly felt a few words of honour and gratitude was in order. To Leeds United Football Club as well as to our fellow visiting supporters.

'We were all mighty impressed that every single one of you defied the means of terror just by coming.

'On behalf of LUSCOS I thank you all for coming to Norway, we really appreciated that you chose to spend time with your fellow supporters in times like these. We hope you all have had a good time, a rewarding visit, and to see you back here again sometime soon.'

The game as expected was a non-event really, but for the record – Nunez scored in the final minute to earn Leeds a 1-1 draw.

We returned to Sandefjord the following summer and it was a much better and more relaxed occasion. It had also been revealed that two LUSCOS members had each paid £16,500 out of their own pocket to bring the Leeds team to Sandefjord.

We arrived at the same hotel as before and headed straight for the bar. Unusually, for a hotel bar, this was the cheapest bar in town, and with the greatest respect, one look at the clientele confirmed it. These were my kind of people and we were quickly chatting away like friends reunited. One particular customer took a shine to me and I have to say, with our long straggly greying hair and beards, we weren't exactly chalk and cheese. Dubbed Santa Claus by our lot, he told us he was an American who has lived here for over ten years. I think him and I had our photographs taken together more than any of the players. That afternoon a fellow traveller from the 1970s (by that I mean he used to go to matches in the 70s, not that he arrived by time machine from the 70s) arrived at the bar. Gary Noble and I were inseparable as we trawled Europe watching the great Revie side. Gaz was with another mate of mine, Paul Taylor, who is the landlord of the Boot Room pub directly across the road from the Castleford Rugby League ground. We were now set for a little pub crawl around town, and wasted no time in getting started.

Just around the corner from the hotel is an Irish bar called Scruffy Murphy's. The landlord is a West Bromwich Albion supporter and immediately slashed his price of £8 a pint to £5 for the duration of our stay, just as he had done the previous year. And once again, he was prepared for us and had even plied the jukebox with a generous supply of Leeds United records – Leeds pennants and scarves adorned the walls. A steady influx of Leeds fans began to arrive from England, Norway and all over Scandinavia and the following afternoon, pre-match entertainment began in earnest. It was a glorious day and with Leeds flags draped all around the perimeter of the beer garden and aided by a DJ playing continuous Leeds songs, the feeling was one of sheer joy, much in contrast to the sad events of our last visit. I noticed 'Santa Claus' walk by at one point and he sat in a vacant chair adjoining Scruffy Murphy's watching events unfold and smiling to himself. He wallowed in the attention he was receiving from some Leeds fans who had met him along the way and I didn't see him turn down any offers of a drink. I passed the afternoon with old friends Baz and Mark and shared a drink or two with Geir Magne Fjellseth and his son John.

Geir loves his English music and his affection for Status Quo is almost on a par with his love of Leeds United – almost. Cato Visdal Mikalsen, who, like our very own Norwegian White Rose member Kjell Skjerven, moved to Leeds to be closer to his heroes, brought a trayful of the customary Jagermeister which we tucked away nicely as Geir Wang followed that up with another full tray. We were grateful for a steady supply of beer filtering through from our old friends, Rune Roalsvig and Rune Reitan. Terje Hansen is certainly worthy of note – he has recently completed 150 consecutive Leeds games, making each journey from Norway. One comedy moment was when, as we stood talking in the sunshine, Boot Room Paul momentarily closed his eyes and fell over. He had endured a long journey here, having to travel across to Liverpool for a last-minute flight where he met Gaz Noble, and then a bus ride from the airport. That and the sun and ale had taken its toll; however, after his very brief catnap he was okay. This game also ended 1-1 with Leeds taking the lead this time through a goal by Jason Pearce.

Apart from Oslo, the airports tend to be quite small and Sandefjord was no exception. As we arrived in the first small bar/cafe I reminded Rich Watson of our last visit here. We had noticed the Leeds squad sat there; the players these days sadly don't tend to mix with fans, preferring the sanctuary of their iPods and gigantic headphones. It is common knowledge that you are getting old when you attend more funerals than you used to and the coppers look about 12 years old, but when you meet a present-day player and he is the same size in real life as he appears from the back row in the top of the East Stand at Elland Road, then you are definitely heading towards the pipe and slippers. Manager Simon Grayson and his sidekick Glynn Snodin were there and came over for a chat.

I had got to know these two quite well over the years and they are on the same wavelength as most of us. Snodin went to get a cup of tea, and he said to me, 'Want a drink Gaz?' 'Yeah mate,' I replied, 'I'll have a beer please,' I winked at Grayson. 'No problem, pal,' said Snodin and he ordered me a beer along with his tea. When the assistant behind the counter gave him the total, Snodin exclaimed, 'How much?' She repeated the total. 'How much is the beer?' Snodin asked, and when she told him he nearly fainted. It was £11 a pint. With Simon and me still smiling, Snodin put my pint down in front of me, 'Here Gaz, I hope it fuckin' chokes yer pal,' he laughed.

The beer had gone up even more than the previous year as we had our final beer in O'Leary's Irish bar close to the check-in desks. As is custom, we all put what change we had on the table to get rid of it and everyone gets a drink (Norway are not in the Euro so people tend to offload their Norwegian Kronas before returning, putting the leftovers in the large charity glass bubbles in the airport). I managed another expensive pint (£10) and a quick chat with Eddie Kelly in the airport before we boarded our flight home.

The Norwegians are indeed a hardy bunch, and one of them once ate himself. Twenty-five-year-old Alexander Selvik Wengshoel was born with a deformed hip and after years of waiting for an operation to have the hip removed the day finally arrived and Alexander even received permission to have the whole procedure filmed. But he then went one step further and took the hip bone home with him and whilst his girlfriend was at work, he took it into the kitchen. He then proceeded to pan fry the bone with chilli and garlic. He then scraped the meat on to a plate and along with a nice potato gratin and a cheeky glass of wine he ate his meal under candlelight. He later described the occasion as 'romantic'.

Chapter 7

Free Wales

The French:
'We have been, we are, and I trust we always will be, detested by the French'

Duke of Wellington.

During the Second World War, a train was bombed by the Germans close to Dieppe harbour in France. Flight Lieutenant Frank Carey: 'We did what we could to save the seriously wounded and move them into the part of the train that wasn't burning. The walking wounded then disconnected the burning part of the train. The French driver had already unhooked his engine and disappeared.'

General Patton, US General, 1945, 'I would rather have a German division in front of me than a French one behind me.'

'In Paris they simply stared when I spoke to them in French. I never did succeed in making those idiots understand their own language.'

Mark Twain, 1908.

Fougeret de Montbron, French writer: 'The English pay us the compliment of hating us as ferociously as possible.' 1743.

'You must consider every man your enemy who speaks ill of your king; and you must hate a Frenchman as you hate the devil.'

Nelson, 1799.

'All the English will be booted out of France, except those who will die here.'

Joan of Arc, 1419.

The Welsh:
Leeds fans live in Wales in huge numbers and Leeds United are one of the best-supported English clubs in that country. Unfortunately, like the French, a large proportion of the population of Wales appear not to like the English, thus meaning that these two nations are very much alike.

So with this Welsh/French problem in mind I have devised a little theory on how we could resolve this to suit all parties and in doing so, help the Welsh economy, saving it from financial ruin by it simply not existing. It's nothing serious you understand – in fact in the words of that brilliant Welsh comic Rob Brydon, 'It's just a bit of fun.'

As the French and the Welsh are very much alike, the idea, as with all brilliant ideas, is simple; sever Wales from England by means of a chainsaw and then place a plank under it and back-flip it across into France. That's the theory; but in practice of course, it would be much more difficult.

So I began making notes and sketches on bits of paper with a view to placing the French and the Welsh together to cohabit as one. Their language is very similar – I for one can't speak either of them. Breton is the name of the language that has previously been spoken by both the Welsh and the French. It is a language brought to Armorica, an ancient French region, by migrating Britons during the early Middle Ages and is closely related to the Welsh language. Interestingly, the Welsh Language Society was formed in 1962 with the intention of promoting the speaking of predominantly Welsh and starting in the early 70s, protesters actively tore down English-only road signs within Wales. The first recorded activity instigated by the Welsh language Society was in Aberystwyth where my mate John, a fellow Leeds United season ticket holder, lives. Breton is a Brittonic language and is now in serious decline, but with the union of these two countries, France and Wales, it is not beyond the realms of possibility that it could be revived in due course.

So, with the language barrier effectively solved, I began to leaf through the 'Hire Shop' section of the Yellow Pages. The first item on my list was a chainsaw and then some sort of staging or large sturdy plank. The Wales Coast Road, which is also the Wales/England border, stretches 870 miles and the distance down to the earth's core is around 20 miles. The world's largest and most powerful chainsaws are mostly powered by V8 engines, and would probably be just about powerful enough, but the two largest blades in the world consist of a circular blade with a 30ft radius and a more conventionally shaped blade which is 30ft in length and has multiple 2ft galvanised teeth and measures 7ft from top to bottom. Either of these awesome machines would have to be slightly adapted to saw off Wales, but the fact that they are both built into a tractor-type body and run on ten-wheel caterpillar tracks would indeed be an advantage.

When I rang to enquire about a chainsaw with a 30ft long blade, the first hire shop hung up. Then I received an email from one particular hire firm suggesting that I should consult a heavy machinery specialist company. However, even if the actual sawing was successful, I would have to devise some type of method whereby a staging plank could be slid underneath what would become the adrift country of Wales, in order to back-flip it over into France before it drifted too far out into the Irish Sea. Rope, similar to those that tether large ocean liners once they are moored, would suffice once it had been strengthened sufficiently. I did in fact play around with the idea of using some form of large, slow moving guillotine, in keeping with the French scheme, to somehow cut away at the surface, but then I remembered that the guillotine, contrary to popular belief, is not a French invention; it was in fact invented in Yorkshire – Halifax to be precise. It was called the Halifax Gibbet and was a sturdy, stocky beast. It had a large wooden block about 5ft long and 1ft thick that held an axe blade like a single tooth. This block was raised 15ft in the air between two wooden posts, before being allowed to drop on to the victim.

Meanwhile, I had been working on a column, which would be needed as the pivotal point of a see-saw kind of manoeuvre essential to the plan. The column itself would have to be built from steel-reinforced concrete and would tower over three miles above ground level and the positioning of the plank on top of it would be crucial. Too near to the south coast and over three million Welsh migrants could find themselves in the middle of the Sahara Desert. Too far inland, it would malfunction and they wouldn't clear England, thus causing all sorts of problems in and around Dorchester.

After several days of intensive research, the small town of Midsomer Norton, just a few miles south-west of Bath and the very town that gave us Anita Harris, was chosen as the perfect location for the construction of the concrete column. So with the minimum disruption possible, groundwork would begin in the centre of the town in readiness for the erection of the column. With safety the utmost priority, a ladder would have to be strong enough, high enough and sturdy enough to scale the concrete column. In the meantime, tenders would be invited from contractors to build a 250 square mile, totally reinforced safety net to go under the 'plank' and cover the entire length and breadth of the proposed operation.

In this case, the four corners of the net would be at Exeter then eastwards across to Southsea, then north to Swindon and then across westwards to Minehead. All neighbouring countries of France will be made fully aware of the impending operation and offered any assistance required and all such countries will be surrounded by extremely high fences to prevent any unfortunate overspill of Welsh people. All fences and subsequent precautions would have to be funded by the individual countries themselves.

Before the actual commencement of the operation, everyone living in Wales and France would have been notified by post of the proposed action and those not wanting to take part in this unprecedented occasion would each have been offered alternative arrangements – for instance; the Isle of Anglesey, being separate from mainland Wales, will not be making the journey to France and will be made available to anyone wishing to remain in the United Kingdom. Those wishing to 'travel' to France would each have received their very own information pack with final details along with specially constructed one size fits all Velcro suits and double-sided sticky pads to be used to secure themselves to a permanent structure before the whole of their country is flown across to the continent. The safety net would be absolutely essential to catch any dislodged entities falling from the jettisoned country of Wales, such as falling sheep, backpackers, or anyone else who hadn't read the information pack.

With the column in place in Midsomer Norton, work would begin on the highly dangerous operation of placing the 267-mile-long, half-of-a-mile-thick staging plank on top of the column and fixing it securely into place, using the toughest metal bolts available. Using a highly top-secret mechanism, the staging would now resemble a very large, somewhat off-balance see-saw.

Much of the south and south-west of England is home to thousands of Leeds United supporters and they would be invited to take part in a lottery competition to win the chance to jump on to the southern edge of the plank. The 2,178 lucky winners required would all have to be declared healthy and be medium- to well-built adults. They would also be required to wear heavy revolutionary lead boots. Fifty-nine children above the age of 16 could also be included but they would have to be supervised by a responsible adult and wear a safety hardhat and high-vis jacket at all times. For technical reasons, all aircraft in the area would have to be diverted or otherwise grounded for the duration. As the crow flies the distance from Wales to the southern part of England is less than 245 miles, therefore allowing the staging to ease under Wales ensuring the perfect amount of polarising required. Consequently, the northern end of the plank would stop underneath the small market town of Llanfyllin close to the junction of the A490 and the A495. The southern end of the plank would teeter over Puddletown just ten miles north of Weymouth.

It was around this stage of the preparations that I received a further email from one of the hire firms saying, 'Further to our recent email conversation, I have discussed this with certain colleagues from that particular industry and they have come up with several suggestions regarding a heavy duty chainsaw and subsequent power tools required. However, they have stated that a chainsaw in the region of over 30ft would be quite impossible. They are open to discussion regarding such a machine, possibly on tracks, but any form of hand held chainsaw of that magnitude is unfortunately out of the question. Please do not hesitate to contact us again if we can be of any further assistance. In the meantime, we wish you luck on your venture.'

Once Operation Leek-Frog was under way, there would be just one chance to get it right. Using a V8 tractor-powered Stihl 12-wheel turbo track system with a galvanised 37ft long and 16in wide steel blade sponsored by B&Q, a specialist team will begin sawing Wales off at a depth of 20 miles starting just a few miles north of the port of Queensferry in Flintshire and continue southwards along the 870-mile-long Coast Path to Chepstow at the southern tip of the border. An experienced support group of 20 will follow behind the chainsaw and using industrial rope and 6ft cast iron posts will tie the severed country of Wales temporarily to the 'new' western coast of England. A second, highly trained group will relieve the first team and continue on to Shrewsbury and beyond. Another highly trained group including many security forces will be in place at Chepstow and begin slowly and meticulously sliding the northern end of the staging under Llanfyllin. Once the plank has travelled the required distance through the loose core of the earth – and to protect the coastal areas of Bristol – a purpose-built steel bridge will enable the plank to sit on top of it thus giving the plank the required angle and at the same time protecting the citizens of Bristol and surrounding areas. The final preparations and any goodbyes between family members will then take place. The Bristol Channel and in particular the Mouth of the Severn will act as a perfect form of leverage once the plank is placed underneath Wales. Then the most important phone call of the entire operation will be made to the Chief of Operations at the Column HQ in Midsomer Norton and once official clearance is given, the countdown will commence. The lottery winners would then jump collectively from a tower specially constructed above the concrete column on to the southern end of the 'plank' and the whole of Wales will fly majestically over the

Bristol Channel, very close to where the English defeated the Spanish Armada in 1588. Precisely three hours and 34 minutes later the whole of Wales will land in France and all machinery must be returned within seven days to avoid further charges.

I don't mind the odd drop of wine, but I will not drink French wine. I won't drink Welsh wine either, and to my shame, I drink very little English wine. But this does not stop the arrogant French promoting their wine as the best in the world. The truth about French wine is eloquently told by an American soldier, Arthur Empey, who fought alongside British troops in 1915. 'Estaminet: A French public house or saloon, where muddy water is sold as beer. Vin Rouge: French wine made from vinegar and red ink. Vin Blanc: French wine made from vinegar without the red ink.'

Perhaps the most unpopular Prime Minister of France, and to date the only woman Prime Minister, was called Edith Cresson. Her reign was brief; it lasted as long as Leeds' 1992 league-winning season, during which she visited London. Angry that men weren't affording her the affection she craved, she announced that one in four Englishmen are gay. 'The Anglo-Saxons', she said at the time, 'are not interested in women. It is a problem with their upbringing – I think it's a sort of disease.' And the most famous French Prime Minister, Charles de Gaulle, fled to the safe confines of London during his country's occupation by the Germans during the Second World War.

Wales, on the other hand, will always remain a friend to England and of course they were our allies during the war helping raise the spirits of the English with early evidence of their famous musical talents, particularly when German paratroopers from the Rhine Valley began attacking parts of England very close to the southern coast of Wales. Not many people are aware of this, but it was from these air attacks that the Welsh composed that very famous song, 'Rhine troops are falling on Minehead'. And years later the defiant Cardiff City fans just across the Bristol Channel would add: 'But that doesn't mean our shirts will soon be turning red.' Although it did.

In a timely conclusion and to reiterate the closeness of these two nations, both did rather well in Euro 2016 in France (once the usual threats of strike by the French air and sea controllers were averted at the last minute). Wales reached the semi-final and their cohorts France were beaten in the final by a 'Ronaldo-less Portugal' and England were eliminated by the smallest team in the competition, Farm Foods. A result that saw Wales's players openly celebrating enthusiastically on camera.

However, I, and thousands upon thousands of Leeds fans the world over, will always be grateful to such legendary Welsh names linked to the history of Leeds United Football Club such as John Charles, John Reynolds, Harold Williams, Gary Speed, some would even say Gary Sprake, Carl Harris, Terry Yorath, Byron Stevenson, Brian Flynn, Gwyn Thomas and Dennis Hawkins.

But France remains an enemy. As does David Jones.

Chapter 8

Julie Andrews, Mozart and Jody Morris

OUR pre-season tour of 2015 saw us visit Salzburg in Austria. This was the very place where *The Sound of Music* was filmed in 1965 and even today images of Julie Andrews twirling about in some mountains are everywhere. As we travelled to our hotel with the characters from the famous musical emblazoned on the side of our coach, a spontaneous rendition of 'Doe, a deer, a female deer' was thankfully short-lived.

On my arrival at our triple room I threw my bag on a bed and headed for the bar. I was the first to return a few hours later and I flopped on to the first single bed and fell quickly asleep. I was soon awakened by one of the other lads who informed me that I was on his bed. I was just about to tell him that *Goldilocks and the Three Bears* wasn't a true story when he pointed to the side of the bed and to his machine and facemask for his sleep apnoea. I hopped off the bed and on to the next one. Next morning after a very humid night with no air conditioning, I glanced over at my first bed to be met by the sight of a large naked human body laid on his side on top of the bed.

I looked at the apnoea machine, which was still on the bedside table and thought to myself how uncomfortable it must be to have to wear that at night. I then noticed two fairly large holes on the right cheek of his arse. 'Christ!' I thought, 'He must have to plug something into his body as well.' and assumed that they were the plug holes. However, as I walked past him to get a shower, I couldn't resist another peak at the plug holes. It turned out that the 'holes' were two Euro coins that must have dropped out of his pocket when he took his shorts off and were now stuck firmly to his arse.

I had a look online at the reviews for our hotel in Salzburg beforehand, and I have to say they were not encouraging. 'The staff are efficient but not particularly friendly' said one and another read, 'The staff are rude and unhelpful.' Another one: 'The walls are really thin so you get to know your neighbours, especially at night when they return yodelling like hell.' One thing that did arise throughout the reviews was the mention of the owner and his wife and the name 'Basil Fawlty' was prominent. We met 'Basil' at our first breakfast and Robbo had told us that he had got the very last room at the hotel and it certainly was busy in the dining room, but Basil didn't like guests, not one bit. And because some of them came down after 9am (the breakfast time was up till 9.30) he became abusive and as sweat poured down his forehead and on to his glasses, he stormed off into the kitchen to roll out some more ham and cheese and refill the coffee pots. A constant stream of more guests got Basil so hot under the collar that he and his wife were falling out each time they crossed each other in and out of the kitchen and plates were thrown, and broken, along with cups and the odd glass.

Later that evening, Big Tony and myself found ourselves in a rather intimate male-only bar, which after a couple of quick stiff drinks we vacated and walked a little further on. As we passed an innocuous-looking doorway, a welcoming and engaging sound of compelling jazz music leapt out at us and dragged us through the door and down the steps to be met by a brilliant jazz set being played on a small stage. We were the last two to leave in the wee small hours. Next morning at breakfast it was disappointing that Basil and his wife seemed more relaxed, and as a consequence, much less entertaining. But there was some form of entertainment at the match later that day against Eintracht Frankfurt. The stadium itself was only a small sports complex and there were only two bars close to the ground, but we managed to soldier on nevertheless. Once inside the ground, I had a beer with Mark Dovey and his son Danny and Liam Cork from Sherburn, who I'd first met a couple of years earlier at Sherburn Youth Club while helping Wub with her new career as a volunteer.

Close to the bar in the stadium was a gymnasium, and inside were around a hundred armed riot police marching up and down in readiness for the Frankfurt Ultras who were thought to be heading to the stadium to confront the Leeds fans. As we drank ice cold beer in the sunshine, Jimmy and Wayne suddenly said, 'They're here!' and hurried towards the gate where about a hundred Ultras, some wearing balaclavas and carrying chains, had forced entry. After tearing down a couple of Leeds flags they were chased across the pitch by dozens of Leeds fans, many with large beer bellies, and out of the ground.

One Leeds fan on his own outside the ground had been attacked by the Ultras and left in a pile of blood, but thankfully he made a full recovery. As the Ultras were rounded up by the police and escorted away, we continued with our beers in the company of many other Frankfurt fans who were there for the same purpose as us – a football match and a few beers.

The following day we headed by coach to Vienna, the home of Mozart. The service stations, unlike at home, have bars in them; which is always a bonus in my book, so we called in at one. However, this particular bar wasn't really ready for 30 thirsty travellers all sitting at the bar with tongues hanging out on a burning hot sunny day. It took us some time as well to work out the system of how to pay for our beers. We were each given a small credit card type thing that was logged in with each purchase and then you had to pay on your way out as you passed through the shop on your way out of the services.

Vienna is recognised, of course, as a city of culture, but quite honestly there is only so much culture one can take of an evening. In fact, in one bar one of the younger lads of our party had said, quite innocently, 'So who's this twat Mozart then?' After a few drinks in a theatre bar we headed off further into town and to some 'proper' bars. Our final day saw us take in a river cruise, which was shit actually, and we then spent the entire afternoon in my 56th Hard Rock Cafe. Earlier on, Andy had been out for a stroll when a man jumped out of a bush and asked him for his credit card. Andy refused and the would-be attacker apologised and went on his way.

Our hotel had a nice little bar in it and we would wind down in there until it closed – our final night was no different. The usual host was there to greet us. We nicknamed him Fabian Delph (after yet another Leeds star to be jettisoned from the club) and although he didn't have a clue who we were talking about – he answered to 'Fabian' every time. He was a cheeky chap however; although the price of alcohol has generally dropped in Austria, whisky was still hellishly expensive in this hotel bar, but that didn't stop Fabian try to shift a few glasses at our expense.

'Which is your favourite whisky?' he would ask, to which I would reply 'Lagavulin'. He would then bring the bottle over and a glass. He did it every night, trying to get me to buy a glass. It is my favourite whisky but at around £12 a glass I stuck vigorously to beer – and my free samples of whisky. On this final night he was going through his usual routine.

This time he poured a few drops into the glass, 'For you,' he said. 'No charge.'

I drank it, and placed the glass back down on the bar. He then began to pour another glass. I asked if this was free also, to which he smiled and shook his head. After a brief stand-off, he poured it back into the bottle and pulled me another beer, still smiling.

At around half-two we finished our drinks off and most of the lads headed to their rooms; Big Tony, Dave and me sat in the large foyer area just chatting. It was then that I noticed three lads trying to open the locked glass doors to the bar. Fabian was still hanging around in reception and had to come across to tell them that it was closed. I had noticed these three in the bar earlier, but thought nothing of it. Despite being told it was closed they began pushing Fabian around and a large security guard came over to intervene. The three of them eventually sat down in another part of the foyer, not far from where we were sitting. It was then that I noticed one of them looking constantly over at Big Tony and saying something to the other two. He then came over and began shouting abuse at Tony, who isn't far off 70 years old, and threatening him with violence. Obviously fuelled by alcohol, the other two then joined him, with the largest one saying, 'There's three of them and three of us, come on!' The third one then joined in with the threats.

Chelsea's academy side had been playing in Vienna and were staying in our hotel. The players who we had seen knocking about the place in their tracksuits had behaved impeccably throughout – but we had no idea at the time that these three nutcases were with the club. It turned out that the tall one was the goalkeeping coach, Bill Thompson, and the one giving Tony a hard time was Joe Edwards, the under-18s manager. The third, surprise, surprise, was Jody Morris. None of us realised this at the time and sensing a hostile atmosphere and with one or two of the other Chelsea party loitering near the reception desk, I went to get some of the other lads. I couldn't wake Rich, who was rooming with me and the hotel was so large that I had no idea where the rest of our lot were, so I returned to the foyer on my own. When I arrived, Thompson had sent Edwards and Morris off to bed and Tony and Dave were talking calmly to Thompson and that was the end of it – until the next morning that is. Tony was waiting in reception very early the next morning as the Chelsea party were leaving, with Morris sheepishly walking out of the lift attempting to be incognito in the middle of a few Chelsea youngsters and began checking out. He spied Tony and muttered an apology but kept his head well down. Joe Edwards had slipped out totally unnoticed, and Bill Thompson was still doing his utmost to keep the peace. But this didn't prevent Tony standing outside the team's coach shouting and demanding that Morris faced him. I was still angry about this altercation when I arrived home and wrote to Chelsea's academy – not so much as a 'tell-tale' but had this behaviour been the other way around and Leeds United Football Club been involved, it would have made national news – there is no doubt about that.

I received this reply a few weeks later:

'Thank you for your letter to Chelsea Football Club.

We have been made aware of the incident that occurred in Austria. Although the staff were on a night off we acknowledge their behaviour is still reflective of the club.

We apologise for any inconvenience caused to members of your party, however I understand that both groups stayed and talked on the night after the argument and again spoke with each other the next morning resolving the matter.

We hope you enjoy the football season ahead.

Yours sincerely,

Hayley Prior

Operations Manager.'

We ourselves checked out a few hours later and flew to Oslo for the second match of the tour against Hoffenheim of Germany, but there was only one topic of conversation as the rest of our lot listened in total disbelief.

We wrapped up the tour with our Norwegian friends and regular faces. Øyvind was once again entertaining the troops with his guitar as hundreds of Leeds fans commandeered an outside bar close to the ground. Both English and Scandinavian Leeds fans sank gallons of ale as Leeds flags were draped all around the pub both inside and out and as usual I received many gifts of brown cheese, and it was also pleasing to see dozens of old Leeds United pictures in a sports bar later in Oslo centre, many of which dated back to the 1960s and 70s.

The scenery in Austria had been fantastic, but the backdrop to the tour in northern Italy the previous summer was just mind-blowing. Massimo Cellino had taken his newly acquired Leeds United on a pre-season tour of Val Gardena, and although the scenery was brilliant, the football was a joke. The first opponents FC Viitorul Constana didn't even turn up, forcing Leeds to field two teams and play against each other. It was also David Hockaday's first game in charge, more of him later. As Hockaday left to take charge of one of the Leeds teams, the Leeds fans split into two groups, one supporting the first 11 and the rest, us near the bar, supporting the second. At regular intervals the Leeds players would look across at the Leeds fans taunting each other: 'You're not singing anymore!' chanted the first-team fans at us, 'We'll see you all outside!' responded the second-team fans. Leeds' next opponents, Gherdeina, did turn up; sort of; with Leeds winning comfortably. Once again, Cellino came into the bar, but when the score got to 16-0 to Leeds with 20 minutes to go, Cellino rushed over to the Leeds bench. Within seconds, Leeds' new keeper Mirco Silvestre was put into the opposition's goal and all the Leeds strikers were taken from the field. We had just witnessed Cellino's superstition for the number 17 and his eccentricity first hand. Cellino came over to the fans again at the end and seemed puzzled that there were so many and of different nationalities, Irish, Norwegian, Italian and even Swiss were represented.

Two fans in particular had an eventful trip getting to the games. Thames Valley Whites members Simon Hyam and Perry Chance set off from High Wycombe and travelled by car, a Renault Megane, through France and Belgium before having their car nicked in Germany, and having to make the rest of the trip by train.

That night a lot of Leeds fans gathered in a bar to watch the World Cup Final. It was between Argentina and Germany which presented us with a very real problem of who to support. The only Leeds connection was that the Argentine manager was ex-Leeds favourite Alex Sabella in the early 80s. Sabella wasn't popular to begin with as he had replaced fan favourite Tony Currie, but his skills soon won the fans over. I remember Leeds' Brian Flynn saying, 'Allan Clarke came in as manager and Alex was seen as an unwanted luxury. I was once sat near Alex in the dressing room listening to Clarke talking when Alex said to me, "I have my own plan Brian, you run for the ball and then give it to me, you keep running and chase the ball and then give it back to me, easy plan eh Brian?" Sabella was the best player I've played with, he had balance, technique and great awareness.'

Meanwhile, in Val Gardena, that didn't prevent us reluctantly siding with the Germans as loud singing ensued, mainly along the lines of, 'Rule Britannia' and 'The Falklands is British'. All the time Kev Morgan was outside with others singing in the square with Leeds fans hanging flags and banners from anything from statues to shop canopies. Once the match had finished on telly, a German couple came over and thanked us for supporting Germany. 'A lesser of two evils love, that's all, don't get carried away,' I said, and with that the telly was turned off amidst German celebrations, and our own songs began in earnest led by Kev Howmuch from Ripon.

Chapter 9

Goats Stories

FOOTBALL mascots really make me laugh out loud. I don't quite know why this is exactly, but every time I see them clowning around and entertaining the crowd I think they are hilarious. It could have been because of the TV programme *It's a Knockout* that began airing in the mid-sixties but sadly is long defunct. I used to howl with laughter, as competitors would encounter oceans of water sprayed and thrown at them, greasy poles, giant custard pies and slippery roundabouts all whilst encased in ludicrous 12ft high gaily coloured foam rubber suits with a huge cartoon head atop. The infectious laughing coming from commentators Eddie Waring and Stuart Hall, both no longer with us, for one reason or another, would have tears streaming down my face. I also won my first ever school fancy dress competition dressed as Yogi Bear in around 1964.

I once met Ellie Elephant, the Leeds United mascot, in the late 1990s. Some people advise against meeting your heroes, but when I rubbed fur, shoulders and trunks with Ellie, I was far from disappointed. Not only that, when I was asked to switch on the Christmas lights in my village of Kippax a few years ago, I was flanked by none other than Lucas the Kop Cat. Again, apart from him/her having extremely thin legs, I wasn't disappointed. Once when I was working beneath the concourse in the East Stand carrying out some much needed decorating work with Paul Hockley and his team, Lucas came and held my ladders – he had brought Sam Byram along with him to hold my paint tin. I'll bet he doesn't get those same job opportunities now he's at West Ham...

In 2005, while Burnley were playing host to Preston North End, a streaker evaded capture from stewards and the police. As he ran away in another direction and taunting his pursuers, he was unaware that he was being chased by a bee. The crowd roared as the streaker was then brought to ground with a superb rugby tackle – executed perfectly by the club's gigantic furry mascot, Bertie Bee. However, Bertie himself would be the first to admit that he's not the most saintly of mascots, occasionally getting up to the odd bit of playful mischief here and there, but his antics pale into insignificance compared to some other, much more ruthless mascots.

The crowd at Bristol City's home game with Wolverhampton Wanderers in 1998 really saw the fur fly when Wolfie was attacked by City's Three Little Pigs on the pitch at half-time. The four furious characters huffed and puffed at each other and stewards then had to drag them apart. One steward even barged into the referees' dressing room asking for help.

But Paul Taylor simply said, 'What do you want me to do, show them the red card?' The pigs and the wolf were all severely disciplined by their respective clubs despite the pigs having nothing to do with Bristol City – they were representing a local double-glazing firm – and Wolfie was also on probation after he had started a fight with West Brom's Baggie Bird earlier in the season.

One famous mascot that everyone remembers is Cyril the Swan at Swansea. He once even brought out his own Christmas CD, a solo number called 'Nice Swan Cyril'. Despite him being a mute swan, it sold out – in the club shop. But he too was never far away from controversy. In 1999 he was involved in what some onlookers described as a 'friendly jostle' on the pitch with Millwall's Zampa the Lion. Friendly or not, Zampa's head ended up being hurled into the crowd. More trouble was to come for Cyril, however, and when he ran on to the pitch to celebrate one of Swansea's six goals, the referee took exception and Cyril was reported to the Welsh FA. At the subsequent WFA hearing, Cyril sat silently in the dock to face the three-man commission. He was supported by his chairman who had to interpret the swan's body language to the commission – who were unimpressed and duly handed Cyril a touchline ban and fined the club £1,000. The media gathered in their masses outside, but Cyril had 'no comment' to make.

Chaddy the Owl, the Oldham Athletic mascot, has won the prestigious Mascot Grand National twice, but in reality he's a very naughty mascot.

In 2003, Chaddy 'kicked ten bells' out of Bloomfield Bear before stealing his boots and tossing them into the crowd. Blackpool Football Club insisted that the owl be banned for the return league game at Blackpool – but Chaddy has always maintained that Bloomfield started it. Two years earlier, Chaddy caused controversy when he was shown the red card in a match against Peterborough United. The linesman repeatedly mistook Chaddy for a player and kept flagging him offside. Admittedly, Chaddy was wearing Oldham's colours – but he was also wearing a gigantic furry owl's head with a large beak and had eyes the size of saucers.

During one game at Huddersfield, someone threw a pie at Chaddy, so, for a laugh, he threw it back at him. The Huddersfield fan then threatened Chaddy with a knife.

'I quickly backed off when I saw he was serious,' said the shaken owl.

Mascotting is a serious business. Spurs fans shunned their very own Chirpy the Cockerel after he dared to shake hands with Arsenal's Gunnersaurus during their FA Cup semi-final clash in 2001.

Deepdale Duck holds the dubious honour of being the first mascot to be sent off in English football. He had to be dragged from the pitch and was later issued with a warning from the Football League. In 1997, he angered Blackburn keeper, Tim Flowers, by leaning on his goalpost during a league cup tie. A couple of days later, Sheffield's Captain Blade staged an on-field protest in support of his fellow mascot.

Everton even banned Deepdale Duck from an FA Cup match at Goodison Park in 2000, fearing that he would incite a riot.

Fulham's Billy the Badger caused a stir at Craven Cottage in January 2008 when he annoyed Chelsea manager Avram Grant by hugging him after Fulham had scored, and a month later his breakdance routine delayed the second half against Aston Villa, forcing referee Chris Foy to lead him from the field.

In 2001, it took seven stewards to break up a pitch-side punch-up between Cardiff mascot Bartley the Bluebird and Robbie the Bobbie at Bury. Bartley, a 7ft furry bluebird with a yellow beak, threw a punch at Robbie who had donned boxing gloves but didn't see the punch coming. Robbie said, 'It wasn't my fault. I was just having a bit of a laugh when I was punched in the face. I wasn't going to take it lying down so we had a bit of a scrap.' Both mascots were ejected from the ground for fear of inciting a riot between fans.

But Robbie the Bobbie has form. He has been dismissed from the field of play for mooning at the Bristol City fans and then belly-flopping in front of them. He did the same to

Stoke City fans and had a fight with Peterborough's rabbit, Peter Burrow, who consequently lost his 2ft-long ears in the melee. Robbie has also been escorted from the ground by two police officers after constantly mimicking a linesman.

It's fair to say that the majority of mascots don't really represent the history of the club or their town or city, but that cannot be said of the famous mascot at Hartlepool United.

H'Angus the Monkey is steeped in history. During the Napoleonic Wars in 1815, the people of Hartlepool found a monkey on the beach. He was the sole survivor of a nearby shipwreck, but the locals dragged the poor monkey away and hanged it, thinking that it was a French spy.

Meanwhile H'Angus the Monkey was running wild; he was ejected from Scunthorpe United for making lewd gestures behind a female steward and ejected at Blackpool for taking an inflatable doll into the ground. Then, in 2002, H'Angus was duly elected mayor of Hartlepool following a promise of free bananas to schoolchildren. However, as he celebrated his new £53,000-a-year job by posing for photographs on the quayside, he was chased off by a large gorilla.

Surprisingly, goats don't figure much in the world of football mascots, with the exception of the grandly named Hennes VIII, who is a real live goat and resides at the home of Cologne FC in Germany.

There is actually a worldwide Fainting Goat Society, but what now follows is certainly not for the faint-hearted. So if you are of a nervous disposition – please look away now.

It all began on the afternoon of 8 August 2002. Shortly after the 1.30pm Hull to Bridlington train left the station, it stopped at signals and it was at this precise moment that librarian Stewart Webb returned to his seat with a coffee and witnessed a bizarre incident as he glanced out of his window. Several passengers gasped as they too watched on as events unfolded. The emergency services were besieged with calls from the public as the realisation dawned on the passengers. A man was having sex with a goat in a field.

After receiving calls and acting on information received, British Transport Police Detective Inspector Dave Crinion led the investigation and declared, 'The police chose not to pursue this line of enquiry because we already had a good eyewitness.' That eyewitness turned out to be a man out walking with his grandson close to the crime scene – the allotments close to Argyle Street. The details are too sordid to reveal, suffice to say, the bloke had his way with the goat and left without paying the bill – or in this case, the nanny.

Seven months later, Stephen Hall, 23, appeared at Hull Crown Court, and after initially pleading not guilty and insisting on an identity parade, admitted the charge and was sentenced to six months in prison.

You would think, wouldn't you, that this type of behaviour is rare. But sadly it isn't. In November 2013, Katana Kitsao Gona, 28, was jailed for ten years in the Kenyan town of Malindi, for having sex with a goat. Amazingly the goat, whose name cannot be revealed for legal reasons, watched quietly in the courtroom as her attacker was jailed for bestiality. Then we have Malam Kamisu Baranda, 20, who admitted to also having intercourse with a goat, but insisted to Jigawa State Police Command that he had asked the animal's permission first.

My good friend and co-author of *Fanatical*, Andy Starmore, once told me of his friends Ken and Denzil who went to a Michael Jackson concert in London, but when they got there, they got in the wrong queue. They were in the queue to see Billy Graham, the evangelist. So they both thought, we might as well go see this bloke instead now. They sat at the back of the auditorium and during the evening Billy Graham asked the congregation, 'Does anyone here believe in ghosts?'

Two Norwegian Leeds fans, Geir & Bjorn with Father Cadfan in 2006.

The spooky rear entrance to Leeds General Infirmary.

A Kippax Branch shirt badge.

The ticket from the game in 1968 that started the (so far) unbroken run of games watched.

The Liverpool team bus arrives at Elland Road in 1979 and not a pantomime horse in sight. By andystarmorephotography@gmail.com.

Possibly the best photo ever: On way to a game in South Africa in 1995.

Seafaring in Amsterdam 1976.

Some of our motley crew on the streets of Amsterdam 1976.

The famous ski slope in Oslo. Two of us tried to go down it on a bin liner.

A simple plan to flip Wales into France.

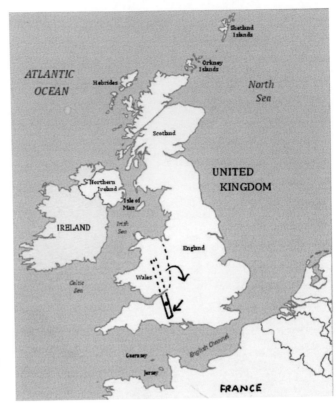

Larksy, Big Tony and Kev in Salzburg 2015.

Para Dave and me in Norway 2015.

My sister Julie, Colin Booth (Huckleberry Hound) and me (Yogi Bear).

Margaret O'Connell behind the smallest bar counter in the world.

Trevor Cusack presents Eddie Gray with a superb personalised glass plate from Waterford.

Mr August as The Horse at Tottenham.

Me and some of the lads near the New Forest on our way to Bournemouth.

The White Rose.

Mr We Beat The Scum One Nil.

Noel Hunt, me and Cato at the Viking Fest in Kippax 2011.

Viking Poster.

Paint it White on stage in the West End.

Massimo Cellino mingles with the fans at Brentford in 2014.

Wub and I during an international break in Dubai.

Me and Cellino in his plush office at Elland Road.

About 40 people put their hands up.

Graham then asked, 'Does anyone believe that they've actually seen a ghost?'

About a dozen people raised their hands.

Graham finally asked, 'Does anyone here believe they've actually made love to a ghost?'

Denzil put up his hand.

Graham then invited Denzil to join him on stage. He then said, 'Right Denzil, can you explain to us all exactly how you think that you've actually made love to a ghost?'

Denzil replied, 'Oh, sorry, I thought you said goat!'

And it isn't just goats.

Thirty-two-year-old Howard Russell contemplated suing his local Greggs bakers in Cheshire after burning his todger while having sex with a hot cheese pasty. After his ordeal, he told the *Sunday Sport*, 'I have been into Greggs many, many times and never have I seen a sign warning you not to put your penis into one of their products, especially after it has been reheated. That, to me,' said a perturbed Russell, 'is a clear case of negligence and I intend to sue.'

Following hot on Russell's heels came another resident of Cheshire. Not to be outdone on the X-rated bake off, 47-year-old water treatment worker Vince Shaw became infatuated with a 95p Tesco Value Range lasagne. But it's probably best that we leave it there.

Chapter 10

Springtime
For Hitler

JANUARY 2007 threw up an unexpected trip to Larnaca on the southern coast of Cyprus. On the 24th, Leeds United were playing Ethnikos Achnas in an exhibition match, so we spent a few days either side of the match baking in the seaside sunshine. It made a nice change to take breakfast in January on the beach each morning – in fact some mornings we even ate something too. And it wasn't long before we found the resort's '£1 a pint' bar too, returning frequently during our visit.

Another favourite hostelry we found was a bar run by a very imposing figure indeed. He was always dressed impeccably in a black suit with matching bow tie and most of the time he would be tucked away in his office, occasionally popping out to make sure things were running smoothly. It quickly became clear that beer wasn't his only business. Thick set and coming in at easily 6ft 5in tall, this clearly wasn't a bloke to be messed with. His name was Big Toni, spelt as in the girls' name, not that any of us ever mentioned it. Nor did we mention the scar that ran diagonally all the way down his face from the top left to the bottom right. Big Toni was indeed a towering figure, but we also detected a lighter side to him as we negotiated some early and late drinking sessions. In return for this, we would entertain the locals with our five-piece band. We would play a whole range of hits from the 60s to the present day. When I say 'play', that's not strictly true; we would in fact mime the songs from the well-stocked jukebox, and our 'instruments' were two wooden stools for drums played by Jonno; two pool cues as the lead and bass guitars with Tony and Macca; and another pool cue was used by me as the microphone for lead vocals, while Little Mick provided extra harmonies with his tambourine – which was in fact the triangle from the pool table.

After three sets the audience would be screaming for more – at least I think they were screaming for more. Regardless, they got their encore and more importantly, Big Toni appeared to like it.

The football match against Ethnikos Achnas, as usual on these trips was pretty tame, ending in a 1-1 draw. The highlight of the game undoubtedly was Leeds' goal scored by Gustavo Augusto Poyet Domiguez, known as good old Gus Poyet to the fans, who was then assistant to manager Dennis Wise, a little bloke from down south.

Four months after the trip to Cyprus, Leeds United crashed out of the Championship and began life in the third tier of English football for the first time in the club's history. The fans needed a decent pre-season trip to boost their enthusiasm and prepare them for whatever lay ahead during the following nine months. Leeds chose Germany. I'd been to several German pre-season tours during the late 1970s, which was West Germany back then, but this was to be in east Germany, kicking off in Berlin, so we packed a bag and off we went.

Once there, we did the usual touristy bit and paid a visit to Checkpoint Charlie and its authentic sandbag walls. To be honest, there was a real sense of history about the place, even though it has obviously changed dramatically over the years. And the American-style uniformed girl with a tight pencil skirt that we had our photographs taken with at 'Checkpoint' was stunning. However, Leeds lost their first game 2-0 against Union Berlin.

The second game was scheduled to be against Dynamo Dresden in Dresden, but the police had other ideas. The match was cancelled on the insistence of the local police and as the German authorities were unwilling and seemingly unable to manage the crowds, the club had to look elsewhere for a game. Some of our long-in-the-tooth members thought it may have been because Dresden had been bombed by the Allies more than any other German city during the Second World War. But the actual reason given for the cancellation was that on the day of the scheduled game, 18 July, a huge pro-fascist march was planned on the streets of Dresden. Couple that with an equal-sized gay march through the same streets and I suppose anything can happen. Add anything up to 500 Leeds supporters into that mix and you've got a tasty weekend in prospect.

The fact is that on over 40 years of pre-season tours, I have seen very little trouble. Of course, there has been the odd skirmish, like in Amsterdam in 1976, when Leeds fans had to run the gauntlet with Ajax fans wielding chains, machetes and meat cleavers which went on for three days. Then there was Denmark in 1981. Leeds United were involved in a tournament in the tiny town of Ikast, but Leeds fans were involved in a tournament of their own. Admittedly, we may have been a tad loud during our two-week stay, prompting local newspaper headlines such as 'Leeds fans spolerer Ikast-borgernes nattesovn' which translated into 'Leeds fans spoil Ikast-citizen's night's sleep' but there were never any serious shenanigans. Unfortunately, this was not how events were portrayed to a chapter of Hells Angels 200 miles away in Copenhagen. One Wednesday afternoon, 100 leather-clad bikers introduced themselves by smoke-bombing a pub that about 20 of us were in. Four days of altercations ensued, but thankfully we are all still around today to tell the tale.

Meanwhile, Leeds fans had to leave Dresden and a hastily planned game against Slovan Liberec across the border in the Czech Republic was to be our next match instead. As I sat on the coach travelling to the border, I had thoughts of what might happen in Dresden that day with the gays and the Nazis, and I couldn't get past the vision of the two groups converging and producing the world's first such march with thousands of them wearing jack boots, marching with arms linked and striding out while singing Mel Brooks's 'Springtime For Hitler and Germany', which contains the immortal line of 'Deutschland is happy and gay', with Mel Brooks leading proceedings in full Nazi regalia. If you haven't seen it already, I would implore you to look up 'Springtime For Hitler' on YouTube – it's hilarious.

We were pleasantly surprised at the exchange rate and even happier at the cost of things once we'd crossed the border into the Czech Republic. We were only spending the day in Liberec, so I thought £70 should be enough as we changed some money at a local greengrocer's shop on the border. Once in Liberec we made camp in a hotel beer garden on a hill overlooking the stadium. We expected the prices to be a little higher with it being a hotel but as we were only here for the day we thought we would push the boat out a little. About ten of us sat around a table in the glorious sunshine and ordered our first beer of the day. After the first round, Kelvin ordered more from the owner and he duly delivered another tray of cool lagers. When he returned, Kelvin offered his money for the first round, to which the owner said something like, 'later, all together', to which

Kelvin shrugged his shoulders and continued drinking his beer. Jeff offered the money next time, then me, then Rich and so on, but still he wouldn't take anything. By now we'd had a couple of bottles of wine as well and we then asked for a menu. 'Well, we're only here for the day, let's live it up a little,' said Ralph.

Several lagers later, we gingerly ordered the bill, which was then passed face down, round the table faster than a hare being chased by a greyhound. But when some brave soul picked it up and read it out, we were completely blown away – we had been sat at the same table for about seven hours and when we reckoned up our bill, the ten of us had drunk enough alcohol to sink a ship not to mention the food and desserts we had gorged on and it came to around £6 each, including a tip. To celebrate, a round of 'Bloody Marys' was ordered. I'd only had a couple of glasses of this famous drink once or twice in my life, but Kelvin insisted I try one from his favourite 'recipe ones' – and it was amazing. Tomato juice, Worcester sauce, Tabasco sauce, no small amount of vodka and a generous smattering of pepper on top. Superb! Some have a celery stick, but personally I think that spoils it.

I have always looked up to Kelvin, and it wasn't just when he accidentally ran me over in his green Citroen Dyane during that pre-season tour of Denmark in 1981 and I ended up staring at the sky from beneath his front bumper. Kelvin had a stroke a few years ago, during which he lost his taste for red wine. It wasn't through choice – he literally lost his taste of red wine as a result of his stroke.

After yet another round of Bloody Marys in the beer garden on the Liberec hillside, we decided to have one more beer and a bottle of wine and then settle up before going to the match. Once in the ground and covering one eye with a hand to bring the players into focus, we watched on as Leeds lost yet again. However, it was an improvement on the Berlin match – this time it was only 1-0. Despite drinking the contents of a small brewery, none of us were really that drunk. In fact, I have never arrived at the turnstile for a match drunk – well at least I can't remember doing so anyway. During the game, Jo Barrett, who was to form part of the committee for our new White Rose branch for the coming season, told me that the Leeds fans back home had been protesting at Elland Road over how the club was being run, and that hundreds of Leeds shirts and scarves had been laid at the statue of Billy Bremner at Elland Road with the overall message of 'Save our Club'. At this point, Leeds still hadn't been given permission by the Football League to compete in the league for the 2007/08 season. Having already been deducted 15 points before a ball had been kicked, on top of ten points taken from us on the final day of the previous season, it was easy to understand the anger from the club and its supporters. Ken Bates, the owner at the time, bore the brunt of much of this anger and news of the protest quickly filtered through to the rest of the Leeds fans here in Liberec and soon there was a massive removal of shirts and shoes as the chant, 'Shirts off if you hate Ken Bates' followed by 'Shoes off if you hate Ken Bates'.

Two more verses followed beginning with 'Sit down if you hate Ken Bates' and 'Stand up if you Ken Bates' which carried on for a good 25 minutes or more.

The final game of this 'German' tour took us to a place called Dessau, a city sandwiched south of Berlin and north of Dresden. It was an eye-opener from the start. Dessau is world famous for its Bauhaus Art Movement. Bauhaus, the gothic rock band from Wellingborough, Northampton, who took their name from that very movement, used the Bauhaus signage from the iconic Bauhaus College Building as their logo. Noticeably, the artists around Dessau are of a different kind these days from those at the Art Movement, with brushes being replaced by bottles and cans. That said, our lot took no time in blending in.

One evening we trawled the many bars to study the local inhabitants in their natural environment. Most were asleep by 6pm, but they would be followed by the next shift, and they in turn would be replaced by the late night shift and so on. It was around 4am when Jeff, Rich and I were joined in a bar by one particular specimen who could only be described as a drunken insomniac and he continued to talk to us until the early morning sun came up. We were all going on a trip to the infamous Colditz that morning so we decided that we'd better get back to the hotel (which was only a few yards from this bar) as the coach was scheduled to leave just after breakfast. But then just as we walked out of the bar into the sunshine our insomniac friend ran across the road straight towards one of our lot, Macca, who promptly turned and ran away.

It transpired that our friend had been boring the arse off Macca in another bar until 3am and when he left to go back to the hotel, the insomniac ended up on our shift. We called our friend Zoonie the Loonie.

An hour later we were on our way to Colditz and an opportunity to catch some shuteye. I stirred a few hours later to hear Kelvin shouting down the coach to Big Mick, 'Oi Mick, I thought Colditz was on a hill? This is like the Vale of York round here.' Apparently due to some translation mix-up, the driver had brought us to the wrong prison and we were outside a prison for Polish women. A few went inside anyway, but I went back to my seat and fell back to sleep. I mean, once you've seen one Polish women's prison, you've seen them all.

The following day, Leeds recorded their third consecutive defeat on tour with a dismal 2-1 defeat to Cottbus – a match that saw Gus Poyet sent from the dugout into the stand and dismissals for Jonathon Douglas and Jermaine Beckford. It was at this game where Little Mick composed a new song as a tribute to one of our star strikers – Tresor Kandol. Cleverly titled 'Kandol in the Wind' it thoroughly deserved to get into the charts. Where's Brian Epstein when you need him?

And so we began our final night where we began; in a bar, and I soon found myself in an argument with Ralph. He had challenged me to a drinking challenge, which I won by downing my pint seconds before him, but he refused to pay me the bet with a flimsy argument that he had not been ready when one of the lads had shouted, 'Go!' I couldn't be bothered arguing about it, so I left and walked down to another bar on my own. In there I sat at the bar with a pint and was quite enjoying the solitude when all hell broke loose. Two lads had been sat in there with Cottbus scarves when one of a group who had been stood at the bar decided to go over and attack both of them. They weren't fighters and promptly left, but then someone took a swing at the assailant and in turn someone took a swing at him. Cue the Long Branch Saloon in Dodge City. Punches were being thrown everywhere and as I sat there at the bar, the only person in the pub with a Leeds shirt on, I prepared myself for the next punch that I felt sure would have my name on the end of it. Unbelievably, it never arrived and after possibly five minutes of trading punches the group of lads went outside and were chatting and shaking hands while sharing cigarettes. If they had been kidding around, they were brilliant stuntmen because I can't remember when I'd last witnessed fist fighting like it.

I rejoined the others, including Ralph, for a nightcap before grabbing a few hours' kip. It was the final night of our trip, and at around three-ish Jeff and I awoke to see someone or something walking into our room (our door had been left wide open as usual). The ghostly apparition passed the end of my bed and as it got to Jeff's bed I noticed it was Coke, who was on our trip and from Wellingborough, just like Bauhaus. I then heard him say to himself, 'Some fucker's in my room.' I shouted to Coke and asked him what he was doing and if he was alright. 'You're in my room, mate,' said Coke, not quite knowing who he was talking to. We put the light on to resolve the mystery. It turned out that Coke had the same room number as us. Well the same last two numbers that is. In fact, his room was four floors below ours. No wonder he looked out of breath, bless him. Our room had been more like a busy terminal during our stay, and leaving the door open didn't help; on another night one drunken lad walked into our room, staggering near the end of Jeff's bed. Then we saw this silhouette fall in three or four stages before collapsing on the floor and falling fast asleep. Jeff threw a spare blanket over him and went back to sleep. The next morning our intruder had gone.

We certainly had plenty to talk about as our coach made its way to the airport first thing next morning – and even now some people still call Coke, 'Casper the ghost'.

Once back in England, it was an education watching some of the lads shepherding a large hoarding along the airport conveyor belt. It had been commandeered at the game in Liberec and had the name of both teams on it – a great souvenir from a great excursion.

I'm happy to say that Kelvin is now doing fine and currently residing in his new home in sunny Spain, and more importantly he appears to have regained his taste for his beloved red wine, so now, with that major obstacle out of the way, the rest of the road to recovery should be plain sailing for him.

Chapter 11

Trevor's Ireland

AFTER our jaunt to Liberec, I had developed a serious taste for Bloody Marys and as we were travelling to Galway for a pre-season game the following year our coach passed through a small town and Big Mick suggested we stay there for an hour. Amazingly, there was a pub called Dracula's, and I thought it would be fun to order a Bloody Mary as a tribute to the Count himself. Unbelievably the bar staff were completely unaware of what one was. They didn't even have any tomato juice! So, instead of savouring the atmosphere of the world's most famous vampire, we all settled down with a Guinness and watched *The Simpsons* on the pub telly.

A girl sat alone at the bar reading a newspaper heard our accents and asked, 'Are you from Leeds by any chance?' It turned out that she had left her Leeds home to move in with her Irish boyfriend just last year. 'It's a small world,' she said. 'Yes,' I replied, 'but I wouldn't want to paint it.'

Galway Bay with its winding, descending streets is an idyllic seaside resort nestled on the mid-west coast of Ireland and street music and entertainment emanates from almost every corner you turn. As we walked past the countless street entertainers, one chap wearing a large white trilby hat and snazzy waistcoat caught everyone's eye. I seem to stand out like a sore thumb at many an event and I have been plucked out of a packed circus audience and subsequently run over by a pick-up truck loaded with laughing clowns, with only a piece of wood to protect me under the truck wheels. And out of a 10,000 crowd at Benidorm in 1979, I was selected to face a baby bull in a mock bullfight while stood on a 3ft high wooden box in the centre of the ring.

During a family birthday event many years ago, I found myself volunteered to take part in a morris dance. There I was, prancing about in a hat, ribbons and bells and involved in a half-hearted stick fight with half a dozen professional morris dancers – and I was completely sober! On a holiday in Dubai I was walking through a large shopping mall when I suddenly found myself designated as an assistant to help an Argentinian mime artist on a foot-high bicycle with a balloon on the end of a fishing rod. So, there I was watching this chap in the white trilby hat on the streets of Galway. He was playing a cut-out cardboard guitar with no strings using a cardboard plectrum while he shouted out, 'Plink', 'Plink' and 'Plonk' at the appropriate time. Beside him he had a cardboard cut-out dog and he was selling blank cardboard CDs for a Euro each (and they were selling like hot cakes). It wasn't long before he signalled to me and handed me a cardboard cut-out banjo out of his cardboard box and we did a duet. I was pretty good too, I have to say. Even though a couple of times I plinked when I should have plonked but I think I got away with it. A 2-0 win later that evening with both goals coming from Jermaine Beckford made our stay even more pleasurable.

From there we headed across to the east coast and to what is the longest-established seaside town in Ireland – Bray. I love it there, and on my recommendation two mates from

Kippax, Kev 'the demon barber' Higgins and Steve 'rave on' Donnelly had made the trip to Bray and they weren't disappointed. The only snag was that Kev is a total jinx when it comes to watching Leeds United. He tends to pick his matches, but every time he does, Leeds invariably lose. When Leeds lost just three games at home one season, Kev saw all three games – those three games were all he watched that season. At half-time at Bray, Kev's unfortunate hoodoo was once again looming over us and we were losing 2-0. I leant on Kev's shoulder and said, 'Why don't you go get yourself a nice pint of Guinness Kev? We'll see you in that first pub on the corner after the game.' Kev duly obliged and was gone. Cue a Leeds fightback assisted by our cosmopolitan contingent. Our defender from Angola, Rui Marques, pulled one back, followed by an equaliser from Canadian Marcus Haber, before Leeds-born Jonny Howson smashed home the winner with five minutes remaining. We then left to meet up with Kev.

Live music was playing all along the seafront that evening, culminating in a sensational show by a U2 tribute band on the main stage. A couple of evenings prior to our visit, a group of Millwall fans had been creating trouble in these pubs and bars but had been quickly dealt with by the locals. This evening however, large numbers of Leeds fans mingled with the locals without the merest hint of trouble anywhere. In one pub we helped one man celebrate his 80th birthday in style. Eric Carlile was secretary of the official Leeds United Supporters' Club for many years and it was a privilege to be in his company yards from Carlisle Grounds, home of Bray Wanderers.

A scenic train ride 14 miles up the coast took us to our final game of this Irish tour against Shelbourne in the Drumcondra district of Dublin. The close relationship between our two clubs is well documented and Leeds United have been regular visitors to Tolka Park since the late 1980s, and even back as far as 1948 when we beat them 10-2, two days before a 4-2 victory over Shamrock Rovers. Leeds were also invited to help celebrate Shelbourne's 75th Jubilee in 1971, winning 3-1. Shelbourne's close ties with their neighbours Home Farm FC have resulted in the odd acquisition for Leeds United, the most notable being Gary Kelly, whose 500-plus appearances for the club was the highest for any player outside of the Don Revie era. Another high profile player to come from Home Farm to Leeds was Nicky Byrne, who also happened to be a singer for some band called Westlife. Paul Huntington scored in Leeds' 1-1 draw with the Shels bringing the curtain down on the 2008 Irish tour, but not before I enjoyed a final night in local pubs in Upper Drumcondra, the Cat and Cage and Ivy House, with some of our group including Brod, Annette and Andy, Rich Watson and Big Ian McKay from Belfast.

Danny Best from Sherburn once came into the Cat and Cage a few hours after a game, and like us, he'd had a few. He couldn't remember which hotel he was staying at; he knew it was in Dublin centre, but had no idea what it was called. The sensible thing to do is pick up a card at the reception of your hotel and put it in your wallet. That's a good idea in theory, but, and I've done it myself, if you lose your card, it's a totally different ball game. I once lost my hotel card in Antwerp, Belgium and although I was only a few hundred yards from my hotel, I didn't find it for about an hour. And one time in Amsterdam, I was in danger of missing the flight home. I'd lost my card and a few of us came out of a late bar to broad daylight with not a card between us. It's usually pretty easy to locate your digs with the help of bright lights and a few landmark signs – but in daylight, everywhere looks different to the night before.

On another occasion, Mark spent the entire evening sat up asleep at a bus stop outside the hotel after an evening on the Guinness. Next morning, he awoke to find that he was surrounded by commuters waiting for the bus into Dublin. To create the illusion that he also was waiting for the bus, he boarded with them when it arrived, with absolutely no idea where he was heading.

I've been a few times to watch Leeds play in Cork, southern Ireland and it's a fabulous city, as is Waterford just a little further up the east coast. My long-time friend and fellow Leeds fan Trevor Cusack hails from Waterford and Wub and I have been lucky to stay on a number of occasions with him and his lovely wife Jean and their two lads, Darragh and Emmet, who are doing remarkably well at sport, particularly martial arts and are both following in the footsteps of their black belt dad. Waterford is a fascinating city and one evening Trevor took me to some of the lesser-known gems hidden away from the average tourist. He took me to a pub that the unsuspecting passer-by wouldn't know was there. It hides behind an old sweet shop and is run by a blind man and only a familiar knock on the front door will allow you access through the shop and into a small bar that has a small black and white television on the dusty bar while the heating is supplied by a battered old electric fire in the corner. The bar was 'busy tonight' as two men sat at separate tables – there were only two tables – with not a word spoken between them. I had been forewarned by Trevor not to order any beer, and to stick to spirits only. There was no draught beer and only a handful of bottles of beer adorned the tatty wooden shelves behind the bar – and all predating the millennium by several decades. Trevor introduced me to the landlord. 'Hello John, this is Gary,' he said. 'He's from Leeds in England.'

'Pleased to meet you Gary,' said John, shaking my hand. 'What will you have?'

'Two whiskies please,' I replied. 'No ice.'

We'd had to knock on the door before we were let in because, although his regulars were trusting and loyal to

John, as time passed, members of the public who weren't so nice began to take advantage of John's failing eyesight and would say they had been short changed or help themselves to something extra over the counter. John was attacked a number of times and robbed of his measly takings.

John held up my ten Euro note and rubbed his finger over it before placing it neatly into an old wooden drawer that doubled up as a till. After a couple of Jameson's we left. To this day, Trevor still regrets that we didn't spend more time in this unique little pub – and that was made all the more poignant a few months later when an intruder tricked his way into the pub and the landlord died as a direct result of a sickening robbery – police said later that the offender had got away with around 20 Euros.

Another attraction in Waterford is Larkin's butchers shop. It is like going back in time as a large old bacon slicer dominates the counter. The till is ancient and still has punt (Irish pound) tabs on it. But there is one thing missing in this delightful shop – meat! In fact, I was told that meat hasn't graced the empty tin trays in the large glass-fronted counter for over 20 years. One year the proprietor didn't order his next consignment of meat and instead just opened the shop to sit and talk to customers about any subject under the sun, from politics to finance and sport to space exploration. Waterford can also lay claim to the smallest bar counter in the world, measuring just 38 inches in length. The 300-year-old pub in the Kilmeaden area of Waterford is run by Gerry and Margaret O'Connell and originally only held six customers in relative comfort.

Trevor and Jean have divided loyalties when it comes to their support of hurling teams. Trevor is a Waterford fan, while Jean is a devout fan of Kilkenny. To make matters worse for Trevor, his family have recently moved from their home in Waterford just across the border into what Trevor dubs as 'enemy territory' – Kilkenny. 'The house is grand,' concedes Trevor. 'It's just that it's in – err, Kilkenny.' Wub and I have stayed at the new house and I can concur that it is indeed grand – fabulous in fact. When we were last there, Waterford were playing a big game against Tipperary. Waterford's shirt bears a striking resemblance to a Leeds shirt so I didn't mind wearing one as Trevor and I made the short walk to his new local pub, The Royal Oak, to watch the match on TV. Although tantalisingly close to Waterford, we were now inside Kilkenny territory and a couple of feet from the pub, which sounded a very loud and raucous pub. Trevor stopped and said casually, 'Oh, by the way, we will be the only two in here wearing Waterford shirts.' Then we walked inside to be met by an instant wall of loud jeers and abuse. It was like walking into a home pub yards from The Den at Millwall. I'm now writing about it, so you can safely assume we both got out of there alive. It turned out to be quite fun, and Waterford won.

They say that football transcends all religious and cultural divides and that is certainly the case where Leeds United fans are concerned. Waterford is the oldest city in Ireland and is also where the Vikings first landed on those shores. Irish and Norwegian Leeds fans now stand side by side at Elland Road and during the Troubles in Northern Ireland in the early 70s, a good friend of mine, Bob Liddle, was on the streets of Belfast fighting in the British Army. He was running a betting book on the Leeds v Arsenal FA Cup Final of 1972 while listening to the match crouched down behind a barricade dodging bullets. It was this same cup final that cemented Trevor Cusack's love for Leeds United and nowadays Bob and Trevor regularly share a beer while attending games.

After one visit to Tolka Park in Dublin in 2010, we headed north to Belfast for a game against Glentoran. Staying in a hotel at the very edge of the infamous Sandy Row, we had a very enjoyable few nights. On the Saturday morning of the game we found ourselves in The Royal pub, which was the local of Alex 'Hurricane' Higgins. On this particular morning however, it was packed, wall to wall with Leeds fans. Butter had come over on the morning flight and was the bearer of some bad news. Our mate Sean Plows had been with some of the lads who went to Salford to watch Castleford Tigers Rugby League Club the night before, but after an altercation with some Salford fans after the game, Sean's ear had been almost severed and he needed major surgery to sew it back on, but thankfully him and his ear made a full recovery. To mark the occasion, a large pig's ear is pinned to the television in our local pub back home, the Moorgate, and still remains there today.

We spent a few hours in a Belfast pub called the Crown situated directly across from the world's most bombed hotel – The Europa – which was bombed almost 30 times during the Troubles. A heavy contingent of Leeds fans was evident and at one point we altered Para Dave's nickname to 'Paranoid' Dave due to the fact that he thought he was being constantly watched by members of the IRA. Para is a Falklands veteran and spent his 21st birthday on board a ship in the South Atlantic.

Regular sightings were reported of an Irish Leeds fan who had travelled up on his own – he is known as Shipwreck and has been following Leeds for many years.

Para Dave got Basher, Rich and me into a servicemen's club near the ground before the game which was frequented by a large number of Leeds fans who were also members of the armed forces. The game itself was a run-of-the-mill 3-1 victory to Leeds, but it was the crowd attendance that was a cause for concern to chairman Ken Bates. The official attendance was given at 4,329 but Bates argued that there were many more people in the ground than the attendance given – and I have to say, given that there was easily 3,000-plus Leeds fans and that the rest of the ground was full also, then the official attendance given was far short of the actual number. Bates vowed never to take his club there again.

We often speak to rival fans about their own pre-season tours and pretty much without exception they know where they are going sometimes months before the end of the current season thus giving their fans plenty of time to plan their trips to go watch them. Leeds United, on the other hand, treat pre-season information as though it was part of the Official Secrets Act and we very rarely have more than a couple of weeks at best to arrange our trips. However, Leeds United surpassed even their traditionally low standards when it came to the pre-season of 2014. After just ten days' notice we were on a trip to a couple of games in northern Italy and due to fly on to a further game against Glenavon, close to Belfast. But news began to filter through to us while we were in the Dolomites that Leeds had arranged a game away at Swindon the night before the game in Northern Ireland. If these rumours were true, it would present a problem due to the fact that we were scheduled to be in Belfast that night in readiness for the following evening's game against Glenavon. Later that day Big Mick, our tour arranger, came into the bar we were in – his face instantly told us that the rumours were true. 'Leeds United don't give a flying fuck about the supporters,' he said angrily. 'There *is* a first-team game in Swindon that first night we are in Belfast. I am currently trying to arrange something.' Mick has often gone far beyond the call of duty arranging our tours over the years, flying in the face of adversity from the club, but this would be a tough call, even for him. Wub has often smiled when she's been on tour with us and we all stand back waiting for Mick at check-in to deal with our documentation and passports. 'Just like a group of school kids,' she has said. To be fair, Mick does everything but wipe our arses on tour, and I'll wager that for a nominal fee Mick would accommodate that too.

On the morning of Tuesday 29 July we touched down at
Belfast airport on our scheduled flight and made our way to
the hotel. It was the same hotel we have used before, right
on the corner of Sandy Row. Then, after a couple of hours
in the hotel bar, we were on our way back to the airport and
a flight to Bristol. We spent a pleasant afternoon around
the sunny waterfront before boarding a train to Swindon
for the game at the County Ground. After the game it was
too late to get a flight back to Belfast, so after a few hours'
kip in a Bristol hotel, sharing a room with Keith – looking
splendid in his pyjamas – we took the first early flight back
to Belfast. After a quick shower in our hotel room that hadn't
been slept in, we had a walk around Belfast before boarding
the bus for a half-hour trip south-west to the game against
Glenavon. On our arrival, the staff at Mourneview Park
couldn't have been more accommodating as they showed
us into the impressive bar underneath the Glenfield Road
Stand and supplied us with a wide range of complimentary
hot and cold food. Coupled with the hospitality of the home
supporters and the inevitable large contingent of Northern
Irish Leeds fans, it made for a pleasant evening, which was
rounded off with a few drinks around Belfast city centre.
Big Tony, Bob, Rich and me ended up in a downstairs bar
of a large establishment where you had to pay to go to the
upstairs bar. But Andy and his mate Karl, assuming it would
be a nightclub, ventured upstairs. Within minutes they had
joined us downstairs – apparently they were the only two
not wearing large pink foam cowboy hats – and there wasn't
a female in sight.

After a few years' absence from the Emerald Isle, we
returned in the summer of 2016 for a couple of games against
our old friends Shelbourne and a weekend game against
Shamrock Rovers and it was as if we'd never been away.
The hospitality was, as ever, superb. I met up once again
with Trevor, Jean, Darragh and Emmet as well as Jimmy

White from Waterford, Patrick Stewart from Dublin and countless others. We even returned to our favourite seaside haunt in Ireland, Bray. This time we managed just two pubs, travelling ten yards in ten hours.

Chapter 12

Bates Motel

'I SHALL not rest until Leeds United are kicked out of the Football League. Their fans are the scum of the earth, absolute animals and a disgrace. I will do everything in my power to make this happen.'

These were the comments of Ken Bates in 1984, and by golly he very nearly damn near did it too.

Following a 5-0 defeat to Chelsea at Stamford Bridge, Ken Bates made this famous comment on 28 April 1984. The result ensured that Chelsea were promoted to the First Division and Leeds United were consigned to yet another season in the Second Division wilderness. The game itself was ended by the referee a full five minutes early as Chelsea fans began gathering on the touchline (and on the pitch itself) in readiness for a celebratory pitch invasion – but they had much more than that in mind. Leeds winger Mark Gavin was amongst the Leeds players attacked as he ran for the tunnel through hordes of Chelsea fans. Peter Lorimer was also playing that day. This was a quote from *The Sun* the following Monday, 'Leeds veteran and legend Peter Lorimer has said that he feared for his life after Chelsea fans invaded the pitch five times during Saturday's game and was kicked by fans. When told of this Ken Bates said, "And how many times has Peter Lorimer kicked people over the years?"'

Chelsea fans soon turned their attention to the 5,000 Leeds fans and the Leeds end of the pitch soon became entirely full of Chelsea fans taunting and provoking the Leeds fans. The Leeds fans responded by smashing the scoreboard to pieces and then began using the debris and stanchions to charge at the high fence that separated the two sets of supporters. At one point a group of around ten Leeds fans charged the fence with an old railway sleeper and the Chelsea fans began to back off. It took over 45 minutes for the police to restore order and with the fence just about destroyed, prevent what could have been a major confrontation.

Twenty-one years later, on 21 January 2005, Ken Bates bought a 50 per cent stake in Leeds United. 'I'm delighted to be stepping up to the mantle at such a fantastic football club. I see Leeds as a great club that has fallen on hard times. We have a lot of hard work ahead to get the club where it belongs, in the Premier League, and with the help of our fans we will do everything we can,' he said. After about a month in charge he told the media, 'Whereas a couple of weeks ago, Leeds had their heads above water gasping for breath, now they are on the surface swimming against the tide. The next job is to get them swimming with the tide.'

I was working up my ladders in the early spring sunshine of 2005 when my phone rang. I didn't get it out of my overalls in time to take the call so it went directly into my mailbox. Later I checked the message but found it very difficult to hear it or even recognise who it was from. I cranked up the volume, and with my ear stuck tightly to the phone I could just about make out the message, 'I've read your books and would like to have a copy of them, I'll try calling later.' Although vaguely familiar, I couldn't make out the voice as it was so low and the caller left no return number. Ken Bates did ring back the following day, and those initial conversations led to invites to his private birthday parties every year since. Of course I get massive stick over attending these functions, but to be honest, I'll eat anybody's lobster or drink anybody's Shiraz for free. Besides, he really is good company – very controversial – but good company.

Bates, of course, is no stranger to confrontation. During his many decades in football, he has crossed swords with the establishment as well as with other directors and players. He wasted no time in ruffling a few feathers upon his arrival at Elland Road either. He mocked Yorkshire folk, and in particular businessmen, for not stepping in to financially assist the club – 'short arms and long pockets' was how he described them. One of the first things he did when he came to the club was make the Leeds United Supporters' Club (LUSC) unofficial, stripping them of any 'powers' they had in relation to the club and no longer allowing them to hold meetings anywhere on the premises of Elland Road. The LUSC is steeped in history, having being instrumental in forming Leeds United Football Club on the very same day that Leeds City AFC were disbanded by the Football League in 1919. They have continued to function ever since, ploughing thousands upon thousands of pounds into the club over those years. After Bates' ruling, LUSC continued to operate from wherever they could, including nearby working men's clubs and even the back room of the Peacock pub across from the ground.

Bates then caused outrage in August 2011 when he called Leeds United fans 'morons' after hundreds of Leeds fans gathered outside Elland Road before a home defeat to Middlesbrough to protest against the club's lack of investment in the team. Bates, who had by now increased his stake in the club to 72.85 per cent to become the controlling shareholder, was unmoved, 'I am unimpressed by the demonstration of a few morons. I aint going anywhere soon. Some fans may not like me, or agree with me, but you're stuck with me.'

The Leeds Supporters' Trust reacted angrily, posting this statement on their website:

'We do not feel it is acceptable to refer to Leeds fans as "morons". We do not want to get into personal battles with Mr Bates or point out the numerous inaccuracies in his words.'

Referring to Bates' claims that he 'saved the club in 2005 and 2007 when nobody else would' the statement added, 'The Leeds United Supporters' Trust is very keen to establish exactly what it is that Ken Bates "saved" the club from and we welcome clarification from Mr Bates.' The Supporters' Trust went on to say, 'Ken Bates did not save us from falling out with the BBC, newspapers, various other football reporters and commentators.'

In another controversial move, he cancelled Radio Leeds' coverage of Leeds United games and replaced it with Yorkshire Radio – which he owned having brought the equipment with him from Chelsea. This affected none more so than my dear old Ma, who listened religiously to every match commentary on Radio Leeds but could no longer continue with this particular avenue of pleasure as Radio Yorkshire was a digital station. I had to laugh recently while having a cuppa with her. She complained that with all the unfamiliar foreign names we have in the side these days she had no idea whether Leeds were attacking or defending. 'In fact,' she said, 'the other night I forgot they were playing.' I replied, 'Don't worry Ma, most of the players and supporters forgot they were playing as well.' Radio Leeds themselves had to operate from that same back room in the Peacock pub, with commentary coming from Adam Pope sitting at a table on a bar stool.

In August 2011, Bates banned the BBC from covering news conferences and banned it from sending reporters or producers to interview players or staff on matchdays, except where the club was contractually bound to make access available. It was banned because of a documentary being made over the club's ownership. Bates banned newspaper reporters on a regular basis – and always kept a very close watch on local newspapers, wagging the proverbial finger if they overstepped his mark. He also refused *The Guardian* newspaper reporter David Conn access to Elland Road to cover matches because of *his* reporting on the ownership saga. He even banned one reporter for life – twice, even having a mock gravestone built with the reporter's name on it. Yet Des Kelly of the *Daily Mail* did secure another interview with Ken Bates in 2010. At one of his birthday parties Ken told his congregation of this interview and started by saying that Kelly had mentioned Leeds fans accusing Bates of being an 'asset stripper'. His guests, who included Jack Charlton, laughed as he said, 'There were no fucking assets to strip.' The interview with Kelly had ended – referring to Bates' one-man crusade against seemingly everybody – along the lines of, Kelly: 'Since when have you been nice?' Bates: 'I am nice, fuck off!' Bates then said, 'The Leeds fans were coming round to the idea that I may have been right after all. What happened when I came to Leeds, it was a disgrace. The place was rotten.

'Behind the scenes it was in a terrible state. Ridsdale borrowed £100m; spent it all on players and had nothing to show for it. He spent nothing on the ground, and we were still carrying out repairs he neglected to do back then. They said that Ridsdale lived "the dream" but he left others with the nightmare.

'Under Ridsdale's chairmanship,' said Bates, 'Leeds United borrowed money on horrendous terms because they didn't think Leeds would get relegated – and then they panicked. They sold the ground for £8m – and agreed a repurchase price of £15m. They sold the training ground for £3m and that repurchase price was set at £5m. These are things that still need clearing up.'

Even a small free Leeds newspaper, the now defunct *Leeds Weekly* didn't escape Ken's eagle eye. I had done a routine interview in the paper discussing the club's souvenir shop and its merchandise, during which I had answered a question as to why Leeds United shirts weren't available in the town centre or why there were no Leeds United shops anywhere in town. 'There used to be several Leeds shops around West Yorkshire, but Ken Bates closed them all except the one at Elland Road,' I replied. 'I have no idea why.'

Before the ink had time to dry on the first publication, my phone rang and it was Ken Bates. At the time, we had just returned from a pre-season trip to Norway. Ken started the conversation, asking me if I'd enjoyed the trip. As I was in mid-sentence answering him, he cut to the chase. 'Do you know why there are no Leeds United shops in town?' I knew instantly that he had read my article. Again he didn't wait for my reply. 'Because they were ripping me off. With just one shop at Elland Road, I can keep my eye on them.' I dared to ask him why Leeds shirts weren't available in the city centre. 'Why should they get all the profits?' he replied.

I remember vividly my first visit to his private birthday party at Elland Road.

It was in the Bremner suite beneath the West Stand and only around 50 people were present. As Wub and I approached the entrance, I said, 'Don't worry, we won't stop long. He won't have a clue who we are and we can just disappear when we want. We'll just have a quick bite to eat and a few beers and we'll be on our way.'

As we both walked rather awkwardly through the doors, we were met by two large, dark-suited gentlemen, who immediately took our coats. Trying hard not to make eye contact with anyone, we each took a glass of champagne from the lady with the welcome tray and headed for a table with food on it. Just as I helped myself to a gigantic tiger prawn I felt a nudge in my back. It was Ken Bates. 'It's Mr *Paint It White*. Is it true that you painted a fire engine white while the firemen were still in it?' he asked. 'Yes,' I said quietly, 'but it was just a publicity stunt for Whyte & Mackay whisky.'

'This is Lesley,' I said introducing her to Ken at the precise moment that we were joined by his wife Suzannah. 'Oh, you must be Wub,' she said. 'It's so lovely to meet you. I've read so much about you.'

We were shown to our table and offered wine. The spread of food all around us was unbelievable – it would have outfaced Henry VIII. There was literally every kind of food you could think of. I sat next to press officer Paul Dews, LUTV cameraman Steve Haughton and the club's resident poet at the time, Gary Kaye, while more wine was poured as a solo harpist played in the background. It was like some sort of weird dream, but I quickly got acclimatised. No players were present and even Dennis Wise, the manager at the time, wasn't present. I was told by Dewsy that after every game, Wise travels back to London so that he can watch his son, Bates' godson, playing football on Sunday morning. Wise's assistant Gus Poyet was never at these functions either. Wub came back to the table with a lobster in a shell that was so big she could have sailed across the Atlantic in it. By now the waiters were just leaving bottles of wine on the table. So much for 'a few beers and we'll be on our way'. At one point, Gary and I had Ken Bates boxed in as we quizzed him on how long he was planning to stay at Leeds and will he be putting any money into the club. Ken then got a napkin and began to write some figures on it. As he was telling us that he would put money in when it was viable to do so, he was scribbling away and then, as we both looked on, he produced two long lines of figures that both added up to a big fat nought. I still have that napkin and to this day I have absolutely no idea how he arrived at nought – in both columns!

A classic example of his use of figures came when he was asked about Leeds' debt of £24.5m when he first took over the club. 'There's not a great deal of debt,' he said. 'We were only £17.7m in debt but former directors have agreed to defer their payment of £4.4m which they are owed and then, if you take away the £3.5m special payment owed to the Inland Revenue to be repaid over two to three years, the figure is down to just £9m.'

Ken was soon up on the microphone addressing his guests, punctuated with frequent swearing and cursing. Politically correct is not in Ken's vocabulary, but he is entertaining. 'Later on,' he said, 'we'll be showing the FA Cup draw, but for now here are my special guests, "Tenors Unlimited!"' With that, three opera singers in immaculate suits and very shiny Italian shoes entered the room and began a full repertoire of operatic favourites. At the time they came on, Suzannah was sat at our table in between Wub and me, 'These are our boys,' she said proudly. 'We used to put these on at Chelsea; we take them everywhere we go now.' Opera is not my favourite type of music by any stretch of the imagination, but these blokes were good. Especially when they sang an opera version of 'Marching on Together'! But then, just as they were halfway through the atmospheric 1990 World Cup song 'Nessun Dorma', Ken signalled for their microphones to be cut. The three surprised singers were plunged into silence as the televisions all around the room instantly sprang to life showing the FA Cup draw. As soon as we had drawn West Brom away, the TVs were switched off and Ken shouted to his deflated singers, 'Sorry boys, carry on.'

Wub, although not quite a vegetarian, is not a big meat eater, but she developed a major taste for the beef Wellington on offer at these parties. As we left the function some hours later, I had a warm glow in my swelled belly, but little did I know that this was just the first instalment of a happy, but unlikely relationship with Mr and Mrs Ken Bates.

Not everything was plain sailing when Ken Bates took over the reins at Leeds United Football Club – far from it. He had upset the fans by replacing the official Leeds United Supporters' Club with his own conception: The Members' Club. This instantly divided Leeds fans; some joining the new Members' Club, others defying Bates and remaining with the Supporters' Club. At times, things got really heated between fans as arguments ensued on a weekly basis. Mr Bates had also upset the media, but it was the fans who undoubtedly bore the brunt of this new regime. Ticket prices went up and season tickets had to be purchased halfway through the previous season.

At Chelsea, he introduced and formed a fans' pitch ownership scheme. Chelsea Pitch Ownership (CPO) basically meant that Stamford Bridge, the home of Chelsea, could never be sold to property developers irrespective of how many shares are owned by one individual. CPO also own the name Chelsea Football Club Limited which in effect means that should Chelsea move to another stadium in the future, as it stands now, they would not be allowed to use the name Chelsea Football Club without permission of 75 per cent of CPO shareholders.

Bates planned to bring in a similar scheme at Elland Road. 'The fans' organisation will grant the club a 199-year lease at £1 a year and give us a 199-year licence to use the name of Leeds United Football Club. That should ensure that any greedy, predatory, property developers won't waste their time knocking on the door.' This scheme, along with his plans to build a hotel at the ground, was never to materialise. The façade at the East Stand is remarkably like the one at Stamford Bridge, both instigated by Ken Bates.

Ken's parties are always held around Christmas time or just after the New Year. One year, it was held in the Banqueting Suite at the back of the West Stand and the place where Wub and I had held our wedding reception after getting married in the boardroom. Ken Bates also has a very good memory. I had mentioned to him previously that I was concerned that the club would sell Luciano Becchio, who arguably was our best player at the time. The next time I saw him, Leeds had just given Becchio a new deal, and as we entered the Banqueting Suite, Ken was falling over himself to get to me, 'I told you we wouldn't sell Becchio, didn't I? You have to trust me.' At another party we walked into the reception area and Ken and Suzannah greeted us warmly as usual, and then Ken said, 'Hi Lesley, I see you're still with this scruffy get!'

It was at one of Ken's parties that I was privileged to meet and chat with Lord Harewood, who was Leeds United president until his sad death in 2011. George Lascelles, to give him his real name, was Her Majesty the Queen's first cousin and was knighted by the Queen as a Knight Commander of the British Empire. His widow, Patricia, Countess of Harewood, took over as patron of the club. I also had a very interesting chat one time with the well-known newspaper reporter Martin Samuel and, surprisingly for a media man, a long-time admirer of Ken Bates and an avid West Ham fan. There was a great sing-song on one occasion led by Simon Grayson and Glynn Snodin, 'Marching on Together'. 'We are Leeds'. I often wonder if Ken knew then that he would be sacking both of them in the next couple of weeks? There was also an appearance once by the infamous 'Yellow Peril', a Leeds supporter from Northampton who later locked horns with Bates after he revoked his disability season ticket. Ken did have a point, after witnessing 'Peril' energetically dancing the night away at his party and him then trying to purchase a disabled season ticket just weeks later. It made no difference in the end as Peril was summoned to be detained elsewhere on another unfortunate matter – for 11 years. It was also at one of these parties that I met Lebanese businessman Ismail Ghandour, who suggested the title for this book.

Brian McDermott's first appearance at one of the parties was interesting. I observed from the next table as Brian looked so natural and unassuming, with the whole of his socks showing and a few inches of leg met the hem of his trousers. His face was priceless when he encountered the Tenors Unlimited; his jaw simply dropped as they had the audience waving their napkins in time to the music, Brian included, albeit awkwardly. He had literally only been here a couple of days then and he really must have thought 'what the hell am I doing here?' when I intercepted him as he made his way to the toilet; I grabbed his ears and kissed him on the top of his head saying, 'Welcome to Leeds, Brian. Please take us up!'

A former chairman at his first club Oldham Athletic in the early 1960s, spoke about Bates: 'You may be surprised to learn that Ken Bates has a few critics (laughs from the audience). But he has done a hell of a lot of good work in the world of football. He was behind the deal that ensured that TV cash is shared equally. He proposed parachute payments for relegated clubs. He was the chairman of the Wembley committee that, at the second attempt, oversaw the building of the new Wembley Stadium.' The audience laughed again when he said, 'And I can assure you that Ken wasn't responsible for the first Wembley project going tits up and swallowing hundreds of millions of pounds.'

While chairman at Wembley, Bates invited Tony and Cherie Blair as guests of honour for a match, 'but then we got a request for five free tickets for his family on the front row and I told them to fuck off,' said Ken. It appears that Bates wasn't a member of the Labour Party; in the Leeds programme shortly before the 2010 General Election, he wrote, 'I have been urged to vote for the Icelandic Volcano Party. They have done more to stop immigration in the last seven days than the Labour Party has done in 13 years.' Obviously, he is never afraid to speak his mind, 'Alex Ferguson's not very likeable and I dislike Wenger immensely. It was me who named him "Arsehole Whinger".'

At 6pm on 30 July 2013, 'I Predict a Riot' by The Kaiser Chiefs finished and silence fell at Yorkshire Radio. The station had abruptly come to an end. Ken Bates and Yorkshire Radio were no more. And shortly afterwards, Ken Bates and Leeds United were no more either as he sold the club to GFH. I remember Wub being a bit sad that he'd left Elland Road and asking, 'Do you think we'll still be invited to his birthday party?'

She needn't have worried and the following Christmas, we were his guests for a meal at the Foundry restaurant in Leeds. It was at this particular gathering that I confronted Gwyn Williams, not my favourite person I have to say, and possibly fuelled by the free Shiraz, I gave the man that Bates had brought from Chelsea as his technical director a piece of my mind. I did lay off him eventually after being calmed down by Wub, but not before I had told him that he looked like Peter Griffin from *The Family Guy* – with about as much integrity.

To celebrate Bates' 50 years in football, he held a grand affair at the swish Chelsea Harbour Hotel, just before Christmas 2015. Despite leaving Leeds United two years earlier, many old Leeds faces were on the guest list. Lorna Tinkler, Eddie and Linda Gray, Mr and Mrs McClelland, Neil Redfearn and Lucy Ward, Mr and Mrs Sutcliffe, Tony Czopczyc and the proverbial pantomime villain, Shaun Harvey. Dennis Wise was there, as was Di Matteo, Graeme Le Saux and bizarrely, the camp astrologer Russell Grant looking resplendent in his familiar colour of purple with a handkerchief the size of a bed sheet protruding from his top pocket and arms linked with a man on either side. We arrived early and after a spot of people-watching in the main reception area, we made our way to the bar. Big mistake; a small bottle of lager and a Baileys over ice cost me a cool £17. I had noticed in the reception that there had been a large gingerbread house and alongside that was a small keg with a tap dispensing free mulled wine. I spent the next half hour draining the keg dry before joining the 300 guests in the main room. The usual standard of fayre was in evidence and a great evening was had by all – although we did have to fight that little bit harder to keep the constant flow of wine that we had become accustomed to. At around 1am, our cab arrived outside and the rear door was opened for us by a very smart man in a top hat who immediately held out his gloved hand. I shook it warmly before climbing into the taxi and heading for our more modest hotel a couple of miles away and a £4 pint of Stella.

Throughout his time at Leeds United, Ken Bates lived in Monaco – a tax haven. He starts his day watching Sky Sports News before tuning into the BBC's *Look North*. After a spell in his Jacuzzi, he would talk on the phone with Shaun Harvey and the then manager, Simon Grayson. He would then settle down with his two newspapers of choice, the *Daily Mail* and *The Times*. He will then make his way to his 'office' – the Café de Paris in Monte Carlo. When once asked if he owned a computer, Bates replied, 'Yes. It looks very nice. I never use it – but it looks nice.'

Ken Bates has been called many names over the years, 'Colonel Sanders' being probably the only one that can be repeated and Leeds fans will always be divided over Bates, with the majority undoubtedly on the anti-side. I personally thought he stayed on too long at the club; his policy of selling the club's top players and not replacing them with like for like was never going to get the club promoted. And his determination to offload established favourites at the club was always going to be unpopular with the fans. Gary Kelly was unceremoniously pushed out of the club in 2007. Admittedly, Kelly was one of the club's high earners, but he told me at the time that I wrote my second book, 'I would have played for nothing for this club.' One of the very few 'one club players' around, Kelly even donated £750,000 of the money he received from his testimonial to build the Cancer Support Centre in his home town of Drogheda, in memory of his sister, Mandy, who had died of cancer at the age of 35.

Eirik Bakke was another player who was forced out by Bates, 'It was me and Gary Kelly that Bates wanted out of the club. But football is more than money. It is about playing, having fun. It was a shame I had to leave, but I had no choice.'

And there were very strong suggestions that still linger today, that Bates did not want promotion. One former Leeds manager told me, 'The perfect scenario for Bates was a play-off final appearance but stay in the Championship. That way the crowds would stay solid because we were near the top and the final money was vital. Also by not going up he did not have to pay the bond holders what they would have been due if we were promoted.' Bates still has an eye on Leeds United and he has opened a new radio station on Elland Road itself. The ingeniously re-titled Radio Yorkshire sits almost hidden away from the public eye above the Subway sandwich shop behind the South Stand.

Nationwide opinion of Bates is also divided. I know many Chelsea fans still hate him to this day; others love him. I was once on the Hawksby and Jacobs show on TalkSport in London and both of them were hugely impressed that an ordinary fan (me) could be invited to his private birthday parties or as Ken Bates sometimes calls them, 'A Party for Friends'.

A few months after Bates left Leeds United Football Club, I returned home one day to hear a message on my answer machine by the man himself. 'Hello. Hello. Are you there? I'll try again later. By the way, have you had your fuckin' hair cut yet?' And there was another time where the message was: 'It's Gary Edwards again – I rang you earlier and you were engaged and now you're on your answer phone. Don't tell me you've hung yourself. If "we" beat Middlesbrough on Saturday, we'll be in the top six – you can then get out there and paint some more fire engines. Its Ken Bates, I'll call you later – this evening, and hopefully you're in, bye.' His wife is the soothing half of the partnership and Suzannah Bates once wrote a lovely letter to Wub thanking her for a Christmas gift of homemade truffles, saying that they were absolutely gorgeous.

Some will always hate Ken Bates, that's for sure, and perhaps with good reason. Others would say Ken sails very close to the wind – for me it's more like he crashes through the waves with every single sail of his ship billowing provocatively in the face of every sign of authority. He thrives on controversy.

That said, I have to say that when I meet him, I like him. He is brash, self-opinionated and at times can be downright obnoxious, but believe it or not there is a very humorous and very generous side.

Unknown to most people he gives to many charities and being born with a club foot, he has learnt to overcome many obstacles during his life, some by fair means, some not. And provided you aren't in the opposite camp to him, he is very, very entertaining.

Bates spoke of big plans for Leeds United, but it's fair to say that not many of them materialised. Plans to buy back Elland Road and the Thorp Arch training complex fizzled out. An ambitious idea to build a hotel within the confines of Elland Road, similar to what he'd done at Chelsea, never got off the ground either. A Leeds United museum was proposed and shelved.

During the summer of 2007, just weeks after Leeds had been relegated to League One the *Yorkshire Evening Post* printed an article claiming that Duncan Revie, the son of former legendary manager Don, wanted to head a consortium to buy Leeds United on behalf of a sheik, reputed to be in the top five richest people in the world. The proposals apparently broke down because of disagreements over non-declaration of United's funds. Duncan wanted to remove everyone from the club including Ken Bates and manager Dennis Wise. Talks were short-lived and Revie left without a deal. I talked to Duncan at great length when researching a previous book and we often talked about his Dad and Duncan's attempt to buy the club. We provided the proof of funds required (£10m) to authenticate a bid for the club. 'I have been absolutely staggered by the reaction of the Leeds fans and my interest in taking over the club. I've always said that they are the most passionate fans in the world and they certainly are. My Dad is still held in high esteem in the Emirates, and that was one of the reasons for this bid to buy the club we love.'

Duncan told Radio Leeds, 'My Middle Eastern backer has upped the pace, proof of funds have been provided and I would like the fans to know that it is my intention to put Leeds United Football Club back where it belongs, in the top flight.'

Bates had taken the club into administration during the final game of the 2006/07 season at Derby, by which time Leeds had been relegated. The business had been bought by a new company, Leeds United FC Limited, of which Bates was chairman, immediately after the club went into administration. Duncan Revie: 'I'm approaching this with my heart, but my financial people are pulling me back and reminding me that we have to think this through sensibly, from a business perspective. We have to be sure that our plans would be workable. It requires a bit of head to go with the heart. That's why we'll spend a few days going over the figures at Leeds before deciding whether or not to make an offer.'

After the meeting between Bates and Revie, the *Yorkshire Evening Post* reported, 'Duncan Revie described Ken Bates as "fairly honourable" but it is unlikely that Elland Road would be big enough to hold both Bates and Revie's backer – a takeover would mean exactly that. It is pretty clear that Revie's vision involves extracting Bates from United altogether.'

Revie: 'My Dad once said to me in the 1960s about Elland Road, "a shed at one end and an old open mound at the other and the pitch is awful," and Dad just kept pointing around telling me that, "one day, son, there'll be private boxes in here, there'll be people coming to lunch at 12 o'clock and not five to three. There'll be sponsorship on the shirts, there will be television worldwide and it will be a complete revolution." I looked at him as if he was mad, but everything he said has come to pass.' Unfortunately, Duncan Revie's consortium did not proceed with their bid.

Revie again: 'I was very, very close. I had a very agonising time, we had the backing of the people in Dubai, who had taken my Dad out there in the 70s, but I did consult widely with other players and with my family, and they said, "Do you really need the aggravation?" I'm sure we would have done a great job, but football is a funny business. But I do feel that we would have got Leeds back to the Championship and then, in time, to the Premier League.'

Then, quite unexpectedly, in 2013, Ken Bates, former travel entrepreneur, property developer and dairy farmer, without consulting Wub or I, sold Leeds United to Gulf Finance House (GFH) from Bahrain. You can read more on this delightful little period in the final chapter.

Dennis Wise did eventually leave Leeds and went to Newcastle as some sort of a scout. Bates said, 'His time at Newcastle was a disaster and I heard about Gus Poyet leaving on Sky Sports News. Then he asked to return as manager. No fucking chance – nobody lets me down twice.'

Chapter 13

White Rose Buds

OUR first official White Rose excursion was Burnley away for a pre-season friendly in the summer of 2007. It was prior to our first ever season in League One (the Third Division) and after a few light ales en route, we eventually converged on the famous Burnley Cricket Club. It was the anniversary of Stick's car accident and so we had a drink to celebrate the fact that he was still with us (some people in the crash weren't so lucky) and one thing led to another until after a good drink we eventually left for the ground, which was only a few hundred yards away. However, one of our new leaders, Annette, led by example, had a few more drinks and never left the cricket club.

One of my favourite coach drivers, who must remain anonymous, was sacked by the company for smoking dope. He would probably have got away with it had it not been for the fact that he was smoking the dope while driving. Another driver we had was doing quite a lot of moonlighting, so much so, that when it came to driving us to an away match, he was always dog tired, having just finished driving someone else to say, London or the like only a couple of hours previously.

Consequently, when he picked us up and we hit the road, it was only a matter of time until his eyes began to close. When they did, an orchestra of passengers behind him would be shouting at him to 'waken up!' to which he would open his eyes startled and shout, 'Hey! I was watching that' just in time to steer the coach off of the grids and the hard shoulder, and back on to the motorway.

Then we had 'Johnny Brakes', who every now and again would jam the brakes on. He would then say, 'they just came on on their own' which obviously, unless there was a major mechanical fault, was impossible. One day he braked so hard for no apparent reason that he sent Big Tony hurtling along the aisle floor so fast that only carrier bags full of hundreds of empty beer cans and bottles blocking the aisle prevented him from being launched at the speed of sound straight through the windscreen.

One of our more infamous drivers was Brad. I liked Brad a lot, but he was a man who, once he'd made his mind up, would not change it. We were once travelling along a country road in Norfolk when Brad couldn't decide which was West or which was East Dereham. Despite insistence from the passengers that 'It is the other way', he ignored them. 'It's not down here Brad, it's too narrow,' he was told time and time again, but yet he continued to proceed down a lane that was just barely wide enough for the coach. The next instant our coach was travelling in reverse at about 20mph chased by a very irate, red-faced farmer in his Land Rover, nose to nose with our coach. All the time, the Fleetwood Mac song, 'Go Your Own Way', was playing out over the radio. You couldn't make it up.

We'd often go miles out of our way when we left a ground and someone would shout, 'Where are we off to Brad?' To which he'd reply, 'I'm finding an off-licence for Edwards.' Bless him. Brad would often drive stood up for a 'stretch'. He also had a fondness for the brakes and one day I was the victim. I was stood up near the back when he braked so hard that I fell forward and I was covered in red wine from the bottle I was holding – it looked as if I'd been shot! This was on the way to Selhurst Park for a match with Crystal Palace and although I had consumed alcohol, I certainly wasn't drunk, but a steward at the turnstile, looking at my appearance with wine stains all down my shirt and jeans assumed I was and I was refused entry. I didn't argue and calmly walked across the road and sat on a garden wall planning my next move.

As I was sat on this wall the owner of the house came out – he was a 6ft plus West Indian. After asking me what I was doing, and me explaining my misunderstanding at the turnstile, he went into the house and brought us both a cold can of Stella which we sat and drank in the scorching sun. When we had finished he said, 'Come on, I'll get you in.' When we arrived back at the turnstile this bloke tried to reason with the steward – I think with the steward being of mixed race he thought he would let me in if he spoke to him on my behalf. But he didn't, so I thanked my helper and after watching a bit of the match through a gate I walked down to the bottom of the road and got a ticket in with the Palace fans. Once inside, I was on the same side as the Leeds fans, but in the Palace half. Periodically I would wave across to Andy and Annette who were of course with the Leeds fans.

Everyone on the coach held Brad in high esteem and that was reflected in the large amount of bottle tops in his whip round. Looking back, I suppose it was all just a gamble to Brad. Whenever we would have an overnight stay, Brad would spend a considerable amount of time and money on the bandits and fruit machines. He would shout and swear loudly if his cherries didn't conform or his apples upset the cart, but he would always buy a drink for whoever was near him on the odd occasion when it all came to fruition.

We had one or two colourful characters at the wheel during our Kippax days too. Big Dave, formerly my brother-in-law, and his sidekick Bill Foster were very often more entertaining than the lads sitting behind them. Another driver who must remain anonymous decided to drink pint for pint with us. It was during our Kippax days and Leeds had agreed to play a friendly against Stevenage Borough to officially unveil their new floodlights, so we set off down south with members of other branches, including the Harrogate and Vine, on board. After the match we stopped off at a small market town for a couple of pints. It was fast approaching 11pm when a lad came in and said that the landlord at the pub further down the street was a Yorkshireman, and wanted to know if we wanted a lock-in. In seconds flat there was about 50 empty pint glasses on the tables and we'd gone to meet the man from Yorkshire. By now we had been joined by the driver wanting to know what time we wanted to leave. We bought him a pint and he came and sat with us. By the time we left the pub at around 2am, the driver had easily consumed at least a gallon of lager. As our coach drove out of the town, swerving violently from side to side, we took out a couple of the empty market stalls and one of the frames was even attached to the underside of the coach causing sparks as we disappeared into the country. It wasn't long before someone wanted a piss-stop and the driver immediately pulled sharply into a lay-by and we were heading straight for a snack-bar caravan. We all closed our eyes as the coach swerved around the back of the caravan and came to an abrupt halt perilously overlooking a deep ditch. When we were halfway home we stopped at the services where we thought the driver would be able to freshen up a bit. But as we were about to leave, we had to wake the driver up who was fast asleep and laid flat out on a table with his arms and legs dangling over either side. Nobody got any sleep for the rest of the journey as we took it in turns at the front continuously tapping the driver and constantly singing songs to keep him awake.

White Rose's Charlie's Angels hit on the idea of a branch calendar to raise funds for charity. It was to be a nude calendar and I have to say there was no shortage of volunteers. I had the dubious honour of being on the front cover with a 6ft-long woollen Leeds scarf covering my prized asset. Charlie's Angels, of course, wasted no time in getting their kit off too, but it was the shy ones who began to take centre stage. We had Keith sorting his pipes and soldier Amos, on a break from fighting evil in Afghanistan, covering his modesty with his large helmet, Andy was wearing only a nice tie while Danny stared menacingly at the camera scaring the shit out of everyone. Smithy used our local photographer Hamish to full advantage and the end product of him sporting a jester's hat in the Leeds colours was genius. And then we had Jeff sat on the coach, using my bottle of wine strategically for his picture and Butter hanging out of his JCB wearing just his Leeds scarf. But I suppose the star of the calendar was good old Basher Bates. Basher is 'ample' in human form and when he was arranging his photograph for the calendar, Bash said to his dad, Andy, 'Will you take my picture with my Leeds scarf on while I sit on my motorbike?' His Dad then walked outside with his camera only to encounter Bash sat on his bike with nothing on but his Leeds scarf whilst the petrol tank hid his privates. That calendar is nearly ten years old but many still refer to Basher as simply, 'Mr August'.

One of the 'Angels' Jo, often gives me a treat when she gets on the coach set for another adventure – a Cadbury's Creme Egg. Once, on the way back from a midweek game, I was enjoying a nice bottle of Shiraz when we pulled up at the services in the early hours and I asked one of the lads to fetch me a Creme Egg or some chocolate mini eggs. On his return he said, 'Couldn't find a Creme Egg so I got you this.' It was a scotch egg!

We have two more Jos on the coach. One who brings a tinful of her delicious homemade chocolate brownies, and the other one who comes up and down the bus with her pink fluffy flashing pen, fleecing us all for a quid for the football card. Jo with her football card is married to Andy (Monkey) and they get on at Barnsley with the rest of the contingent, Paul, Ben, Jack and co. Monkey then attacks us from the rear wanting a pound for raffle tickets and then, as we are still reeling, Jo Barrett attacks from the front wanting the bus fare. It's like travelling aboard a working men's club on wheels. Monkey and Jo are the parents of Maurice, who is a two-foot stuffed monkey. He doesn't say much, but I'll bet if he did, he'd want a quid from us all. Before Jo and Monkey were married and their relationship was in its infancy, Monkey took Jo to her first match – away to Luton. Stu (Sticks) Hayward was in the disabled section and was getting abuse from some Luton fans. Andy Marshall told Monkey that they had better go help Sticks. 'Okay,' agreed Monkey, but Jo said, 'No fighting!' and went off to the toilet with Andy's wife Annette. While they were gone, Leeds scored and as Monkey and Andy embraced, Andy accidentally punched him in the eye and when Jo returned she looked at Monkey's emerging black eye and she went nuts. Brad, the driver, loved nothing better than throwing the coach around roundabouts and invariably, Monkey was in the toilet when he did so, resulting in quite a lot of extra liquid being splashed on Monkey. So, on one pub stop at Towcester he decided to go to the toilet when everyone got off – but while in there, Brad, oblivious to Monkey being in the toilet, moved the coach. A rather wet Monkey arrived at the pub to a reception of loud cheers, led by his wife Jo.

Toilets, Brad and Monkey go hand in hand so to speak. On one very long midweek away match, courtesy of the league's 'random' computer, Monkey got on at Barnsley and didn't notice we had two drivers on board and when the coach set off and Brad made his way to the toilet at the back, Monkey shouted, 'Fucking hell Brad, who's driving the coach?'

We have several characters within our ranks. In 2010, Martin Bland, who comes from that famous Leeds fan stronghold – Huddersfield – changed his name in order to stand in the election for Leeds Central. Of course, many people before him have changed their name in pursuit of their political dreams. Mad Cap'n Tom became a pirate whose policies included 'rum t'be tax free' and with the promise of changing the name of the iPad to the iPatch. In 1987, ex-boxer Terry Marsh contested the South Basildon election as 'None of the above' and the Monster Raving Loony Party provided a candidate in a Mid-Derbyshire election under the name of Mr R.U. Seerius. A Sussex constituency were given a pledge to save the dodo, despite the fact that it had been extinct since 1681. Baron Von Thunderclap also promised to make sub-aqua hang-gliding an Olympic sport. But none of these come close to our Martin; he planned to stand in the Central Leeds constituency and in preparation changed his name to, 'We Beat the Scum 1-0'. He had planned originally to name his new political party by that name, but time ran out, so he decided instead to change his name and stand individually. But first he needed a £500 deposit and that came from the most unlikely of sources. Ken Bates was amused by the name and the whole concept, and agreed to give half of the money required for the deposit. Leeds' press officer at the time, Paul Dews, met our new candidate a week later on the steps outside Leeds Town Hall and handed him a brown envelope with the full amount of £500. Game on. He was now ready to stand against heavyweight political campaigners such as Hilary Benn, using the campaign slogan: 'Lose your vote with a smile'. Unfortunately, 'Mr 1-0' as he is known on his official match tickets from the club, didn't win and lost his (Ken's) deposit, which he had pledged to donate to the Leeds Candlelighters charity in honour of Leeds fans Kevin Speight and Chris Loftus who were murdered in Istanbul in 2000, had he retained it.

Joshua Tetley's much loved brewery, and workplace of Wub's for almost 40 years, closed in 2011, and as Big Si says, 'The only Tetley's to come out of Leeds these days are the Tetley coaches carrying Leeds fans all over the country.' Several branches, including ours, use the Hunslet-based company and after the fleet has set off through the early morning mist, the coaches can be seen hours later all travelling in different directions, along country lanes to secret locations and pub stops dotted all around the final destination town. One really annoying aspect when travelling away is the constant 'phantom' roadworks where speed is restricted to 50mph with no apparent signs of any work being carried out – these restrictions often last for anything up to 50 miles in distance.

We found ourselves encased in one of these stretches as we travelled south once to a match at QPR. We had only gone a few miles when we had to adhere to the enforced 50mph limit. The only trouble on this occasion was that our coach couldn't get up to 50 miles an hour – in fact it was hard pressed to reach 20mph. This hadn't escaped the eagle-eyed amongst us and Bob shouted rather politely to our driver TJ, 'What the fuck's going on with the bus TJ?' To which TJ just shrugged his shoulders and said, 'I don't know Bob, it appears to be knackered'. TJ is a 6ft well-built black man and nothing ruffles his feathers. Danny, our leader, rang the coach company for a replacement bus to be sent out only to be told that they didn't have another bus and we would have to continue as we were. Minutes later, after TJ himself rang them to fully explain the severity of the situation, they miraculously found two spare coaches in their yard. We had originally arranged to stop at a pub in Putney before going on to the match, but decided to have our pub stop in

Alfreton, Derbyshire, giving the replacement coach time to catch us up and swap over. We had stopped here on previous visits to places such as Derby and Nottingham, so TJ tapped it into his satnav. However, we soon found ourselves in a very tight residential cul-de-sac at about half eight in the morning and TJ had to do a 36-point manoeuvre to turn around. On about the 23rd turn, our windscreen was literally inches away from the front window of a terraced house. At that precise moment, the owner of the house opened his curtains to witness a 50-seater coach full of football fans and a large black man behind the wheel an inch away from his living room all staring back at him. Then in a brilliant comedy moment the man in the house closed his curtains and then slowly reopened them slightly and peered back out through his window – we were still there, staring into his house. With his curtains now closed again we completed our manoeuvre and trundled out of the cul-de-sac closely watched by a nosy neighbour as she stood in her front garden a little further down feeding the birds. I should say, 'overfeeding the birds' as by the time she'd finished gawping at us, she must have emptied the whole contents of a large box of seed on to her small bird table which resulted in a few overweight sparrows struggling to take off again.

After a few hours in the pub, we returned to our replacement coach and a chuckling TJ; it transpired that the other driver of this replacement had used the same satnav details as us and ended up in the same cul-de-sac as us, with the nosy neighbour still witnessing the whole thing and apparently still pouring seed. A few games after this trip, a game at Wolves in December 2015, sadly TJ left the company, but we have many fond memories of a great bloke, who still makes an appearance now and again on our coach as a passenger.

Back in the day when we could have alcohol on board, Big Si would gently sip his chilled gin and tonic, while the rest of his Airedale Terriers, Andy, Dave, Lewis and Fez would make do with a few lagers. Big Tony, however, overdid it on one return trip from Charlton Athletic – his trip, as we stood outside the coach at the services, took him headlong into the unforgiving large metal hub of the front wheel of the coach which combined with bolts the size of a small tin of beans left many cuts and bruises on Tony's head. Little Dave saw Tony stumble, but unfortunately could do nothing about it, and as Tony, almost in slow motion, tripped and on his way to head-butting the wheel, took Dave out too, pinning him to the floor. Tony's injuries would normally require medical attention, but with the alcohol acting as an anaesthetic, he was fine.

These days of course alcohol is not allowed on the coach, but confusion reigned when the ban was first brought in and the rules were somewhat hazy; for example, whether or not you were allowed to drink on the way back from the match or not. One time, we were unexpectedly pulled over by an over-zealous traffic cop, causing absolute mayhem on board as what seemed to be an endless supply of beer and lager bottles and cans, cool boxes, barrels, casks, a small dray wagon, boxes of wine, vats of sherry and a medium-sized distillery were hurled backwards towards the secret compartment we used to have on the coach. It was an impressive operation that would not have looked out of place in *The Great Escape* or even episodes of the long-forgotten but brilliant *Hogan's Heroes*. Never mind all those tons of soil in the films, we shifted the contents of a small high street off-licence in just two minutes flat. The cop apparently had over-reacted and stopped us by mistake, but we left him with his superior officer tearing a strip from him. The 'TSSST!' of the opening of cans and bottles as we resumed our activities was delightful.

In September 2015, Les Rowley, who had been the producer of the stage play *Paint it White,* approached me with an idea to travel on our coach to an away match. Now working for the new TV channel, Made in Leeds, he and Mark O'Brien thought it would be a good idea to do a 'fly on the wall' documentary of our branch in full swing as it was on the road.

So one Saturday morning at 6.30 the crew arrived at my house, six hours before our kick-off at Huddersfield Town. I had stressed to Les beforehand that I'd like to be at the pub as soon as possible to meet up with the rest of them. Despite moving my living room clock forward on two occasions when they weren't looking, they were still at my house for around two hours. Eventually we made our way to the pub. The Hope Inn in Leeds is where we meet up for every away game. The landlord, Gary, as mentioned earlier, runs the Hope Branch, but both branches meet there for a drink before the game, before departing in our separate coaches.

The TV crew continued to film once at the pub and Gary gave a great interview outside in the car park where the original signage 'Leeds United AFC' from the old West Stand at Elland Road dominates the Hope Inn car park. Interviews continued in the pub with young and upcoming Leeds fan Harry Todd, son of Phil.

Another outdoor interview took place with Monkey, Maurice the Monkey and Nigel. Once on board for the short trip along the M62 the cameras continued to roll. Baz was sat next to me as the crew slowly made their way up the coach from the front to conduct interviews with different members. Baz, not normally quiet, then said to me, 'They'd better not come to me. I don't want to say owt!' Slowly, the crew approached us and then walked past us and went to interview Fez a row back. 'Why haven't they asked me owt?' Baz said. It was a brilliantly funny moment. A good mate of mine for many years, Baz is one of the best Leeds fans I know and has been watching the club for as long as I can remember, and it's about ten years since he missed a game either home or away. Les Rowley came to sit just behind me and sat beside Big Tony who explained to him how he has written many popular Leeds songs, then proceeded to sing one, to the rousing tune of Davy Crockett – 'Johnny, Johnny Giles. King of the United – Leeds!' Les's face was priceless. As the crew continued around the bus gleaning stories of the fans' commitment to our club, we quickly arrived at Leeds Road, Huddersfield. How they must hate that name. The Made in Leeds crew had hoped to continue filming inside the ground, but Sky TV and their regulations prevented them from entering the stadium. Instead, they went for a cup of tea until the game had finished. One of the first fans to be interviewed after the game outside our coach was our old friend Belfast Bill – Mark Cosgrove. I've mentioned my long-time friend and top-drawer Leeds fan from Glengormley, Northern Ireland, many times in previous recollections, but suffice to say that in 1982 he won the *Shoot* football magazine Fan of the Year and even today, Mark remains one of the club's most loyal supporters.

Three of our apprentices, Danny, Danny and Tommy T-dog, who we call The Inbetweeners, were sat in the Hope one morning, taking the piss out of his mobile phone which must have been one of the first ones ever made. The screen on it is smaller than a postage stamp and when young Tom took it off him, he was in fits of laughter over it, and then he tried to scroll down. 'It's broke,' he said, 'you can't scroll up or down.' Baz snatched it back and said, 'You don't scroll on this one – use the menu thing.' 'It's ancient,' said Danny, and Baz shouted, 'At least I can place a bet on it.' 'What, on that? Can you hell!' said Danny. 'I'll bet you a fuckin' fiver that I can bet on this phone!' said an irate Baz with not an inkling of what he'd just said.

Young Tom was a bit off colour on one trip and Baz said 'here drink this'. It was rum and brandy – and it perked Tom up no end. I just happened to say to Baz that Don Revie used to give his players sherry and a raw egg when he was in charge and a while later we were talking about Baz's remedy for Tom and Baz said, 'You can do what Revie used to do and give 'em chilli and egg.' I told Baz that it wasn't chilli. 'Oh aye, sorry, sherry trifle, that's what you want.'

One morning as our coach picked up in Leeds, Kjell, our resident Norwegian got on, and Ady shouted, 'Hey it's Jager-Man (Jagermeister)!' Kjell responded in a flash saying, 'Hey, it's naked man!' referring to a time on our way back from a match when Ady decided to strip off and have a run round the car park.

At a cup match at Bradford in 2014, Hockaday's last match in charge, I was stood in the concourse with Smithy just before kick-off when one of the balls that the teams were knocking about with came rolling up a tunnel near us and landed at Smithy's feet. He picked it up and stuffed it up his t-shirt. A young ball boy came and asked him for it back to which Smithy said, 'No'. The ball boy left and returned with a steward who asked him for the ball, again Smithy said 'No'. The steward went away and before he returned with a copper we went up into the stand with the ball still under Smithy's shirt. After the match Smithy walked back on to the coach still with the ball up his t-shirt and when he got it home he gave it to his son Arran, who took it to school the next day where it ended up on a high roof and has remained there ever since.

I feel like I know Dodworth 'doddath' roundabout like the back of my hand as we've been picking up there now for decades and they're a different breed, them flat-cappers. I chuckled one day as we were ambling down the M1 and two cows were embroiled in a bit of passion in a field. One of our Tykes said, 'Did tha si them two? Just doin' it 'an that aat i'oppan. Tha'd a' thowt thu'da got hiddy or somat wunt tha?'

We were blessed to have a young lad called Reece Hopkins who used to travel with us; sadly, he passed away a couple of years back at just 25. He was a major part of our branch and everyone has their own fond memories of him. He used to bring his own big bottle of 'special' coke which after consuming you would not be able to drive for several days. When I saw him drinking his coke I used to think of the old Coca-Cola advert in the 1970s when the New Seekers sang, *I'd like to teach the world to* (change the word sing for drink) and repeat.

We've had one or two early set-offs in our time too, and one morning it was pitch black and I could just make out these two pointed things sticking up in the seat in front of me. As it got a bit lighter I noticed they were ears, like dog's ears. I had to look twice and then discovered it was Andy Mitchell sat there and he had a Scooby Doo onesie on – it takes all sorts I suppose. When it did eventually get light, Amos said to Andy, 'I've been trying to work out for ages what you were mate,' and Neil, sat next to Amos just shrugged his shoulders. On his tours of Afghanistan and elsewhere with the forces, Amos will have seen it all; but waiting for daylight and discovering you're sat with Scooby Doo going to Watford won't be on that list.

I don't want to blow my own trumpet here, but I'm a pretty accomplished musician – by that I mean I can play the egg slicer. I brought it along one day and got out my small amplifiers and opened my small song sheet at 'Marching on Together' and served up a passable rendition of our anthem. Well I thought I had, but on the way back home the egg slicer was nowhere to be seen and I found the amps a few seats down. But also missing was my ham sandwich. Baz was the nearest, but he wouldn't admit to it and even after ringing Crimestoppers and *Crimewatch* I never saw my sandwich again.

It doesn't happen too often these days but it's great to travel home on the White Rose with Tricia's Northern Soul banging out of the speakers, and we have a right good sing-song and sometimes even a dance. Jonathon and Jenny, and over the years Christine and Ann-Marie. And when we pull up at the last services, it is an education watching two of the Jos and Viv get off, light up, and send smoke signals back home with what they want for their tea.

Leeds are blessed with some of the best supporters' branches in the country and I have great memories of travelling with the Pontefract Whites, after the Kippax was disbanded, and the Knaresborough Branch with Graham Ive, who I used to travel with to England games at the old Wembley Stadium. Then there are the Harrogate Whites, with Stella, Charlie, John, Jimmy, and Geoff among many others. On one trip with the Harrogate branch, we were on our way home from a game at Bristol City and snow was falling heavily, and poor old Stella got a tad annoyed at everyone throwing snowballs at him at the services, but once we resumed our journey, we were confined to the middle lane as the inside and outside lane were white over, and the trickle of traffic was progressing in a very slow, single file. It was difficult to see out as the wipers were no match for the huge dollops of snow clogging up the windscreen, and the driver even suggested that we may not get home and would have to pull over somewhere for the night. All of a sudden, like some sort of ghost ship, a huge shape overtook us – it was the Leeds team coach, and as if raised above the snow, it continued effortlessly into the distance. A brief attempt by our coach to follow in its tracks was quickly aborted and we were soon back in the middle lane trudging along. Eventually the weather did clear up and before too long we were met on the horizon by the welcoming bright lights of quite possibly the best city in the world – Leeds. I've enjoyed being in the company of other branches too, Mick and the Vine Branch need no introduction of course and the Hope Inn are up there too with Gary Barass at the helm. And now the White Rose, a very well-run branch by the two

Jos, Monkey and Danny has emerged as a well-established branch of the official supporters' club, and we still have one or two other former Kippax foot soldiers in our ranks, such as Terry 'Jacknife' Ford and John West.

Even the police seem to have mellowed over recent years. One came to me and Baz as we stood near the front one night at Bristol City. He wore a baseball cap, flak jacket and jack boots and we thought we'd done something wrong, but instead he just said, 'I've never seen fans like this,' looking up at the Leeds fans, 'they are amazing!' Baz replied, 'You a Leeds fan then mate?'

To which the copper said, 'No, I'm West Ham, but I've never seen anything like that!' as he looked up again at the masses behind the goal.

Unfortunately, there are still some bad apples in the police force – and that includes the Humberside lot. They are nasty and arrogant and some Hull City fans are just as nasty. During a recent game at the KC Stadium, Leeds defender Beradi was stretchered off, but as he was being carried behind the Hull goal, he was verbally abused and had objects thrown at him. During that same game, Hull police launched an unprovoked attack on Leeds fans with pepper spray, using it indiscriminately on men, women and children until Leeds stewards reasoned with them to back off. Outside after the game, as those same police filed arrogantly passed the Leeds coaches, one fan near us shouted, 'where's your spray?' to which one of them smiled and patted a canister fastened to his belt. Further on, our coach stopped at a garage, along with Birdy and the Worksop lot and four motorcycle cops came in. I was in a queue behind one of them and said to the shopkeeper, 'Get him a pepper steak slice on me mate.' Luckily the cop took it in good fun (the older ones generally do) and smiled at me and wagged a knowing finger in my face.

Chapter 14

The Vikings Are Back... This Time With Their Boots

THE Moorgate pub is our local boozer run by Bob and Tracy. It's a Samuel Smith's pub, which means there is no television, no music, definitely no singing and it's cheap; just over £2 for a pint of strong lager and under £2 for a pint of hand-pulled bitter. It's got a traditional sporting taproom, rugby, cricket, boxing and Leeds United photographs adorn the walls and we just love it – and so too do hundreds of Norwegians. Well, why wouldn't they? Used to forking out an average eight quid a pint – they absolutely go mental when faced with two quid lager – and bloody good lager at that.

Over the years I've made friends with countless Scandinavian Leeds supporters and on regular visits to Leeds United games, large groups of Norwegians shun the bright lights of the bustling Leeds city centre and travel in fleets of taxis seven miles eastwards to our village of Kippax, and the Moorgate. Tim Harland, a former landlord of the Moorgate, had made friends with many of the Norwegians, and as I knew many Norwegians too, the foundations were laid for a football match between a team from Kippax and a Norwegian side. On the eve of a Leeds United game, the Gate taproom is awash with jolly, noisy Englishmen and women together with Norwegians creating a scene reminiscent of a rowdy inn in merry olde England. I've lost count of how many times our Norwegian guests go to the bar for drinks and thrust a £20 note into the hands of the bar staff and refuse any change, simply saying 'get these a drink' and pointing along the bar to anyone who happened to be stood in the vicinity.

Amongst the jostling crowd most evenings is Tore Pedersen. Now a very successful football agent, Tore played in the Premier League for Wimbledon, Oldham Athletic and Blackburn Rovers and was a Norwegian international with 47 caps. He also played for Eintracht Frankfurt, Sanfrecce Hiroshima and a number of Norwegian clubs, but above all he is a staunch Leeds United supporter. I never tire of relating the story he once told me about when he played at Elland Road for Blackburn. Leeds scored at the Kop end and Tore, one of the conceding defenders, was seen by Rovers' captain Colin Hendry silently celebrating the goal with a clenched fist. When confronted, Tore denied all knowledge, but Hendry had seen, more than once, the tattoo on the inner wrist of Tore – a Leeds United tattoo.

One evening in the taproom and with the atmosphere in full swing, a football match against the Norwegian Leeds fans was arranged. We set the date of the game for 3 December, the day before a Crystal Palace match at Elland Road.

The Viking game had attracted a great deal of attention from the local media such as Radio Leeds and Radio Aire, and two days before the game, Paul Robinson from the *Yorkshire Evening Post* rang me. Snow had fallen heavily in Kippax all week and showed no signs of letting up and Paul wanted to know what the chances were of it still being played. They were slim.

I cannot recall snow as thick since we were young kids sledging down the hills of the local Billy Wood and despite the best efforts of Kippax secretary Dave Easen and a band of spirited volunteers including Chris Rollinson, Dan Ogden and some fine organisational skills from Sean Plows on the morning of the game, the snow fell even faster and as we were shovelling it away, it was falling in huge clumps. There wasn't a 'snowball in hell's' chance of it being played. The *Evening Post*'s award-winning photographer Steve 'Fritz' Riding gallantly turned up and after snapping a couple of photos of the snow white pitch, he left, vowing to return when the game was eventually played. But for now though, it was beer time.

The impressive Kippax Welfare clubhouse is above the dressing rooms so therefore conveniently overlooks the football, cricket and rugby pitches around it. Its steep, creaky wooden steps lead up to a large concert room area and on each table the Norwegians had placed a bottle of their local firewater, Linie Aquavit. Aquavit is a potent Norwegian spirit infused with aniseed and many other ingredients. Linie is Norwegian for equator and even to this day Aquavit is loaded in barrels on to ships and sailed from Norway to Australia and back thus crossing the equator twice before being bottled for distribution. Apparently this procedure allows 'constant movement, high humidity and fluctuating temperature that cause the spirit to extract more flavour and contribute to accelerated maturation'. The room quickly filled up and old faces Big Tony, Bob, and Andy from Castleford were already busily trying out the local fayre, which just happened to include a wide range of Sam Smith's ales. This concert room has housed some fantastic events; regular Northern Soul nights with hundreds of scooters converging for the weekend. We had our very own Kippax night to raise funds for the Don Revie statue in this very club in 2012 attended by organiser Jim Cadman, Allan Clarke and Terry Yorath and hosted by top-class comedian Jed Stone. Jed is a proud Scouser, but a Leeds United season ticket holder. It was a phone call from Jed one Sunday morning that sent me into total disbelief. A good friend of Jed's, ex- Liverpool star Jan Molby, had telephoned him to tell him of the death of our very own Gary Speed. Yorkshire and England's Chris Silverwood hails from Kippax and held his testimonial evening in this room and there have been top tribute evenings in honour of local rugby league legends the late Roger Millward MBE and Malcolm Reilly OBE, both sons of Kippax, and countless other celebrities from the sporting world; but no one has witnessed anything like what happened when the Vikings came to Kippax on 3 December 2011.

The disappointment of there being no actual football match that afternoon quickly subsided into oblivion amidst huge waves of alcohol. TV and stage actor Gary Dunnington, who played me in the adapted play *Paint it White,* had accepted my invitation to attend – and we were both speaking fluent Klingon within a matter of hours. Along with Tore Pedersen, other Norwegian stars were present. Former Leeds player Alfie Haaland soon joined in the fun. Meanwhile, Leeds defender Ben Parker arrived with a signed football, thanks to the club's player liaison officer Stix Lockwood, but as Ben entered the room he immediately encountered the mayhem and quickly became enveloped in the massive wall of sound. I was alerted to his arrival and made my way through the crowd to thank him, but by the time I got there, Ben had left, leaving the ball with the nearest person to him.

The ball and dozens of autographed Leeds training tops and shirts were auctioned with proceeds going to young Kippax resident Noah Woolford, a fantastic little kid who has cerebral palsy – and a braver and happier chap you will never meet. A few weeks later I was having a drink with Noah's dad, Andy, and he told me that I had a few pints paid on at the bar by him. Thinking it was because of the donation to Noah I thanked him but told him it wasn't necessary. 'No, mate, it wasn't for that,' said Andy. 'I watched you fill in the football card the other day. And I put down the same results as you except for one that I changed.' The football card is run by Kippax FC and the punter has to correctly predict who will win from a selection of the following week's fixtures. I've never won a cent and in fact, I don't even look at the corresponding teams in the left-hand column, except for a quick glance to see if Leeds are on, and then I literally put anything down, home win, away win, draw, who cares? Andy wrongly assumed that I knew what I was doing and followed my lead – changing just one of my predictions at random. The following week he won a few hundred quid!

Meanwhile at the club, Alfie Haaland was up on one of the tables dancing and singing, 'We are Leeds! We are Leeds!' This was met with a deafening chant from the floor, 'Alfie! Alfie! Alfie!' and in reference to his well-publicised feud with Roy Keane, 'Alfie's gonna get yer! Alfie's gonna get yer!' with which Alfie happily joined in.

Alfie Haaland won 34 caps and was a Leeds player from 1997 to 1999 and also played for Nottingham Forest and Man City. Alfie had an ongoing feud with Roy Keane who played for Leeds' arch enemies from across the Pennines. In 1997 Keane fouled Haaland during Leeds' 1-0 victory at Elland Road, but in doing so he injured his own anterior cruciate ligament. Keane was booked as he was stretchered off and was out of the game for almost a year. However, the pair clashed again in 2001 and again Keane launched a horrific challenge on Haaland for which he was sent off and fined £5,000. In his autobiography, Keane admitted that the foul was an act of vengeance and for the criticism that Haaland had given Keane back in 1997. On hearing of this, the FA fined Keane £150,000 and banned him for a further five games. Although Alfie admits to bearing no lasting bitterness towards Keane, he further endeared himself to the Leeds faithful by declaring, 'I really dislike United and I can't stand any of their players.' He was also photographed posing in front of anti-United graffiti.

Other prestigious guests present in Kippax were Eirik Bakke who played for his country 27 times and wore the Leeds shirt 143 times. Also Gunnar Halle, who played for Oldham in the Premier League as well as Wolverhampton Wanderers and Bradford City, and of course Leeds United, and gained 64 international caps for Norway.

As the evening progressed, one lad picked up one of the bottles of Linie, poured it into a pint glass and promptly drank it down in one go – he then collapsed in a heap on the floor. There was an overwhelming lack of sympathy for the curled-up heap but eventually when someone observed that he had no pulse, an ambulance was called, and by the following Monday, he was fine. Throughout the evening we were entertained by our regular musician Øyvind Bratlie Skaare, a valuable member of the travelling Vikings, as he belted out his excellent repertoire ranging from hits from Oasis to the Stones and the Beatles to David Bowie including of course the full catalogue of Leeds United anthems. It was no reflection on Øyvind's playing that many people by now were unconscious and others were simply asleep in their seats, some with amusing little illustrations on their foreheads.

The evening, not surprisingly, just disappeared before our very eyes and before we knew it, Nick was calling time and we had to trek through the thick snow to the nearest late-night pub. Our overseas guests had made their way back into the centre of Leeds in taxis and despite the adverse weather, it's a pretty safe bet that they reached their destination long before we navigated the half mile walk to the Commercial Inn. First of all, I slipped and managed to find possibly the only piece of exposed concrete in the whole of Yorkshire, resulting in a quite impressive shiner and a four-inch graze down the right-hand side of my face. I was quite the gentleman as I was falling by grabbing the nearest person to me, Gill, who ended up on her arse too, as did the actor Gary Dunnington who fell into a nearby ditch just behind me. When we finally reached the pub we dried out while quaffing our final drinks of the night as Gary ordered a taxi to take him back to his home near Leeds. We found out later that for some reason Gary got out of his taxi at the Moorgate, just a mile away, and had to order another one to complete his journey home.

The following day, matchday, I was surprisingly alert and looking forward to the day ahead. I had arranged to meet Alfie Haaland and show him around the pubs in Leeds before making our way to the game against Palace. I don't mind admitting that I felt 10ft tall as I walked into Spencer's pub with Alfie as he was immediately recognised. It was quite a few years since Alfie had played for Leeds, so therefore it was extremely pleasing that he was greeted by Leeds fans young and old as we went into the West Riding pub and everywhere else we went, including the special buses for fans taking us to Elland Road. Once in the Kop, it wasn't long before most of the fans spotted him stood beside me and the familiar chant of 'Alfie! Alfie!' resonated all around us. He responded by standing on his seat and waving his Leeds scarf enthusiastically around his head. When Leeds scored the winner in a 2-1 victory, he hugged me and others so excitedly that I thought he was going to burst. It was a memory that I will always cherish. I've 'stood' in the Kop now for many years, and it's more or less the same crowd that gather in our area every season, the Darlo lads, Mick, two Pauls, Bremner, Candy Man, Phil, Ste, Whistling Jack Smith, Vince, Gaz, Ray, Lee, Mark and quite a number of Norwegians are always in attendance. Cato is usually a few rows behind me and I've shared more than the odd beer in the Revie Bar with Ottar Kualheim and his mates.

By the time of the next visit by our horned comrades, the weather was much kinder and this time the game went ahead as part of what we now called our Viking Fest. Steve Riding from the *Yorkshire Evening Post* finally got his pictures and in attendance were two Leeds legends, Peter Lorimer and Eddie Gray. The visitors, Kampen 01 Ball, had arrived once again bearing gifts and sporting Viking helmets. Before the game they visited the Kippax dressing room and offered them a bottle of Jagermeister, to which the hosts duly obliged by unscrewing the cap and passing it around. Rather like liniment for the inside.

As the two teams ran, or rather wobbled out, to the welcome of an enthusiastic crowd, Kampen were wearing a white kit sponsored by Norwegian rapper and Leeds fan Lars Vaular who had just released a tribute record to Gary Speed but some of the Kampen team had forgotten to take their horns off. After a quiet word from the referee, Tony Denton, the helmets were removed and taken to the sidelines. In the early stages, Kippax AFC had the upper hand but an ambitious bicycle kick by 'Chewy' resulted in him falling flat on his arse and the ball dropping conveniently to enable an easy pick-up by the Norwegian keeper. Chewy did manage to convert a couple of chances later as Cato Visdal Mikalsen, a White Rose member and a Norwegian guest player for Kippax, also grabbed a brace while another Norwegian guest for Kippax, Geir Wang, put in a workmanlike performance, reminiscent of David Batty. As did Andy Liddle who was reminiscent of Elvis Costello without his guitar and in goal

Daniel 'Hoggy' Hogden performed admirably with gloves that looked like they were straight out of a Persil advert. The Norwegian trainer was probably the busiest man of the entire afternoon as he ran on to the pitch continuously with a bottle of Jagermeister to revive his players who were going down faster than Robert Pires. The game itself, a slightly one-sided affair, ended with a final score of 14-3 to Kippax, although that scoreline was disputed by the Scandinavians, who claimed that they had scored early in the second half but the referee had missed it. 'It could have gone either way before half-time,' a Kampen player told a Norwegian reporter afterwards.

My good friend from Waterford, Trevor Cusack, was over for our little Viking get-together and brought with him a couple of special guests. Noel Hunt had a brief and troubled period as a Leeds player, but he remained popular with the Leeds fans and he turned up at the club with a signed Leeds United shirt which was auctioned off and readily snapped up in true Viking style.

Noel's mother, Maria, also turned up to join in the frivolities. Maria is the nanny for Trevor and Jean's two boys, Darragh and Emmet. Also present was Noel's stepdad Anthony and his sister Sharon. Leeds United at the time were managed by Brian McDermott and were playing the next day so there were certain restrictions on players, but Noel was given permission for a brief visit to deliver the shirt. After the game, the traditional speeches and thanks took place and Rune Roalsvig spoke on behalf of his fellow Norwegian comrades along with Per Kristian Hansen, thanked the Kippax Football Club for its hospitality, especially Richard Marchant and Richard Seymour. Then, quite embarrassingly, I was called to the stage, promptly dressed in a fur-collared cloak with a Viking helmet placed upon my head and was then presented with two certificates that pronounced me as an 'Ennobled Honorary Viking of the 1st Degree for his display of courage, brotherhood and manlihood.' I was honoured and more than a little flattered, as I humbly unscrewed one of my horns, filled it with Jagermeister and toasted our esteemed overseas guests. Smithy took the other horn and followed suit.

I then proceeded to swan around the club in my cloak and crown of horns and Heidi Haigh, a top fan in the Leeds ranks, struggled to stifle a snigger as she politely asked me for a photograph.

The evening continued as Big Tony climbed upon the stage and crooned the night away with a couple of old favourites such as, 'We all live in a white Scratching Shed' and one that always brings a tear to the eye, 'Wee Billy Bremner the pride of Leeds'.

Tony was still singing as Nick called last orders and once again wheeled his wheelbarrow full of takings down the stairs and towards the bank.

Many of the Norwegians were over for a game against Bolton at Elland Road in 2014 and the next day came to support us in a charity event. It had come about one Sunday afternoon when I was joined in the Moorgate by two of my good old mates from Castleford, Big Tony and Bob. It was one of those days when the beer tasted good, too good. In fact, we sat there from lunchtime and we were still there at closing time that night – almost a 12-hour shift. I didn't feel too bad the following morning, a bank holiday; but as I cooked myself a couple of rashers of bacon, I suddenly had a flashback to yesterday in the pub. Did Bob and I really agree to shave our heads for charity? A quick text to Bob confirmed this and a couple of months later we arrived in separate cars at the Commercial Hotel run by Leeds United legend Peter Lorimer and his wife Sue, the venue for our impending deed. Thankfully, we were well supported and many friends and family turned out. Both Bob and I had long hair, mine was grey and straggly and to be honest I couldn't wait to see the back of it. Bob, on the other hand, and despite being a few years my senior, had a decent head of hair and as a result was visibly more nervous than me as they prepared the executioner's chairs for us. Our good friend and local demon barber Kev Higgins had kindly agreed to perform the task and within minutes it was all over. Eddie Gray had come to lend his support as did two of my very good friends from London, Leeds season ticket holders Stew and Steve Heasman. Friend of the Kippax, Marie, had earlier plaited part of my frayed locks and cut it off as a souvenir, not exactly a lock from one of the Fab Four. Leeds United had lost to Bolton 5-1 and in order to salvage something from their weekend some of the Vikings had gone to support Hunslet Rugby League Club, the famous 'Hunslet Hawks'. They arrived back at the Commercial just as the last strands of hair were falling from mine and Bob's heads. Hunslet had been stuffed 66-2, but thankfully the sight of the two of us sat there looking like two aliens from Roswell seemed to cheer them up. Steve Riding from the *Evening Post* was present again to capture this rare occurrence. As we circulated to allow people to stroke our bald heads my Ma, Dad and Barb also took photos. Mark Dovey had his photo with us, as did our old boxing mate Mark Liddle. Smithy, who suggested Macmillan as one of our charities was there with his Dad, but it was my little grandson Charlie who found it difficult to take on board. His mum Vicky and dad Ste tried to explain, but as Charlie stroked my head all he could say was – 'Gone.' Our hair loss was charity's gain and Macmillan along with our other charity Diabetes UK, suggested by Wub, benefited to the tune of almost £3,000 thanks to the generosity of everyone involved on the day and online.

Chapter 15

Whites! Camera! Action!

IT was late in 2009 when I received an email from a chap called Les Rowley. He was interested in putting my first book *Paint it White* on stage. Naturally, I thought it was a wind-up, but a few days later I met Les in Leeds. It emerged that after reading the book he saw the potential of transforming it into a stage play and he had already spoken to people, actors and such like, who he believed could fulfil this. I have to admit that I found the idea intriguing and curious. Les takes up the story: 'It was never intended for me to walk into a coffee shop in North Leeds and come out with a notion of putting *Paint it White* on stage. Here was a confluence of circumstances that fell into my lap over a cappuccino when catching up with an actor friend of mine called Gary Dunnington in the spring of 2009. We had been friends for many years and while my career took me into journalism, Dunnington, a local lad from Halton Moor, had gone to London to become an actor. Over the froth of the coffees we discussed opportunities for the theatre in Leeds and we were perfectly placed having both relocated from the capital. On the one side there was pure art and the possibility of putting on a northern version of Chekhov or Brecht; but on the other the accessible nature of fringe theatre, which in my opinion was missing from the Leeds landscape.

'At the opposite end of the literature scale in the classical sense was a book I had read called *Paint it White* by Gary Edwards. I enjoyed it very much and the idea was thrown into the ring as a counterbalance to Shakespeare and his ilk. From a producer's prospective it made perfect sense. The idea, once the antithesis of what you do in theatreland, became the forefront of what would take up two years of my life. Damn those buttons that you push!'

Les continued, 'Gary Dunnington was the perfect casting and the first piece of the jigsaw. He fell into my lap because casting is very hard. In football terms it was like finding a striker of John Charles' standing. With Gary Dunnington, he not only possessed the skill as an actor, but physically he had the menace and the voice of Gary Edwards, who as a person, I am guessing could look after himself in a tight spot. If it had been Wayne Sleep I was having coffee with, then this project would not have seen the light of day. Casting was all important and Dunnington knew enough similar theatrical evacuees to assemble an incredible and talented array of acting talent. In no time at all I was surrounded by names all falling over themselves to get involved. Actors are a world apart and it was very reassuring that they believed in what I was trying to do.

'There comes a time in every project though, when you have to commit and push the right buttons. There's a feeling in the sub-cockle region of your wallet when this is done but with confidence in your ability then the feeling and the trepidation does not last any longer than the entire period of the play. Ultimately, before I could go anywhere with this select group of actors, I had to be sure I had a theatre to perform in. Leeds isn't blessed with a rich vein of venues and once the main protagonists all counted themselves out, then I had to build a theatre in central Leeds all by myself – and therein lies another story.'

He added, 'However, along with Gary Dunnington, we added Cathy Breeze who would play Lesley, the long-suffering wife of Gary Edwards. Cathy had recently returned from London where she had been playing in the Cameron McIntosh production of *Les Miserables*. What a CV she had and she accepted the offer of *Paint it White* immediately. Along with Nigel Collins and Jonny Dixon as well as Rayner Bourton and Alun Lewis as co-directors, you could say I got lucky.

'Rehearsals began in August 2009 in a small church hall in the Hyde Park area of Leeds. During the day the hall offered refuge for the down-and-outs and misfits of the area, yet for £100 a week we transformed a working script into a fully functioning production. They transported the book of Gary Edwards into a stage version of the glorious period of fun, laughter and nerves and by the opening night in October 2010, the team had done it.'

Les continued: 'Busloads of fans came from every corner of Yorkshire to be there for a theatrical first. Seated on wooden timbers in a makeshift theatre in Unit 17, a capacity crowd of 150 people witnessed the opening scene of Dunnington painting over a red square and chatting about his addiction to Leeds United. *Paint it White* had triumphed over the council. We'd triumphed over the nearby offices with an electrical generator that could have powered Peter Ridsdale's ego, and we had a sponsor to pay the wages. I can't say any more than a full house, it's a producer's dream and my gamble had paid off. Of course, many people visit the theatre and support shows which do not quite cut the mustard in terms of entertainment, but *Paint it White* was everything it set out to be. I would have been disappointed if the crowds had stayed away, but the play was good. It was so good even that the prestigious West Yorkshire Playhouse stepped in to have it performed at their theatre once it went nationwide.'

Les continued: 'The greatest praise, however, didn't come from the critics (although they were very generous), but from former Leeds player Peter Lorimer. He had come to see the play during the first week and liked it so much that he was ringing me for tickets for his friends. You know that something is right when Hotshot himself comes back for more.'

A couple of weeks after we had agreed to go ahead with the project, a mate of mine, Mikey, came to me in the Moorgate and said, 'I've just seen a bloke reading *Paint it White* in a pub in Burley and couldn't resist telling him that I knew you.'

It turned out that this bloke was Gary Dunnington, the man who would be playing me. That felt weird, it really did. 'What did he look like?' I had to ask. 'Nothing like you mate,' Mikey replied.

Then, one Saturday morning, I was making my way to Spencer's pub for a drink before a home game when I was approached by this lad walking a pushbike near Lands Lane precinct in the city centre.

'Gary?' he asked.

'Yes,' I replied, slightly puzzled.

'I'm Gary, I'm playing you in *Paint it White*.'

I was gobsmacked. He didn't have a hair on his head and not the remotest sign of a beard. We had what I can only describe as a bizarre conversation and we shook hands and I continued on to Spencer's.

A few days later, Martin White, my postman and a long-time mate from my school days, handed me a large thick envelope and I spent a few hours of a dark November evening sat in my back garden beside my chimenea with a glass of whisky, reading the script for the stage version of *Paint it White*.

It was a weird experience, but exciting and I have to concede that I felt a small tingle of pride as the shadows of the fire danced along each page as I read through every act.

If I'd had a pipe and a smoking jacket, it would have made the perfect scenario.

As the following months passed by I heard very little from Les, planting doubts in my mind that it was never going to happen. But all the time, the production was in session with a mix of a small, but highly experienced and distinguished group of actors and directors. The actors were plucked from stage and screen. Gary Dunnington has played in *Coronation Street, Sharpe, The Bill, Holby City, Casualty, Heartbeat* and *Doctors* as well as countless stage productions including two years in New York. Cathy Breeze (who played Wub) was a truly special addition to the cast, coming fresh from stage productions such as *Les Miserables, Oliver* and *Wizard of Oz*. Her TV credits include *EastEnders, The Royal, Holby City* and *Dalziel and Pascoe*. Cathy sang at Elland Road for the Queen during her Silver Jubilee in 1977 and sang at Wembley during Euro 96. In 2005, she was the voice of Madame Winnie Bago in *Wallace & Gromit: The Curse of the Were-Rabbit*. She again appeared on the big screen in the very popular *Inbetweeners*. She was cast as 'Neil's Northern Bird' in a very funny film. I dragged Wub to watch the film at our local cinema even though it wasn't really her cup of tea but I knew Cathy was in it, and Wub didn't so I waited for her reaction.

I didn't have to wait long; in an early scene, Cathy is seen on the dance floor of a nightclub in Crete with Neil, but even then Wub hadn't realised it was Cathy, not until the scene developed a more amorous take and the pair became entwined in a moment of passion with hands and tongues everywhere. As Cathy uttered the words, 'Come on baby, let me have it!' in a very broad Yorkshire accent, Wub shrieked, 'Oh my God, that's me!' She then sank down into her seat as everyone in the cinema looked round at her.

Jonny Dixon was only 22 when he appeared in *Paint it White*, but had already made a name for himself in *Grange Hill* before landing the role of Darryl Morton in *Coronation Street*. A solid contribution and highly polished performance in the play came from Nigel Collins who had starred in theatres up and down the country in productions as diverse as *Up and Under*, *The Hobbit*, *Great Expectations* and the lead role in *Postman Pat*. As well as TV roles in *All Creatures Great and Small*, *Coronation Street*, *Emmerdale*, *Heartbeat*, *Brideshead Revisited*, *Harry's Game* and alongside Rod Steiger in *Glory Boys*, he also appeared in two films: *Resurrected* and *The Nature of the Beast*.

Two well-known show business faces were brought in by Les as co-directors. Alun Lewis was best known as Darryl Stubbs in *Birds of a Feather*, as well as writing a couple of scripts and as Vic Windsor from *Emmerdale*. He also appeared in various other roles including a tough detective in *The Professionals* and a gay furniture dealer in *Minder*. Alun plays guitar in the band known as the Woolpackers, who had a number five hit with *Hillbilly Rock*, a trio consisting of other Emmerdale favourites, 'Terry Woods' on guitar and lead vocals and 'Zak Dingle' on drums.

Rayner Bourton created the role of 'Rocky' in the original and first ever production of *The Rocky Horror Show* which has toured on four continents and he directed the first ever National tour of New Zealand. Rayner wrote and co-produced *Let the Good Times Roll*, the biographical musical charting the phenomenal success of The Rolling Stones which was shown right across Britain including London's West End. His other credits include numerous stage productions and appearing in *Britain and on the Continent*, which he directed and produced. He has staged corporate events featuring Pans People and had a book published in 2010 called, *The Rocky Horror Show: As I Remember It*.

Behind the scenes of *Paint it White* was a highly professional crew consisting of stage managers, Ollie Micklem and Steven Robinson, who also carried out the lighting sequence along with Ross Pomfret and the make-up and costumes were in the capable hands of Misha Homayoun-Fekri and Onai Bikishoni. The long-term plan was to put *Paint it White* on at a small venue in Leeds with a view to taking it out on the road if expectations were realised.

We had great support from the folk at my local pub, the Moorgate, who duly arrived in a 50-seater coach and converged in a nearby hotel bar just around the corner from the small theatre situated in the Clarence Dock, a canalled area of Leeds close to the Royal Armouries. After we'd had a few drinks with the Kippax entourage, Wub and I made our way early to the theatre, both nervous but looking forward to it. As we arrived at the stage door, I met Gary Dunnington and I was blown away by the transformation. He had a grey tatty wig on and had grown a beard for the part; he looked uncannily brilliant. He was puffing frantically on a cigarette and was obviously nervous. 'How you feeling mate?' I asked.

'I'm fucking shitting myself mate,' was his immediate answer. 'I just want to get this right.' This from an actor who had trodden the boards across the Atlantic.

Tetley's (Wub's place of work from 1973 right up to its closure in 2011) were the sponsors of the play and had kindly given me a free bar, for which I was obliging – reluctantly of course.

We took our seats and waited for the show to begin. Inside, the sell-out crowd applauded and cheered as Gary Dunnington appeared on stage and I couldn't help but look around for my friend's reaction. Happily, it appeared to be good. Almost immediately, the first comedy moment arrived – and it wasn't in the script.

Gary did his first few lines but then stopped. There was silence and he disappeared behind the screen – he had forgotten the next line. Instantly, from the very back of the theatre, Rayner Bourton, the director, shouted out the line in question. Gary picked up on it, and from then on he never put a foot wrong throughout the whole set of shows. He was brilliant. As were the rest of the cast. The show went at a fast pace and was packed with classic one-liners like one scene featuring one of my hearses; as the cast, dressed in undertakers' attire, contemplated going into the funeral business for themselves and offering a service as *Marching off Together*. Then the audience almost burst with laughter as 'Peter Ridsdale' appeared as a clown, complete with bright coloured wig, large shoes, the lot.

Just as everyone was wiping the tears away, tears of a different kind appeared all around the theatre as Gary sat alone on stage with one spotlight shining down on him, talking to the statue of the legendary Billy Bremner. This solo performance alone received a standing ovation as Gary urged Billy to, 'Please come back to Elland Road, we miss you Billy!' after another home defeat.

After the final show in Leeds, a small party was thrown for anyone who cared to attend and we danced and sang with the cast on stage to 'Marching on Together' and other classics. Two of my mates, Stew and Steve Heasman, had travelled up from London to see the show and brought with them a friend who was dressed in typical 'theatre-going' attire complete with scarf and looked a proper 'luvvie'. 'I really enjoyed that,' he said. 'In fact I'd give it seven out of ten.' Stew looked at him and said, 'You must be joking, that was a ten out of ten if ever I saw one'. Afterwards, the cast and crew retired to the nearby Palace pub, where more drinks were slung down the gullet, and Stew and Steve earned the nickname 'The Sway Twins' from Les Rowley. It became a bit noisy and boisterous towards closing time and in true showbiz fashion the entire entourage were asked to leave.

On the way home we had my nephew Scott in the back of the car and he said to me, 'What a brilliant night, I'm so proud of you. And you, Auntie Lesley, your driving is at least an eight out of ten.'

To the enormous credit of the production team and cast, the show had gone from strength to strength, attracting rave reviews from the local media critics and public alike and the following year the show received more lavish plaudits up and down the country as it embarked on a national sell-out tour which included an appearance in London's West End, and two shows at the prestigious West Yorkshire Playhouse. The two shows in Leeds were said to be the favourites of Les Rowley – he called it the Wembley Stadium of the tour. The nationwide tour began at the Phoenix Theatre, Castleford on 13 October 2011 and just before the first show kicked off, Les said this about taking the show on the road: 'On its first run on the fringes of the main theatre circuit, audiences laughed and cried in all the right places and with Leeds United there was always going to be more crying than laughing. You don't need to be a football fan to enjoy this play. It's been a long road but the production has passed the theatrical litmus test and taking it on the road is another step up the ladder for something that started with my first Leeds United game in 1970.'

The cast had seen one alteration to the original line-up. Because of prior commitments, Nigel Collins couldn't make the nationwide tour and his place was taken up by Dan O'Brien. Dan was 'Mr Whiteside', the teacher in the children's TV series *My Parents are Aliens*. Other TV roles included *Dr Faustus*, *On the Piste*, *Mr Toad* and *Much Ado*. He also starred in the film *The Tragedy of Macbeth*.

Before the show was due to arrive in Grimsby, the *Grimsby Telegraph* announced Dan's impending arrival: 'An actor who is anything but alien to the stage will be painting the town white when he heads to Grimsby. Dan O'Brien who plays Mr Whiteside in the long-running children's series *My Parents are Aliens* will be getting to grips with Leeds United play *Paint it White* at the Caxton Theatre. Barnsley-born O'Brien is currently on our screens in repeat episodes of the popular children's show and is also a veteran of several of John Godber's productions including *On the Piste* and *Perfect Pitch*. He has just returned from Austria where he has been filming *The Tragedy of Macbeth*. O'Brien, 48, had a promising goalkeeping career with Sheffield Wednesday before deciding on acting as a profession. He now lives in Dewsbury, West Yorkshire, and is married to the actress Jacqueline Naylor. Rehearsals for *Paint it White* begin in Leeds at the end of September and O'Brien is excited at the prospect of turning in a match-winning performance as a number of Leeds fan characters. He said, "I'm looking forward to it. Theatre is my first love and even though I have been working in TV for seven years I have never strayed far from my theatrical roots. I would say I am strongest as a stage actor." The producer, Les Rowley said he thinks Dan O'Brien will be brilliant for the play.'

Family friends of ours, Ken, Margaret and Jill Crow attended one of the shows at the West Yorkshire Playhouse and were 'well impressed'. The *Yorkshire Evening Post* called it 'Top of the League Stuff!' and their reviewer Steve Riding wrote this: 'There's a saying in football which basically boils down to "never go back". I'm pleased to report that it doesn't apply to *Paint it White*. Based on the book by Gary Edwards, the stage play went down a storm with audiences during its debut three-week run at the cosy Clarence Dock Theatre last year. Now it has returned, mixing with the big boys of the theatrical world with a two-night stay that's part of a nationwide tour. And the good news is that the production is an even slicker, funnier affair this time around. *Paint it White* follows Gary's ups and downs during more than 40 years of following United. The cast of four, Gary Dunnington, Jonny Dixon, Cathy Breeze and Dan O'Brien are superb, energetic and very funny. Cathy in particular excels with her facial expressions that had the audience in stitches. A host of one-liners have been added to the original script and there are poignant moments too, none more so than when the Gary character talks about late Leeds legends Don Revie and Billy Bremner. Laughter, emotion and football – what more could you want out of a night at the theatre?'

This review by the Playhouse's S.E Webster was along similar lines: 'Paint it White was naturally going to meet with a warm reception at West Yorkshire Playhouse in Leeds. As theatregoers walked over pieces of white paper shaped like splattered paint at the entrance, it became immediately clear that we were in for a night of light-hearted comedy. Like the game of football itself, the play attracted all ages and many a Leeds fan. The Courtyard Theatre itself was an ideal setting; the balconies and seating were all reminiscent of the stands at a football ground. On stage, subtle hints at location were employed. For example, a pub corner and the use of a central screen, which alternated images related to the comic narration and to football, visually reinforced the theme of football in Leeds.

'Gary Dunnington, the male lead, with his authentic Leeds accent and casual dress of jeans and a Leeds United shirt, looked relaxed and comfortable on stage, with a clear control of space and soon built a strong rapport with his audience; within minutes of the play's opening, members of the audience were verbally pronouncing their support and clapping loudly. Dunnington had great chemistry with his fellow cast. Dan O'Brien and Cathy Breeze gave commendable performances, whilst Jonny Dixon was flawless throughout. All four actors succeeded in achieving maximum comic effect as they impersonated various other individuals in the world of football, the media and the personal life of Gary Edwards. While there were many references to past Leeds United players, managers and games to all of which Leeds fans could relate, there was also a great deal of comedy that engaged members of the audience less familiar with the detailed history of the football team.

'The action also touched on real-life issues such as marriage and divorce, meaning that the play did not become superficial in its portrayal of football. Thus, the performance did not exclude anyone and instead could be enjoyed by all.

'As the play drew to a close, the actors stood together in Leeds United shirts and scarves listing all the major successes that the Leeds team has enjoyed over the decades. Although the closing scene arrived somewhat abruptly, it worked highly effectively in creating a complete and 'united' atmosphere. Thus, overall, *Paint it White*, filled with comic inspiration and based upon a very interesting true-life story, can certainly be considered a success.'

As the show zigzagged across the country in all directions it racked up an enormous amount of praise. Here's a random selection of some of the reviews it received:

> 'Hamlet spends nearly three hours struggling to bring the audience on to his side, to appreciate his suffering and strife. It takes the Gary Edwards character the better part of 30 seconds.'

> 'When we witness Edwards' first trip to Elland Road, Old Gary plays Young Gary, shuffling across the stage on his knees with a chirpy childlike smile on his face as he's introduced by his dad and uncle to the working men on the kop, the *Express*-reading Tories on one side of the pitch and the enemy "over there".'

'The play – like the book – is typical football story telling; a half whimsical, half deadly-serious treatment of the sport as something epic akin to warfare.'

'As well as playing his wife Lesley, Cathy Breeze also plays Gary's first wife as they spend more time fixing a date for their wedding amid Leeds fixture congestion than they actually spend married. Later on, he lives the dream and scores big time by managing to find a woman (Lesley) who works for Tetley's and marries her.'

And my favourite, by *York Press*:

'A frankly insane level of devotion to an often forlorn cause.'

There was an interesting story connected with the play when it appeared in Malton, North Yorkshire. Initially, it appeared that it would not go ahead as planned; once again producer Les Rowley takes up the story: 'Professional touring theatre companies only survive on accruing income streams. Every penny helps since not one single channel of revenue is sufficient to pay for everything. Wages of actors, technical staff, lights, cameras, vans, accommodation, scenery – it soon amounts up. So in the case of the Leeds United-themed play that went to Malton in November 2011, it survived on ticket sales, programme sales, a cut of the drinks bill and sponsorship from Tetley's Brewery. It's a model that works but difficult to put in place because the producer (me) has to get this just right if he isn't to fall out of pocket. The theatre isn't just about the art (although he'd like to think so), it is about a product which he hopes people will buy into – the measurement of which is bums on seats. Happy bums.'

He added: 'We always knew that *Paint it White* was going to do well in certain areas other than Leeds. Leeds United is a very well-supported club with many of its supporters' branches scattered far and wide from Cornwall to Carlisle, Scotland to Shropshire and Darlington to Devon, and as soon as the play was purchased by the West Yorkshire Playhouse, I set about working out which towns would take the play as part of a nationwide tour. Initially we thought it too expensive to take the show to Malton as we had pinched some of their audience for shows in York and Scarborough. This is where a team behind a proposed new food store and petrol forecourt for the town came to be the same people who effectively brought *Paint it White* to the Milton Rooms in Malton. GMI Holbeck Land immediately saw the play as an ideal night out for the people of the town. It already has a Leeds United Malton Supporters' Club so we always knew the audience was there and it was quickly added to the schedule. Without the vision of GMI Holbeck Land the play would not have visited Malton. They had a genuine reason for providing entertainment to the community since they were behind the proposed food store and garage. Their vision for that site, north of the town centre, mirrors what they saw in bringing *Paint it White* to the Milton Rooms. It gave the residents opportunity, choice, commerce, work and cheaper ticket prices. Malton saw a production that was selling out each night and I hoped that they would remember the evening with affection.'

Les continued: 'The show was a huge success and the people of Malton came out and enjoyed a fantastic evening and afterwards I had a drink with Garry Cooper, the creative force behind the Milton Rooms, who told me that through sponsorship, Malton could become a staging post for more top-class plays as they had seen that evening. After the success of *Paint it White* I have been approached to write and produce another play about the life of Don

Revie called *The Revie Era Touch*. If and when it reaches the point of rehearsal, then my first call will be to book it into the Milton Rooms.'

This was the Malton *Gazette & Herald*'s tribute to that evening in Malton: 'Judging by the Milton Rooms audience's reaction at the recent performance, most were well aware of the ups and downs of Leeds United over the last 50-plus years, but this was an entertaining look through the eyes of Gary Edwards (played by Gary Dunnington), a fervent supporter. Edwards explained his was a passion, not a disorder.

'We heard much of his love of white and his hatred of all things red – something to do with a certain Lancastrian club – which included throwing away a new set of red saucepans bought by his first wife, repainting the red rose sign on the M62 Lancashire border and refusing to travel on red buses or paint anything red.

'The passion led to several postponements of his ill-fated marriage because of clashes with United matches – home or away – but the marriage broke down after only weeks, but fortunately before the start of the next season. He advised a child to take care of the "3 r's" – readin', writin', and Revie! Distance to away matches was measured by the number of cans of Tetley's consumed en route in one of Gary's hearses. There were colourful reminiscences about overseas fixtures, and the excitement of hearing that a match in Belgrade (rumours of no pubs) had been switched to Amsterdam. Edwards and his mates established the Kippax Leeds Supporters' Club at the local pub and were visited by a colourful, mad professor (Cathy Breeze) wanting to know more about the fan culture and whether or not they were (as they showed us) "John Travolta wannabees".

'The show was riddled with rude remarks about Margaret Thatcher and the football folk of those days – Carlton Palmer, Jonathan Woodgate and Brian Clough all fared badly – and the character of Peter Ridsdale (Dan O'Brien), complete with red nose and wig was hilarious.'

It continues: 'A serious, moving tribute to Billy Bremner included reference to a pilgrimage by Edwards to Bremner's birthplace in Stirling – only to find it had been demolished. We saw Gary, encouraged by a TV presenter (Trisha Goddard) make a marriage proposal on the pitch at Elland Road in front of 30,000 spectators and an amusing talk with a counsellor about his obsession. The show closed with a rousing chorus highlighting Leeds' achievements and failures over the years. (In light of my given first names) I was disappointed at the lack of reference to John Charles, one of the all-time Leeds greats, but this was a truly entertaining production, full of light, sound, music and laughs. Congratulations to Garry Cooper and his team at Milton Rooms.'

One of the obvious highlights of the tour for me was the glamorous appearance in London's West End. This is an extract from the show's preview: 'Tonight, the northern cult play, *Paint it White* comes to Leicester Square. Transport for London might want to think twice about letting any of their red buses near Gary Edwards when he's in town.'

Once again the show didn't disappoint and reviewer Natasha Hotson wrote: 'The War of the Roses is still being fought in Kippax near Leeds, where a die-hard Leeds United fan refuses to take a red bus "'Cos them's the colour of our enemy at Old Trafford" – and he's on a one-man crusade to "paint everything white". Based on the cult autobiography by painter and decorator Gary Edwards, Les Rowley's stage adaptation takes us from Gary's first match in the 1960s through to the glory days and the recent fall from grace. Still, Edwards sees the funny side – the portrayal of Peter Ridsdale is hilarious, even if you don't know who he is. And while there is a soap star-studded cast, the centre-forward of the show is undisputedly Gary Dunnington. It would be easy for the leading man to come across as a teensy bit selfish as he watches every match bar one since 1968, but he manages to somehow garner the respect of his audience for his uncompromising devotion to the beautiful game. This play is a must-see for all football fans from both sides of the Pennines and beyond.'

Wub and I attended a couple of the shows ourselves, being guests of the Scarborough branch of the Leeds Supporters' Club when the show went on at the town's historic Spa Theatre on the seafront. When the show appeared in Nottingham, Leeds United were playing at Elland Road the same night, so the disappointed, but loyal, Nottingham Whites contingent headed north for the match and missed the play, which incidentally still played to a full house. Wub and I travelled down by train to watch the London show and seeing the billboard announcing 'Paint it White – tonight' outside Leicester Square Theatre was a proud moment indeed. The 15-date tour ended in Halifax at the Square Chapel Theatre on 9 November 2011 and was attended by a contingent of the Halifax Platoon of the Leeds supporters. Among them were Heidi and 'Captain' and 'Big Brian'. These good people have been friends of mine for well over 40 years and I was really saddened when Big Brian died early in 2015.

After the final show in Halifax, all the cast and crew met with the audience in the bar, chatted and signed autographs. For the final time, Wub and I said farewell to a very talented, hard-working team who had all become friends over the last couple of years. It had been a great, yet extremely humbling experience for me.

Of course, I'm no stranger to the grease paint. In 2006 I played a starring role in a wonderful film called *The Penalty King*. It featured household names such as Clare Grogan, Nick Bartlett and Sam Beckinsale. Directed by Leeds fan Chris Cook and produced by Twin Track Films, both based in Brighton, it features a Leeds United fan who goes blind, putting an end to his amateur days as a footballer. However, inspired by his hero Billy Bremner, he returns to the pitch with comedic effect. My 'starring' role incidentally consisted of around ten seconds, and even then I was mostly obscured by my fellow thespian and Leeds legend Peter Lorimer who was sat in front of me in a crowd scene, taken at Elland Road.

My first major speaking role in the film industry came in 2014 in *Boy Called Bremner* (Yorkshire Films). I only spoke twice, one of them an expletive, but my role this time consisted of *two* appearances amounting to somewhere in the region of maybe 45 seconds in total. I still check my telephone at regular intervals to make sure it is working.

Boy Called Bremner was a terrific film about a young boxer in Leeds called Bremner, written and directed by Leeds fan Jason Lumsden. Ex-amateur boxer Lumsden won the majority of his 40 fights and brought together this cast for his first ever film venture. It features a starring role by Grumbleweeds favourite Graham Walker as Bremner's booze-fuelled dad, Jimmy, who has a horse called Radebe. Whenever he goes AWOL, Jimmy is found asleep at the foot of the Billy Bremner statue at Elland Road. Jason's own lad, Sonny, plays the title role and there is also an appearance by *Shooting Stars'* Charlie Chuck. The 'bad boy' in the film is played superbly by Tony McDevitt, one of Jason's old boxing mates – Tony was also responsible for key behind-the-scenes work and casting. Also making a cameo appearance is my long-time acting colleague Peter Lorimer.

Much of the film (including my two scenes) was shot in the Burmantofts area of Leeds and one day during a scene involving drugs and guns, the cast were surprised to be surrounded by armed police officers who had been tipped off by a member of the public that there was a shooting taking place. The actors were ordered through megaphones to 'drop their weapons' and lay face down on the floor. Which they did alongside the crew and cameramen with their big fluffy microphones.

Graham 'Grumbleweed' Walker, who featured in a hilarious 'nude scene' at Burmantofts, was diagnosed with cancer in 2011 and was ill throughout the filming of *Boy Called Bremner*. Sadly, Graham died just weeks after completion. Another actor, Richie O'Coy, also died shortly after filming. But both left a lasting legacy in a film that played to sell-out major cinemas.

In my role as a Z-list celebrity, I was once asked to open a fish shop and almost immediately became embroiled in a 'cod war'. Ady and Sharon kindly chose me of all people to officially open Regent Fisheries in Horsforth, Leeds. All went well until I was out a short time later with family friends Cheryl and Melanie. They had read about my little appearance at the Regent in the local paper, but their reaction wasn't the one I was expecting. I was asked in no uncertain terms why I hadn't mentioned the other fish shop just down the road. Because they had 'been going to that one for years'. This wasn't the end either.

One day I was queuing in my local, and I have to say excellent, fish shop (The Fish Shop, Kippax) when Martin the owner began talking very loudly from behind the counter. At first, I took no notice but then heard him say to someone in the queue, 'What do you think of that then?' He put a magazine on the counter and pointed to an article. It was the *Fish Fryers Gazette* or something like that, and in it was my little event at the Regent. 'Him there, (me) has only been promoting someone else's fish shop.' He diverted his attention to me. 'What's up with my fish shop then?' said Martin. At first I thought he was joking, but he was deadly serious and continued, 'Aren't my fish and chips good enough for you then? Why didn't you mention my fish shop?' I was gobsmacked, but I had to defend myself. 'Well, you never asked me,' I replied.

Some while later I was out enjoying an Indian meal at Westbourne Spice in Otley with Cheryl and Melanie when the subject of the Regent once again came to the surface, but almost as if it were planned as we were discussing it, a van pulled up outside the window. On the side of the van were the words 'Regent Fish Shop'. I couldn't believe my eyes when in walked Ady and ordered a takeaway. As he looked around he saw us at our table and came over. I introduced him proudly to Melanie and Cheryl and you could have knocked us all down with a feather when Ady went to pick up his curry at the counter saying, 'I'm gonna enjoy this. Best food you could wish to eat!'

Chapter 16

Clown Princes

THE legendary footballer Len Shackleton was an England international who began his illustrious career in my very own village of Kippax. During the mid-1930s, Shackleton played for the very impressive Kippax Legionnaires, a side long defunct, but still held in high esteem by locals of a certain age. Shackleton went on to star for Arsenal, Bradford Park Avenue (making his debut against Leeds on Christmas Day 1940), Newcastle and Sunderland before hanging up his hob-nail boots in 1957. Shackleton was known as the 'Clown Prince' because he would 'entertain and amuse' fans. I am proud to have been associated with a very select group of 'clown princes' both at football matches and in the real world.

First up is someone who for the purpose of this particular section shall be called 'David'. Complete with his distinctively tattooed forehead, this man is a true legend. He came into a bit of money a few years ago and asked me for a quote for some decorating at his house. He wanted an estimate for a complete redecoration of his staircase and hallway throughout. It's a fairly old house and all the paint on the woodwork was to be burned off back to the original wood – a complex and lengthy process. A couple of days later David accepted my quote and we set a date for the work to be carried out. 'Let's go for a drink,' said David, and off we went. Although David was constantly inebriated, he could name the Leeds team of the 60s and 70s off by heart and used to be a regular at Elland Road back in the Glory Days. These days he prefers a pint or a large vodka and tonic – or both.

Two days later, David called unexpectedly at my house, 'Me staircase won't need burnin' off now mate,' he said. Thinking that he had decided it was too expensive to have it burnt off, I said, 'No problem, I'll give it a right good sanding down and see what we can do.'

David chuckled, 'Thing is mate, I got a bit pissed up yesterday and fell asleep when I got home.' He still seemed a little tipsy as he continued, 'We had two fire engines at ours for about an hour.'

'What happened?' I asked, pretty much knowing the answer already.

He laughed again, somewhat embarrassed, 'I fell asleep, dropped my cig and t' next thing my front door is being smashed down and these firemen came charging in. "What the fuck's going on?" I shouted, and then I saw flames everywhere! Anyway mate, half of the staircase and doors have gone. Everything is charcoal. Can't get upstairs, 'cos there isn't any. I'm having to use the downstairs toilet.'

I asked him where his wife was and was told that she'd been staying at her sister's for a couple of days. 'I don't think she'll be right happy when she gets home,' he said.

That was a massive understatement.

I found out later that a neighbour had alerted the fire brigade after hearing smashed glass and then seeing huge flames billowing and swirling out of two or three windows. Most of the house was engulfed in thick black smoke. The neighbour feared that David and his wife had been overcome by the fumes and lay unconscious – or even worse. This all happened at around 2am.

His wife is quite a patient lady – she has to be – and she's put up with a lot over the years. I arranged to go and have a look at the damage the next day and when I did, I was met with total carnage. 'It's gonna take a few coats o' paint innit mate?' David said to me, without the merest hint of sarcasm.

As I looked around I saw that half the wooden staircase had indeed disappeared, all the surrounding curtains had gone, the staircase carpet was non-existent and you couldn't see out of the black windows. Even the TV, which was yards away in the corner of the living room, was coated in black soot. The ceiling was black and every light fitting, bulb and light shade was either melted or disappeared altogether. 'What do you think then?' he asked, looking around at the devastation.

I was speechless and just as I was about to say something, in walked his wife to the overpowering stench of smoke. As broken glass crunched under her feet, her mouth was wide open and the colour of her face was the exact opposite to that of the staircase walls. I beat a hasty retreat, saying that I would call back. I was going to say, 'I'll alter the estimate to an insurance estimate – smoke damage,' but immediately thought better of it. None of us saw Dave again for about three weeks.

In fact, the next time I saw him he was pushing an old wheelbarrow with a squeaky wheel in the direction of his house transporting a gigantic television, one of those with the huge back to it – it was easily 3ft 6in square. He had obviously begun refurnishing the house and someone had given him a telly.

It transpired that he had spent the past few weeks staying in a 15-room establishment. In fact, it was the boarded-up derelict old school at the top of the hill. Since the wife kicked him out – for his own safety – he had been sleeping rough in one of the classrooms – complaining to himself about the 'noisy' pigeons who shared his temporary accommodation.

When he had finally been allowed to return home, his first job was to get another telly. This particular one, he had found at the bottom of someone's drive.

Talking of temporary accommodation, on a previous exile from his home he once talked police into giving him a warm cell for the night and a bacon sandwich before sending him on his way the next morning. The prison was the HMP Wakefield – one of Britain's top security prisons.

David lives drunk – and once on an all-inclusive holiday in Spain, his wife had locked him in the apartment in an attempt to cut off his never-ending free supply of booze, before going out with the people in the next apartment. Undeterred, David peered over the balcony which was four floors up, and weighed up his options. He figured that if he could make it down to the tree two floors beneath, it would soften his fall and he could then go on to the bar. He climbed on to the wall and without hesitation launched himself towards the tree. He landed on the tree, which buckled momentarily beneath him before rising up and catapulting him 3ft up in the air before he plummeted headlong on to the tarmac beneath, knocking himself out. He was just coming round a few minutes later when a security guard arrived by his side. David was helped to his feet and, still stunned, slowly made his way to the bar ten yards away, leaving the security guard staring at him in total disbelief. Although totally drunk from the whole day and evening drinking, David could remember every minute of his freefall to freedom. His wife had good cause to try and prevent David from getting anywhere near alcohol. He is known to the lads as 'The Exorcist' – wherever he is, all spirits disappear instantly.

His wife certainly deserves an award; even on their wedding day they arrived at church driven by David's mate in an old, untaxed Austin Allegro. 'It's dear enough getting married as it is,' David famously said, 'without forking out for an expensive wedding car.'

Next in our hall of fame is someone who used to work behind the bar at that very pub David frequented and in keeping with our last contender and concealed identity, we'll call this person 'Charlie'.

One quiet afternoon, two lads walked in to the taproom and ordered drinks. On receiving their pints one of them asked, 'Have you got any dominoes mate?' Handing them over the bar, Charlie said, 'I'm sorry, but we haven't got any domino boards to play on, but there's a couple of spare loft hatches under the coat stand there, one of those should do.' Of course, those 'loft hatches' were indeed the domino playing boards, but the two lads began their game without saying a word.

The first ever visit to a horse race was such an adventure for Charlie, rushing up excitedly to the course bookmaker and saying, '£5 on Wensleydale Warrior please.'

'Is that to win sir?' asked the bookie.

'Of course I want it to fuckin' win!' snapped Charlie.

At Pontefract, as with other courses, some jockeys fly in or out by helicopter in order to ride a horse elsewhere on the same day. This intrigued Charlie.

Late in the afternoon, as a chopper landed in the large grassy area in the middle of the surrounding track, Charlie, on noticing a tiny jockey (Steve Cauthen) running to board the flight remarked, 'What's going on there?'

'He's in the 5.15 at Wolverhampton,' someone said.

Charlie thought for a few moments before coming out with this absolute classic: 'Where does the horse go?'

Next up is 'Smithy'.

I think we all know a 'Smithy', but this fella is different class. His lack of knowledge is natural and totally unrehearsed, which makes him a total expert. The first time

I remember witnessing his gift was in the coach park after a game at Nottingham Forest. Our coach found itself at the very back of a long line of departing coaches, much to the annoyance of us all on board. As we trundled up a steep hill, Smithy, in an attempt to lift our spirits said, 'Don't worry lads, we're not the last coach, look, there's one in front of us.'

One morning in the Hope Inn pub in Leeds we were all having a pint before traipsing over the Pennines for a game at Blackburn. We were in a fairly heavy discussion about the unexplained and UFOs and stuff like Area 51 and Roswell. 'Well I think there's something in it,' said Mick, 'all this secrecy over abductions and such. Definitely.' Just then we all noticed that Smithy had gone uncharacteristically quiet. It looked like he was in some sort of a trance and then, just like a typical scene from The Grapes smoke room in *Early Doors*, he said, 'I think *I've* been abducted.' We all looked at him in complete silence as he continued, 'It was a while back, but I'm sure I've had my complete brain sucked out of my head.'

Still silent, but now stifling sniggers, we listened as he added in graphic detail, 'I was just sat there and then I felt everything being sucked out of a little hole just here,' he said, feeling the back of his head.

Smithy genuinely enjoys his status as a champion idiot, and he actually becomes quite competitive about it – possessive even. This belief I have in him was put to the test one day when his crown was brazenly challenged by a young upstart – let's call him 'Tommy'.

A young, enthusiastic Leeds fan, Tommy is an integral part of our platoon that travels by Kipper's Mini Bus to every home game from our pub, the Moorgate. As a show of trust, Tommy is occasionally afforded the job as second in command of the group, behind Smithy of course. Tommy is a very likeable bloke and could best be described as Prince Charming with a severe bout of Tourette's syndrome. Nestled in the corner of the bar is the pub swear box. There is absolutely no need for this particular revenue for charity to be chained down in any way, especially when Tommy is in residence. On a routine session, Tommy single-handedly keeps the box so full that it would take four men to lift it. After one of these sessions, Tommy was catching forty winks upstairs on his bed when there was a constant knocking on his front door. Thinking that it was those pesky kids from up the road resuming their weekly antics of knocking on his door and running away, he ignored it – but the knocks became louder. 'That's it!' thought Tommy and stormed into his bathroom and filled a large jug. Opening the front bedroom window, he then unleashed almost a gallon of ice-cold water down on to the delivery man who had arrived with the Chinese meal he had ordered half an hour before lapsing into a coma on the bed. He likes his takeaways does Tommy. One evening, after watching Leeds get soundly beaten at home to Brentford, he was stretched out on the settee watching one of his many exercise DVDs when there was another knock on his front door. Zipping himself up, he made his way to the door. 'Good evening sir, your curry,' said the Asian gentleman. 'Cheers, mate, how much is it?' said Tommy, scooping up some money from the coffee table. After paying the man and closing the door, Tommy went to get a plate from the kitchen when there was yet another knock, this time to the front window. It was the delivery man again. 'Fuck off!' shouted Tommy, rushing up to the window. 'I've fuckin' paid yer!' Just then the Asian gent held up a brown bag containing his chicken tikka masala and three chapattis.

During the pub quiz one Sunday evening the answer to a question was Toto – 'Africa'. Tommy, who was stood just outside the doorway having a cigarette, began miming the answer to his own quiz team through the window. He stuck two fingers up behind his head and began tapping his open mouth with the middle three fingers on his other hand. The answer Tommy was attempting to pass on was 'Tonto'. Another occasion saw Tommy galloping up and down outside the pub window slapping his arse to indicate 'Centaur' as the answer to another question.

This and countless other episodes saw Tommy surging up the league table of Idiocy and within touching distance of the Clown Prince Smithy, who up until now, has remained unchallenged for several years. And as if to further demonstrate his superiority, Smithy recently had a tussle with a tube of glue, having to retrieve the top from his glued-together lips with a sharp craft knife.

I suppose I could induct myself briefly into this select hall of fame due to an incident that occurred in my own house. Wub was sat on the settee and I was sat in my usual chair, both watching the telly when she said, 'I see it's the tenth anniversary of Eric and Katrina.' I thought for a while, I must admit I don't always listen to what my love is saying some of the time and I thought I'd missed something. 'Who's Eric?' I asked. She looked at me and said, 'Are you serious?' I nodded and she shook her head. It turned out that she was referring to 'Hurricane Katrina' that engulfed New Orleans ten years ago. Doh!

But now, ladies and gentlemen, brace yourselves and prepare to witness the king, a true professional a true legend in every sense of the word, and perhaps the most infamous member of the LUSC Kippax, our very own Ginner – the Champions League Champion version of the Clown Prince. But, be warned, the following exploits are not for the squeamish and kids (or adults for that matter), don't try any of this at home. We'll start at the very beginning.

Similar to one of our other candidates Tommy, Ginner was a very good goalkeeper prior to two accidents when he fell out of a tree and later fell off his scooter which put him in a coma for six weeks. He was an expert at one-on-one goalkeeping and played for the Station Hotel in Crossgates,

Leeds. He wouldn't train and wouldn't take advice from the manager, or anyone – and when the game got to half-time, Ginner would immediately walk off the pitch and into the pub and would stay there till closing time. He was known as the undisputed champion drinker in the area and when his Friday wages expired, usually on a Sunday, he would cadge money from anyone to continue his consumption crusade with Tetley's. One of Ginner's schemes to raise cash would be to get money in advance to do people's gardens and, almost without exception, the garden would not get done. He would drink 20 pints as a matter of routine and could sink five or six pints in less than two minutes (for money of course). His other famous stunts to raise funds included drinking pints of urine and bill poster paste and eating underpants. Ginner always maintained that Freddie Walker's underpants, which he consumed greedily in the Scarborough Taps one evening after a home game, were the best that he ever ate.

Ginner didn't go to many Leeds home games, preferring instead the away games where he could tap money for beer from complete strangers in the pubs around the ground.

He worked for a while as a grave digger at Whitkirk Parish Church, but he subbed off the vicar that many times that he had no money to come at the end of the week. He would often go for a pint with the vicar, where his code 'more tea vicar' meant 'your round vicar'. Another of his codes was 'what about the water level?' which meant, 'get me a pint' – or – 'have you got any cans in?'

One of Ginner's best mates, Frank Rounding, once helped Ginner to dig some graves when it had been snowing. This was in 1982 and £25 a grave was not a bad little carner, but Ginner was not as daft as he made out; there was a 6ft stick which was used to mark the depth of the grave, but Ginner had sawn off a foot at the end so that he only dug a hole that was 5ft deep. His party piece would be to jump up out of the hole, screaming like Kenneth Williams, scaring the kids and their mams as they were passing from school. After certain funerals he would hold out his cap to the mourners for a tip.

Eventually, the vicar refused to sub Ginner any more, saying, 'I only employed you through respect for your father and I am not giving you any more money in advance to drink with.' To which Ginner responded with, 'Fuck off then you four-eyed bastard, you won't get a better grave digger than me!' To which the vicar began walking off and Ginner went after him saying, 'If you're not going to employ me any more do you know of any other churches that will? Don't you know anyone in Belfast or New York? There are plenty of murders there. I could be planting four a day, not four a week!'

I myself have always had a fascination with hearses, and used to collect them. Once during the early 1980s when Ginner was doing a bit of painting and labouring for me, I took him home in one of my hearses, but before I dropped him off, we called for a pint in the Melbourne pub close to where he lived in Killingbeck, long since demolished to make way for the original home of cardboard eggs – Burger King. Just to digress for a minute, it was here our daughter Vicky (Spoon) met her future husband, Ste. Spoon worked behind the counter, which as a vegetarian at the time had its obvious problems.

As Ginner and I sat in the dark, foisty, dingy, sticky-carpeted best end of the Melbourne, he saw someone he knew at the bar and went over to him. He returned shortly afterwards and I said to him, 'Give me your glass I'll go get some more beers.' 'Oh hang on a minute,' said Ginner, and went to the bar and came back with half of a broken pint glass. 'What's happened there?' I said. 'Mick at the bar there offered me a quid if I ate my glass, he let me off with this bit,' said Ginner. On the short trip back to his house, he insisted on lying in the back of the hearse, banging on the windows and shouting at people as we passed.

Whenever he took a job on, he would give 100 per cent and worked his socks off, literally, I kid you not – he would often eat his sock or socks if someone offered him a pound. He worked up in Scotland many times and Frank would often go with him, 'He was a celebrity up there. The best grafter they had ever seen and he would stand on his head in the street and all the kids used to prod him,' said Frank. 'One day he got bored and swam across a large river and disappeared and police were out for hours on end searching for him. Two days later he turned up back in Leeds with a holdall full of money. He had been working 12 hours a day up there for three solid months so his money had mounted up. He said to me, "I work to get money for ale not to stuff mattresses with," so the following night he, with a couple of hangers-on, got the train to London, followed by a ferry to Ostend, where they went on a three-day bender and spent the lot.

'My Mam and Dad loved Ginner,' Frank continues, 'but my old man had a habit of bringing him home when they were both pissed, for Sunday dinner. Ginner would eat everything put in front of him and then afterwards would eat the fat, bones, the lot. He would then wash up and tidy the kitchen as payment for his food. My Mam liked him in small doses, but once he'd done his chores, he would sit there in complete silence until opening time arrived at 7pm when he would instantly rise to his feet and go to the pub.'

Ginner continued to frequent the Crossgates area as ever in his trademark shorts and vest, even in the middle of the harshest of winters. I still recall, however, that Ginner could dress with a bit of style when he wanted. Admittedly, not very often, but when he did, it was notable. I can still close my eyes and see him strutting his stuff with his Northern Soul dance routine wearing a full-length black leather coat floating effortlessly on the dance floor of the Astoria in Harehills at the various Lambretta Club of Great Britain functions.

Ginner was married twice and both his wives were, as you would expect, on a similar wavelength to him. When he married his first wife, Ann, he wore a beer-stained white suit and she wore a cowboy outfit. Then the hired stripper appeared and Ginner danced with Ann with no shirt on as she whipped him with the stripper's whip, which she presented to Ginner afterwards as a wedding present.

Frank recalls his Mam seeing Ginner and Ann every weekend trying to walk home from the pub. Ginner in his white suit, wide tie and flared pants and Ann in her cowboy hat and billiard ball set of teeth. Later that year, Ann fiddled £15,000 out of the social security system and received a prison sentence, while Ginner received no punishment on mental health grounds. Sadly, Ann died a few years after their legendary marriage, and he kept her in an urn in his back garden.

Ginner did marry again, soon after, but it was the start of a sad decline for Ginner. Her name escapes me to be honest, but I remember meeting her at their home when I agreed to do some decorating for them. Ginner had been in regular work as a labourer and wanted me to spruce their house up a bit. On the very first morning I was there, she offered me and my mate, Jim, a drink. 'Yes please,' I replied, 'two teas please, milk and a bit of sugar in each, ta.'

'Oh, I can do better than that,' she said, before disappearing into the kitchen.

'Looks like we're getting some biscuits as well,' said Jim.

She returned carrying two mugs full of what I believed to be a concoction of Tia Maria, Cointreau and barley wine, with maybe a dip of a tea bag, and neatly warmed up in a saucepan.

She was seeing another bloke, which normally would present a problem, but even when she admitted to bringing him to the house when Ginner wasn't home, he responded by simply saying to him one day, 'Jeffrey (that was his real name), the next time you come round here, I'll knock your fuckin' head off – unless you come bearing gifts.' Ginner by that stage had fallen completely out of love with his second wife and the next time Jeffrey arrived he brought three two-litre bottles of White Lightning cider for Ginner, and continued to do so thereafter.

In 2013, Ginner died of a heart attack. To be honest, it was always expected, but was a shock when it occurred nonetheless. He had no family.

His funeral was at Cottingley cemetery, in the shadow of Elland Road, and was paid for by two of his mates. It has been described as being like a trip to a brewery, attended by such stalwarts as Andy (Bungalow) Holmes, Bernie Heaslip, Carl Cooney, Gary Barrett and countless others.

Many people say to this day, that it was the best funeral that they had ever been to. And just as Ginner would have loved, almost everyone was inebriated, and fittingly the vicar delivered a sermon about eating underpants, socks, glass pint pots, whisky glasses and chair legs.

Inside the Station Hotel there hangs a plaque dedicated to Ginner, one of this country's finest ever characters. Of course, there have been other contenders for the title of Clown Prince, like a builder working at my house a few years ago. He failed to turn up for several days and used the excuse that he had been beaten up outside a pub and had to be put in a seduced coma. But none come close to the legend that is Ginner.

Chapter 17

The Crazy World of Massimo Cellino

WHILE Leeds were winning the league championship in 1992, an Italian by the name of
Massimo Cellino was busy buying his boyhood
club Cagliari. Twenty-two years later, like a dangerous
asteroid, he would collide with Leeds United Football Club.

This wasn't his first attempt at buying an English club;
in 2010 he offered to take over West Ham for a little over
£100m but was thwarted by the Premier League's fit and
proper person test because of two criminal convictions. The
first of these, in 1996, resulted in a 14-month suspended
sentence for deceiving the EU and the Italian Ministry
of Agriculture out of £7.5m and a 15-month suspended
sentence was given following a charge of false accounting
while in charge of Cagliari FC in 2001. After West Ham,
Cellino attempted to buy Crystal Palace and then QPR,
before turning his attention 200 miles north up the M1.

In February 2013, Cellino was arrested and spent 16 days
in Buoncammino Prison following charges of embezzlement

in relation to the redevelopment of Cagliari's Is Arena Stadium. The arrest warrant for this particular charge described Cellino as, 'A man of marked criminal tendencies and capable of using every kind of deception to achieve his ends.' The now decaying Is Arena Stadium, with an average of just 5,000 fans, down from 40,000, was covered in graffiti by fans calling for Cellino to leave in 2014, and by the time he arrived at Elland Road in January, a further charge of embezzlement was hanging over him.

But, largely due to the demise of the club resulting from the dreadful Ridsdale/O'Leary saga plus the eight years of non-ambition by Ken Bates and a takeover by Arabs masquerading as competent business bankers in Bahrain, the Leeds fans saw the arrival of Massimo Cellino as being the long-awaited light at the end of the tunnel. The fact that in 2012, Cellino had moved his side's home games 500 miles from Calgiari to the Italy/Slovenia border in Trieste, and that their fans had to travel 6,920 miles to watch the remaining eight games of the season, mattered not a jot to punch-drunk Leeds fans and Cellino's string of other misdemeanours were conveniently obscured by the fact that a man with 'loadsamoney' was finally coming to Elland Road. Inheriting his father's agricultural empire, the 'King of Corn' is reportedly worth over a billion but he claims not to know how much money he actually has. He first visited England in 1975 working as an 18-year-old dishwasher for the Regent Palace Hotel and it was then that Cellino developed his love for English football – he remains a Tottenham fan to this day.

His arrival at Leeds, subject to Football League approval, was greeted with jubilation by the majority of Leeds fans. His opening official statements gained further admirers: 'I will buy Elland Road immediately. It has to be done. And then the following day I will buy Thorp Arch (training ground).'

A rival consortium, Together Leeds, had tried to buy Leeds United at the same time as Cellino. After losing out to Cellino, prominent members including ex-Leeds commercial director Adam Pearson and Welcome to Yorkshire's chief executive, Gary Verity, had hoped to join forces with Cellino in some capacity, but, after first saying that he would talk to them, Cellino said that he did not want to enter into a partnership. 'I'm driving the bus,' he said, 'I have no plans for any other investors. I want the fans close to the club, we don't need anyone else. I want the fans to become owners of the club, because who owns the club? It's the fans. We are just here temporarily. I'm here to clean up and let the fans feel as though they own the club.'

It quickly became apparent that Cellino can change his mind in an instant.

Initially, the previous owners, Gulf Finance House (GFH) of Bahrain had seemed like a breath of fresh air when they bought United for around £50m with Ken Bates netting £32m of it. They instantly won the fans over during their honeymoon period by 'propping up' the club financially and appearing to inject the odd million into the club here and there.

Three directors of GFH, Salem Patel, David Haigh and Hisham Alrayes, all became directors of the club. Haigh, a self-confessed Leeds fan, said, 'We are a Dubai-based, regulated bank owned by a Bahrain-based regulated bank that is listed on the stock exchanges in Bahrain, Kuwait, Dubai and London. So when it comes to transparency over where the money comes from, who are our investors, who are our shareholders and directors, it is very clear and it is incredibly transparent. We have bought the club with cash. There is no debt.' Patel said, 'Any club would love to own its own stadium, currently Leeds United do not own their stadium or Thorp Arch training facility, but it is part of our plan to buy them both.'

It was looking very much like the best Christmas present that any Leeds fan could have wished for. Ken Bates was initially to remain as chairman until the end of the season and then take up the position of president of the club. But many Leeds fans, quite understandably, were concerned that Bates could step back into a more active role in the club when he became president, but GFH moved quickly to quell such fears by saying, 'Ken Bates cannot regain control of the club under the terms of the agreement that we have signed with him.' And Leeds fans were even further delighted when, in 2013, Ken Bates was sacked over a jet. GFH claimed that Bates was using a private jet to commute from Monaco to Leeds which they said was not agreed to in his contract. Bates contested this, saying that he was entitled to do so under the terms of his contract and had authority to do so. But in July, while on holiday in Italy, he received a hand-delivered letter informing him of his dismissal.

Leeds fans clearly enjoyed this turn of events, but barely two months after purchasing Leeds United, GFH announced that they were looking for investment into the club. Then just one month further on they gave formal notice that they had begun negotiations to sell the club. A year later it was still trying to sell the club to an unnamed British investor. It quickly became apparent that GFH were haemorrhaging funds at an alarming rate and had racked up debts said to be around £100m. The transparency that David Haigh had talked about was about as clear as a bucket of tarmac and the wall of silence that surrounded the boardroom at Elland Road was deafening.

The only noises about Leeds United were coming from outside the club with legal wrangles ranging from Sports Capital, one of the consortiums that tried to buy Leeds instead of GFH, suing them for £33m, to a startling revelation that the Iranian government had part-funded the takeover by GFH, contravening all international sanctions as well as defying a United Nations Security Council resolution.

Massimo Cellino arrived at Elland Road at the end of January 2014 amidst huge publicity and with a pending court case once again hanging over him, as well as numerous others on the horizon. The pending case of not paying tax on a yacht called *Nelie* was seen by the Football League as contravening their 'fit and proper person's test' and he was banned before he'd even pulled his chair under his desk.

GFH were in total disarray and then, like a ghost from the past, Ken Bates re-entered the ring.

'GFH claim to be a multi-million-pound bank, so why did my wife, Suzannah, have to lend them £1m to pay the players' wages last year?' Bates asked. 'And why are they scrabbling around today to pay tomorrow's wages? It's hand-to-mouth all the time.' Bates continued, 'I have been asked and agreed to join a consortium to purchase Leeds United.'

That consortium consisted of David Haigh and the club's main sponsor Andrew Flowers, but the possible return of Bates was met by a not unpredictable response from the fans, and the internet was awash with scathing comments.

Counte of Monte Frisco asked, 'How does this correspond with Bates' comments at the time of the sale (to GFH) finding the right strategic buyer to take the club forward with proof of funds needing to be shown?' And then a further question, 'How did GFH pass the Football League's own "fit and proper test" with regards to the ongoing funding of the club and proof of funding issues?'

Jimbo609 added: 'I can't see how Ken Bates can have too many complaints about GFH – he sold the bloody club to them in the first place!'

And deanolofts1981 simply asked, 'What the fuck is going on?'

Things, however, in the world of Leeds United rarely happen as they should, and Cellino's ban was overturned on appeal by Tim Kerr QC, thus ending Bates' interest in the club and allowing Cellino to take control at Elland Road. But, and certainly not for the last time, the Football League, who said they were 'disappointed' that Cellino had won his appeal, had Leeds United in their sights and Cellino immediately went on the offensive. 'The Football League are really tricky. They made trouble at a time I couldn't walk away and I submitted myself to a trial – a humiliation. I don't want to be here if the league doesn't want me, but who are they anyway?

'Me, I sort out the fucking problem at Leeds. I prefer to play by the rules, not to cheat. Leeds fans who are tired of eating shit. They accept me with enthusiasm and that gives me a lot of responsibility. I'm the richest man in the world to these fans and I can challenge anyone, everyone. I am proud to be a guest of Britain – and the best place in Britain is Yorkshire. This club is being shown as something it is not, like we are not proud. We should be proud. Leeds is a very big club. We have incredible, crazy fans. I feel the football business in England is afraid of Leeds United and I quite like that.' Cellino often tried to defend the club, like the time he refused Sky TV in to cover a game at Elland Road because of too many Leeds games being on Sky and having to be re-arranged more times than Michael Jackson's face, forcing thousands of Leeds fans home and abroad to cancel or alter their travel plans. Cellino only let the Sky team in after the league intervened and threatened a points deduction.

At first Leeds fans were supportive of their new potential saviour, and Leeds fans even travelled to the Football League HQ at Preston to protest outside with flags and banners. And with GFH desperately clinging on to Leeds United's shirt-tails with a minority share of 25 per cent and decreasing by the hour, Cellino's initial investment of £25m had to be almost doubled as he inherited a debt of more than £22m.

'We're not in hospital,' said Cellino. 'We can survive. The club is a little bit ill, that's all.'

And Cellino, it appears, also didn't want to look at those books that Bates apparently didn't want Duncan Revie to see in 2007 – Cellino just wanted to get started at Elland Road. And he did, but he openly criticised GFH saying, 'You can see what's been happening here – it's been done by people who knew they weren't staying and now I have to clean up the shit. GFH made big mistakes, but not on purpose. The men who were here in the name of GFH did a really, really, bad job.'

At Cagliari, Cellino had sacked 35 managers in 21 years earning him the name of *ll mangia – allenatori* which translates to manager eater, and even in his attempt to buy West Ham in 2010 Cellino had said that his first job would be to sack the club's manager, Gianfranco Zola – even though he was a long-time friend of his. By the time he breezed into Elland Road, Cellino certainly wasn't about to rest on his laurels, and within days of him arriving at Leeds, and even though he had yet to officially take charge, he sacked the club's current manager Brian McDermott and sparked off an incident that dominated Sky TV's transfer deadline programme and was covered by the media the world over because of the bizarre circumstances.

The evening had started off with fears that Leeds' star striker Ross McCormack would be leaving the club and going to Cardiff City and as the 11pm transfer deadline drew closer, all eyes were glued to the transfer window countdown on television. At around 8.30pm, McCormack announced that he would not be leaving Leeds and was happy to stay at the club. But the next few hours turned out to be nothing short of incredible, and even in the unpredictable world of Leeds United, beyond the realms of belief. A mere 20 minutes after McCormack declared his intention to remain at Elland Road, a breaking news announcement began running along the bottom of the TV screen, 'Brian McDermott sacked as manager of Leeds United.' It transpired that McDermott had been dismissed during a telephone call at 6pm from a lawyer, Chris Farnell, representing the Cellino family and that he would be receiving a letter revealing all the details. McDermott said he'd never heard of the lawyer and had never spoken to him before. It was also rumoured that former Middlesbrough player Gianluca Festa, a long-time friend of Cellino's, was to be the next Leeds manager.

This was earth-shattering news to Leeds fans, and immediately sparked a deluge of phone calls and social media comments and hundreds of fans converged on Elland Road at around 11pm. Cellino was spotted getting into a taxi and the drama began as Leeds fans linked arms and blocked all exits from the stadium's car parks, preventing the taxi from leaving. The taxi remained within the confines of Elland Road for an hour prompting a desperate tweet online from Stanningley Cars saying, 'Please let our taxi leave, the driver wants to go home, and he is close to running out of petrol.'

Meanwhile, McCormack, a close ally of McDermott's, after hearing of the dismissal, appeared to change his mind about staying and it looked very much as though the deal to go to Cardiff for £6m was on. An hour later McCormack said that he had decided to remain at Elland Road and 'help the club' as the deadline that Leeds fans have hated for many years passed without McCormack's departure. McCormack said, 'Brian telephoned and told me he was gone. It's sad times at the club and I'm absolutely gutted. I had a really close relationship with the manager and I was looking forward to continuing at Leeds but things have changed a lot quicker than anyone could have imagined. I'm very happy and content at the club, but a big part of that was Brian and I think he was a little surprised in terms of how quick it has happened, although he always had an inkling it would happen.'

Eventually the police arrived at Elland Road to break up the human barricade, but massive protests would continue the following day and there was a further twist to this crazy event to come. Removed from his post, McDermott did not attend the match at Elland Road the following afternoon and David Haigh the club's managing director asked Nigel Gibbs, McDermott's assistant, to take temporary charge against Huddersfield. McDermott phoned Gibbs to wish him and the players good luck, and Leeds also asked academy coach Neil Redfearn for his assistance. Cellino did not attend the match either, a 5-1 victory, including a defiant hat-trick from McCormack; instead he had apparently spent hours trying to contact McDermott. Rumours had begun circulating around Elland Road long before the final whistle that Brian McDermott hadn't been sacked after all, and shortly after the game the club attempted to clarify the recent buying of the club by Cellino and the apparent dismissal of McDermott by producing this official statement:

'Following recent media reports and speculation, GFH Capital would like to confirm that it has agreed to sell a 75 per cent stake in the club to Eleonora Sport Ltd, a company owned by the Cellino family who have years of experience in football and who plan to invest substantially in the club including the reacquisition of Elland Road. Eleonora (named after Cellino's daughter who introduced herself to the Leeds fans by posting pictures of herself on social media with some rather seductive poses, although fully clothed) will be working on completing the required Football League approval. The Cellino family is a well-known Italian sports family, who have owned Serie A side Cagliari since 1992. They come to English football with an ambition to support Leeds United financially to take it to the Premier League and a belief that the club can sustain top-flight status. Since the agreement, Leeds United is in discussion with Eleonora Sports Ltd on a number of issues concerning the club matters including the structure of the management of the first team.'

The club also added, 'The club would like to make it clear that Brian McDermott remains our first team manager and he has not been dismissed from his post as has been suggested and we look forward to him continuing in his role with us in taking Leeds United forward.'

But earlier, Cellino had told a different story, telling *sportingintelligence.com,* 'I spoke with Brian earlier in the week and gave him the chance for the challenge. I don't know him, but I told him I would be coming in and he would have the chance to build something special and work with a lot of money. In the end we didn't have any choice though, because he did everything to get fired. He gave me no choice. He started an argument with everyone. He was talking with the papers, with everyone, which was not fair. He made it impossible. I want a coach for the club, not a manager.'

But then in the next instalment of the unfurling drama, he categorically denied wanting to remove Brian McDermott from the club. In an interview with the *Sunday Telegraph* he said, 'I want the coach back and have been trying to call him. How could I sack anyone anyway? I need approval from the Football League before I own the club. GFH are still running Leeds United. They did not want Brian as manager but didn't have the courage to sack him. I never wanted Gianluca Festa to replace Brian as manager. Festa was not here to coach the club, just to make the translation with the players; Festa has never run a club before. I have never had him coach a team in Italy before, so why would I want him to coach a major club like Leeds? I like Brian and he is my man.'

Festa had been thrust into the limelight just four days before the Huddersfield game when Cellino unbelievably tried to force Festa into the dugout alongside Brian McDermott.

As McDermott began preparations for an important home midweek league game against Ipswich Town it was reported that Cellino wanted his lifelong friend Gianluca Festa to sit alongside McDermott in the dugout. This was much against McDermott's wishes and understandably he refused to allow the man tipped as his successor to sit alongside him, and in doing so thwarted a clumsy attempt to place his apparently preferred manager alongside existing manager McDermott. As would later become blatantly apparent in so many ways, Cellino has little, if anything, in the way of tact, and in my opinion, can best be described as a loose cannon, unpredictable, headstrong, a definite crackpot and by his own admission 'not normal' and he's certainly not blessed with the greatest of football knowledge; but his passion for the game is undeniable and he genuinely seems to want to do the right thing. But he seems to look at everything as a toy to replace whenever he sees fit. He will not listen to anybody. His toys, in this case, his managers or as he calls them, head coaches, are replaced at an unprecedented rate. He is a sole trader, of that there is no doubt; he has installed his sons Edoardo and Ercole on to the board of directors and surrounds himself with 'yes men' and its pretty apparent that he continues to run the club unilaterally.

There is definitely a family trait though; in April 2016, Edoardo was suspended by the FA and fined £5,000 for gross misconduct on the social media network, Facebook. He was found guilty of calling a fan a 'spastic' and a 'moron'. He was also ordered to complete an education course. Then, in the same month, his brother Ercole was accused of calling a female fan a whale and told her to stop eating. He then used the hashtags of 'Gestapo' and 'SS' on Instagram.

Massimo Cellino is obsessed with superstition. He hates the number 17 and even instructed Brian McDermott to remove the number 17 from the squad list for the new season. His fear of 17 apparently came from a car crash in his homeland, Sardinia. On 17 June 1984, a Fiat 127 pulled out of a petrol station and wrote off Cellino's Ferrari. Cellino ended up in a coma and has been fearful of '17' ever since. He even ordered David Hockaday not to play Paddy Kenny again because he was born on the 17th – that and the fact that he was one of the highest earners. Cellino also hates the colour purple; because as a Catholic, he associates the colour purple with the robe worn by a priest in the weeks preceding the Church's remembrance of the crucifixion. But he sought the help of a priest when he believed that someone had put a curse on Leeds United. 'We are not winning at home,' said Cellino, 'so I brought in Monsignor Philip Moger of St Anne's Cathedral in Leeds, to bless the field and the dressing room and afterwards a black crow flew away.' Leeds immediately won their first game at Elland Road for eight months, beating Cardiff City who they had not beaten for over 30 years. Leeds' legendary manager Don Revie brought a gypsy to Elland Road in the 1960s to remove what he thought was a curse on Leeds United and shortly afterwards Leeds won their first major trophy.

I met Cellino briefly for the first time when I was outside Elland Road about to go into an evening of support for former Leeds favourite Brendan Ormsby who had recently suffered a rather bad stroke. Si Turnpenny and a few of the lads and me were just walking into the East Stand concourse when Cellino appeared out of nowhere. It transpired that he had been having a beer in the Peacock pub just across the road from the ground. He hadn't been at the club very long, and he had been seen in pubs with fans all over Leeds. Social media was awash with photos of people with Cellino who Leeds fans hoped was the new saviour of the club. Outside the East Stand he asked us where we were going, saying 'no game tonight'. It was too complicated to go into the details of Brendan's evening, so we didn't. Besides, he looked in a bit of a hurry and when a brown car pulled up, he shook our hands, called us 'crazy' and got in the back, saying that he was 'going for a beer in the city'. To call us crazy seemed a little strange, considering his high-profile arrival at Elland Road.

There is little doubt that the arrival of Massimo Cellino was met with high expectations and hope from the majority of Leeds fans; he appeared to be a man of the people, quickly demonstrating his flamboyant style by appearing at the Leeds United end-of-season dinner-dance by guesting on guitar with the Leeds band, the Pigeon Detectives. He loves his music and plays in a band himself, the Maurilios; he is friends with the band Kiss and on his arrival had described Leeds United as the Highway to Hell. But his spontaneous visits to city centre pubs and bars would become less frequent over the following months as the encounter with his new manager at Leeds remained in the spotlight.

Brian McDermott had arrived at Elland Road in April 2013 as a popular choice replacing Neil Warnock who appeared to have suffered from a severe bout of deafness. As results began to go against Warnock, and pressure mounted on him, he repeatedly said that he would only leave when the fans told him to. But despite constant chants of 'Warnock time to go!' he couldn't hear them. Warnock was a lot smaller in real life than I thought, and typically when he left the club, he blamed everyone but himself. 'There is a cancer at the club,' he said, and accused United's staff, individual players and the local media of undermining and complicating his reign as boss. I did, however, agree with Warnock's comments on United's technical director Gwyn Williams. 'I never did work out what his role at the club was,' said Warnock.

As McDermott travelled to his new role at Leeds he joked that he had never driven this far north before and feared he would run out of petrol at one stage. He had arrived ahead of his wife to sort out their new house in the Harrogate area, 'I had never really seen Yorkshire before, but it's beautiful, it's stunning,' said McDermott.

He called into an off-licence close to his new home for a corkscrew to enjoy a bottle of wine on his first night in his new North Yorkshire home, but they didn't have one. Luckily, also in the shop at the same time was a Leeds fan who recognised McDermott and welcomed him to Leeds United. Then, on hearing of his dilemma with the corkscrew the Leeds fan disappeared and returned with a corkscrew of his own and gave it to Brian, whose offer of £20 was turned down by the happy-to-help fan.

But by the end of May 2014, Cellino could wait no longer and he dispensed with Brian McDermott's services by 'mutual consent'. Admittedly things hadn't been going too well for McDermott and the all too familiar lack of funds and investment into the team certainly hindered his plans to progress. But typically, McDermott remained dignified throughout and issued this statement: 'It has been my great privilege to manage this great club and I have enjoyed the challenge immensely. However, it is clear that Massimo wishes to implement a new structure that he feels will work more successfully for Leeds with a coach rather than a manager. Massimo wants to bring a new energy to the club, so that we can return to where we belong as a healthy football club. I say thank you to all my staff and players, but especially to the incredible force that is the Leeds United fans I offer my heartfelt thanks. Your support for me and the players was always an inspiration and I urge you to get behind the team and the new owner next season to get us back to where we need to be, fighting for trophies and competing at the top table of English and European football. It won't be easy, but Marching on Together we can get that wish. I wish Massimo and all my friends at Elland Road every success in the future.'

Cellino responded: 'Brian is a great manager and a great guy. He has been unfortunate to work in such difficult circumstances. I did not fully understand the mess he had to work in and the broken promises he had to deal with. He has been a gentleman to deal with, his main concern and priority at all times has been the welfare and protection of Leeds United. His honest efforts to guide us to the safety of mid-table when faced with so many difficulties is appreciated by us all. Brian will always be a friend of Leeds United.'

Kind words indeed, but Massimo Cellino's next decision was baffling in the extreme.

David Hockaday was a virtually unknown manager in non-league football and currently unemployed. His only managerial experience had been at Forest Green, who he led to relegation, only for Forest Green's rivals Salisbury City to be found guilty of financial irregularities and relegated instead of Forest Green. The following season, Hockaday's team were yet again embroiled in a season-long fight against relegation and survived yet again – this time on goal difference. After a run of six defeats from the first seven games the following season, Hockaday left the club by mutual consent.

Eight months later, eagle-eyed Massimo Cellino spied this unemployed little gem and took him to Elland Road as his new coach. There were several reactions from the Leeds fans; bewilderment and disbelief possibly best described the mood.

While every Leeds fan viewed the appointment with surprise, Hockaday countered, 'Is it a surprise? No it isn't; because of my background and the fact that I'm a very experienced British coach. I tick all the boxes and intend to take it with both hands.'

A few weeks after his appointment, Hockaday took charge of the team for the two-match pre-season tour to Val Gardena, nestling in the Dolomites in Italy. Standing under an umbrella beneath torrential rain, Hockaday explained to Leeds fans gathered outside the bar that the other team hadn't shown up, but because of the amount of

Leeds fans that had turned up, a game between two Leeds team would take place. As Hockaday left to take charge of one of the Leeds teams, Cellino ambled into the bar. He didn't say much, he just posed for a few photographs and left. Just one month into the season, and with two wins from six games, Hockaday was sacked. Cellino said, 'I would like to thank David for his efforts but the results since the start of the season have meant we needed to act and make this decision. I was going to sack David after the Watford defeat, but decided to give him a last chance. As a club we will now begin our search for a new head coach. Neil Redfearn will take temporary charge.' A month later another head coach was wheeled in by Cellino.

'I had to hire Darko Milanic,' said Cellino. 'A former Slovenian international with 47 caps for his country, many as captain, and he has gone on to become a very successful coach too. I don't know why I've chosen him. Coaches are like watermelons – you find out about them after you've opened them. His particular qualities? He's good looking and he doesn't talk much. He's very pragmatic, I like him. He is a very cool guy.'

Darko, who can speak five languages and was the club's first ever foreign coach, took charge of his first game at Brentford and he was like everyone else; upstaged by Cellino. Midway through the first half, Cellino left the comfort of his director's seat and somehow found himself in with the home fans and amongst some of the club's disabled fans, including Leeds disabled fans and my mates Stu Hayward and his brother Rob. Then, after James Tarkowski missed a penalty for Brentford, Cellino made a bit of a nuisance of himself and was asked by stewards to leave that area. He then made his way to the away end. I was stood with Big Tony right at the back of the upper stand in the gangway when Cellino sauntered past us without a care in the world. As surprised Leeds fans had their photos taken with him, he made his way down towards the front and in the middle of the Leeds fans. He stayed there for the rest of the game – a 2-0 defeat for Darko.

Cellino mixing with the fans hadn't gone unnoticed by Darko, 'I have already seen how great our fans are. They get behind the team and really care about the club. I like that and I want to make those fans happy. Leeds is a big club and famous across Europe.'

When he first arrived, Darko had said, 'I am essentially cautious,' and this became a heavy burden around his neck. Peter Lorimer observed, 'People who'd watched him in Austria and Slovenia said he was quite a negative coach and having watched his first six games in charge, I can't disagree. The games which rang alarm bells with me were the defeats to Rotherham and Wolves. In both games we were 1-0 up and cruising to an extent. But in both those games we sat back in the second half and allowed the opposition to come on to us. I've no idea why.'

Darko didn't win any of those six games, prompting Cellino to publicly call him a loser, and after just 32 days in charge he was sacked, making Brian Clough's tenure at Elland Road in 1974 seem like a lifetime. But even Milanic's departure was shrouded in uncertainty. He claimed he had not been sacked and would not terminate his own two-year contract. So he remained on 'gardening leave' so long that he attended two Christmas parties for staff at Homebase Garden Centres.

Before offloading Darko, Cellino said, 'I want to apologise to the supporters, they deserve better. I am disappointed, I understand football and I can understand the fans calling for Redfearn.'

Neil Redfearn had been there when required by the club; in 2012 following the sacking of Simon Grayson, Redfearn took over as caretaker manager. Then he returned without any fuss to resume charge of some of the country's finest young prospects in his role as reserve, development and academy manager, and then he had to take charge of the first team once again when manager Neil Warnock left the club in April 2013. Then, when Brian McDermott arrived, Redfearn was immersed back into the academy.

A week after Milanic's 'sacking' Neil Redfearn once again sat in the hot seat and in December 2014 as expected and after meticulous investigation, the Football League obtained papers from an Italian court which cited Cellino as dishonest and his appeal was overturned and he was banned.

But even that didn't stop the manager's revolving door spinning yet again and in May 2015 Redfearn was once again rejected by Cellino. This was particularly hard to take for most Leeds fans as under Redfearn, things had definitely looked to be going in the right direction. I met with Neil Redfearn while working on this book and over a green tea and an espresso he talked candidly about his time at Elland Road. Much of what we talked about, for obvious reasons, will remain private, but it was evident that he has lost none of his love for the club he has supported since he was a boy, or the 'tremendous fans'. He spoke fondly of the youngsters he brought through at Leeds and how he still talks to all of them on a regular basis. 'There were distractions from Cellino and he interfered constantly,' said Redfearn. 'He was president and he thought that he was within his rights to do so. There are huge differences between Italian and English football and he couldn't and still can't grasp that. I just buried myself in the development of the young players at the club and everyone knows how brilliant they are.'

During his second stint in charge of the first team, Redders took on an assistant. Steve Thompson had played with him at Bolton and they remained great friends, but more importantly for Leeds United, they were an instant success. After hovering precariously above the relegation zone up to, and over the Christmas period of 2014, Leeds began climbing the table in earnest and talk switched from relegation to possible promotion via the play-offs. Then, however, totally out of the blue, Cellino got out his big stick and rammed it back through the spokes of the Leeds United wheel. He ordered the club's sporting director Nicola Salerno to suspend Steve Thompson with immediate effect.

'On the very same day we became mathematically safe from relegation,' said Redders, 'and knocking on the door of the play-offs, Tommo was suspended, by letter, with no reason given. The club made up stories to get rid of him – most probably to undermine me. He did absolutely nothing wrong – on the contrary.' Salerno himself was then relieved of his duties by Cellino just days later. 'There was total confusion once again at the club and then Cellino came to me and told me not to pick striker Mirco Antenucci because if he scored any more goals we would have to give him a 12-month extension on his original contract. Mirco was playing well and that was my only concern. In my mind, Cellino shouldn't have offered him that deal in the first place and my only concern was the playing side and results. I was put in charge to pick the best team and that's what I did. I guess I knew then that my days at Elland Road were numbered.'

Steve Thompson spoke out about his suspension many weeks later saying, 'We were second bottom when I joined and we were knocking on the door of the play-offs when I was suspended. It was complex there, with something of a divided dressing room with players who just weren't good enough. You had foreign lads smoking before training which was something I just wasn't used to. I remember Redders saying to me, "The better we do here the worse it will be for us." I thought that was strange at the time, but he was right. One Thursday morning a letter was left on my desk informing me I had been suspended. There was no explanation. The most frustrating thing was the word suspended which implied that I'd done something wrong, which couldn't be further from the truth. I think it was done to try and undermine Redders, and I really felt for him.'

More turbulence was to follow the day before a game down at Charlton. Six players – four Italians, a Frenchman and an Albanian – all declared themselves injured. 'They kept coming to me on the Friday and saying that they weren't fit,' said Redfearn, laughing. 'It got to the stage where some of the academy staff were taking bets on who would be next to come in and see me. Cellino was currently on one of his bans from the Football League and I wasn't supposed to speak to him. But I knew in my heart that these players weren't injured, but it couldn't be proven otherwise. I knew that something was going on, but I had to see the season out with as much dignity as possible for the sake of the supporters. I know without doubt that had I been left in charge there would have been something special happening at Leeds. I put a lot of hard work in, along with other people and there definitely was light at the end of the tunnel, with excellent young players coming through the ranks. Leeds United is my club, always will be. If I got the call to return I would – but obviously circumstances would have to change.' Then, as he expected, Redfearn was told his services would no longer be required and he was stood down on 20 May; the same day as Uwe Rosler arrived to take up the baton.

Towards the end of our conversation, we were joined by Neil's partner and herself a former footballer, Lucy Ward. Lucy starred for the Leeds United Ladies as well as being an under-21 international for England. She then spent 17 years on the education and welfare side of things at the Leeds United academy. She was dismissed from her post on the same day as Neil and one week on from our meeting she would fight Leeds United and Cellino in court over unfair dismissal and sex discrimination – and win. A couple of weeks after that, Leeds' former assistant manager Nigel Gibbs was awarded a six-figure compensation settlement for unlawful dismissal. Hot on the heels of this came an out-of-court secret settlement to the club's former kit suppliers Macron, who sued for damages after Cellino ended their shirt-making agreement in 2014, breaking their contract. Before the start of the 2015/16 season, Cellino also ditched shirt sponsors Enterprise Insurance and Leeds played in an unsponsored shirt that season, which was popular with quite a lot of fans. 32Red written in blue became the new sponsor in 2016/17 and due to my aversion to the colour red I instantly developed my own form of dyslexia meaning that now when I see the sponsor's name, I only see blue.

When Rosler took the reins, he backed himself to thrive under Cellino and said, 'I'm not suicidal. This is the chance of a lifetime. I'm looking through a glass half full.' The week before Rosler's appointment, Cellino had held a bizarre press conference which baffled everyone in the room with random, nonsense ramblings and at one stage he just got up and walked out for a cigarette, leaving newly appointed managing director Adam Pearson to take charge. Pearson eventually unveiled Rosler a week later without the presence of Cellino. Leeds fans were genuinely confident of good things ahead; Rosler seemingly capable of injecting new ideas and Pearson with an apparent control over Cellino's regular outbursts. But Cellino supported Rosler, and at the end of the September said, 'I like him more than any other coach I had here before. He needs to relax, and let the players relax, but believe me; I'm going to let this work. Next season we will be in a better position for promotion.'

Just over two weeks after this message of support, Cellino sacked Rosler after just 12 games, saying, 'We thank Uwe for his efforts and commitment, but we were just trying not to lose, we were not trying to win. Uwe said when he came that his football would be like "heavy rock music" but it was more like country and western.'

Adam Pearson then walked out on Leeds United a week later and the much-needed stability that Pearson had undoubtedly brought to the club evaporated into thin air as Cellino once again took centre stage. The same day, 19 October 2015, that Cellino sacked Rosler, he appointed Steve Evans of Rotherham.

Then Cellino was banned again for yet another tax evasion, this time relating to a Range Rover. Once more Cellino appealed and subsequently the case was quashed, and at the time of writing he still remains at the helm with the Football League continuously looking into further cases of tax evasion, embezzlement and breaking league rules over transfer deals.

As pressure grew on Cellino, the fans mounted a challenge on his leadership. No expense was spared as an advertisement placard was placed immediately outside of the main entrance outlining Cellino's failed promises and calling for him to leave. This was removed by Cellino's lawyers, but that did not stop the heavily funded group from projecting 30ft messages on to the main stand calling for Cellino to leave. The images were beamed on to the East Stand throughout the Middlesbrough game and for the following home game against Bolton, a plane flew over the ground unfurling a banner saying: 'Time to go Massimo'. The protests continued with marches and banners as fans marched from the city centre carrying a coffin announcing the imminent death of our club. Extravagant advertisements calling for Cellino to leave appeared in newspapers and there was also a big leafleting campaign, outlining Cellino's broken promises of 2014, 'If we don't go into the Premier League in two years then I have failed. And if I fail, I go away and you never see me again.'

Massimo Cellino agreed to meet with me just a few days after our final game of the 2015/16 season. It had been another disappointing season, once more testing the fans' resolve to the absolute limit. Yet for this last, worthless, game at Preston, 5,600 Leeds fans took up their positions in the away end for what would be the largest away following for the entire weekend in the whole of Britain.

It was generally regarded as being the last game that Steve Evans would be in charge. After the final whistle, Evans led his team over to the Leeds fans and openly wept as he basked in the adulation heaped upon him by the travelling hordes. After initially claiming that he was confident of an extension to his existing contract, he said afterwards, 'I fear this will be my last game.'

All the players and staff set off on holiday straight after the game (except Evans, he remained to continue scouting for players) and all were told that they would receive a text in due course informing them of any change in the head coach and with details on when to return for training.

'Hello my friend,' said Cellino, peering over his glasses as I entered his office. 'Come, come, please sit down.' He reached out and shook my hand. I had met him briefly on a couple of occasions before, and I was certainly not his biggest fan, but seeing him sat dwarfed by this huge chair and sat behind an obscenely large desk, I wanted to just cuddle him, or throttle him, I wasn't sure. He looked tired and worn out. He was not making my job of taking him to task easy.

'I'm here to ask what are your plans for my football club,' I said as I sat down smiling.

'I love this club,' he said, in a typical Italian-style shrug of the shoulders with his open hands gesturing towards me. 'But the Football League!' His arms became animated. 'They hate me! I am not scared of them. Who are they? I am not bothered about them. I fight for this club, but the fans, they fight me, I don't like that. I want to be friends, but they fight me.

'I came to Leeds because this is a great club. I thought my life would be easy here. But no.

'Can you imagine staying here when the Leeds fans want to kill me? They call me a bastard and tell me to "fuck off". I think that they are so used to eating shit that they don't believe I can make things good here. I am not a bad person. It hurts me. Sometimes I do things without thinking, I make mistakes sometimes – but I don't do it on purpose.'

He puts his head in his hand and throws his glasses on the desk. I point to my left.

'That crowd here love Leeds United with everything they have got and if you ever witness that ground brimming with 40,000 of the best fans in the world, it will make your hair stand on end. You could be part of that,' I say, but Cellino shrugs again. 'I sometimes wish that I hadn't bought this club,' he concedes. 'There is a lot going on behind the scenes.'

I continue to tell him of my love for Don Revie and what this club owes to him, his assistant Les Cocker and his trusted backroom staff of Syd Owen, Bob English and Cyril Partridge. I tell him that because of these great men I, and thousands like me, have been supporting this club ever since for over 50 years, many even longer. He looks me in the eye and smiles, 'You must be fucking mad.' But he throws his glasses down again, 'That's what I need – a Don Revie.'

Cellino's green-windowed office is situated beneath the words 'Leeds United' emblazoned high on the East Stand façade situated on Lowfields Road across from the statue of Don Revie. I imagine that Cellino would look out at Don every day and when he glanced down, for a few days only, he would also have seen the 'Cellino Out' advertising board situated deliberately just outside the East Stand entrance, until it was removed by Cellino's lawyers.

'I told the Football League to wait for the facts,' Cellino continues, picking up his glasses again. 'They ban me but I tell them to wait for the third time. The first time is nothing – it means nothing. The first time is just a practice but the Football League tried to ban me on that first meeting. Now that third meeting is done – I am not guilty. I told them to wait.'

Cellino is right; over the few days surrounding our meeting, news from Italy claimed that the third hearing proved that Cellino has no case to answer and that he is innocent. The day after our meeting, the league begrudgingly announced: 'At its meeting today, the Football League board discussed matters relating to the pending disqualification of Leeds United president Massimo Cellino, in light of this week's verdict in the Italian court. The board determined that Mr Cellino's disqualification – under the Owners' and Directors' Test – will no longer apply if the written judgement of the court, which the league is yet to see, confirms that Mr Cellino has been acquitted of this offence following recent changes to Italian law which have decriminalised certain offences with retrospective effect.'

I tell Massimo that the Football League have always hated Leeds United. He seems a little surprised at this. I tell him that I have watched Leeds United since I was ten years old in 1966 and assured him that they and the Football Association despise our football club and they always have.

He shrugs his shoulders again, 'They threw me in jail when they thought I had done wrong in Sardinia. I did nothing wrong but I went to jail. While I was in my cell, my team Cagliari won; they hadn't won in a long time. After a week they come to let me out but my team win while I was in jail so I say, leave me here, my team win while I'm in here. Then a week later they come to let me out. I say again leave me here, my team win again while I'm in here. I was happy in my cell playing my guitar and smoking my cigarettes. My team win about six games and then they come and say I must leave now. So I go back to my club and we fucking lose! I asked them why they lock me up? They say, "Because you're a dickhead." I know I'm a dickhead, I say, but that is no reason to lock me up.' He then threw his glasses again and they landed in an ashtray piled up with dead cigarettes. 'I can be the best arsehole in the world,' he shrugs his shoulders again, 'but, I'm not a bad person.'

I dare to ask about Steve Evans, and will he still be here next season. 'I like Steve. He works very hard and is a nice guy – he is honest. But I have to sack him. I cannot work with English managers (Evans is Scottish). British coaches (he lunges his arms forward as if demonstrating the long ball) they are no good. I must look for a foreign coach. Where am I going to find a manager in England who is actually a coach? And Sol Bamba, he talks too much.' I point out that he *is* club captain. 'He won't be next season,' says Cellino.

Stix took a photo of us both as I left and Cellino shook my hand again saying, 'I like you Gary, you remind me of my father.' Make of that what you will.

Steve Evans had arrived at Elland Road looking like a cross between an inflatable Freddie Starr and Eddie Izzard and the fans' opinion was clearly divided. While manager at Rotherham in October 2013 he said, 'Leeds United are not a big club. Don't get me wrong, they used to be; now they're run by puppets, watched by blinkered seals. If they ever offered me a job, I'd turn it down. I want to be the captain of a cruise liner not the *Titanic*.' But for the few months he was at Elland Road, the longest so far under Cellino, he came across as a nice, honest bloke. After just managing to squeeze into the manager's chair he lost four stone in as many weeks. Partly due, he said, to cutting down on beer and drinking wine instead, and he stopped having late-night meals. I admired his loyalty right up to the end. With his present contract quickly coming to a close and not knowing if it would be extended Evans continued to work tirelessly for the club. This was in spite of the fact that Cellino cruelly left his manager in limbo, making no attempt to contact him whatsoever; similar to what he had done to both Brian McDermott and Neil Redfearn. Evans returned from a short break in Dubai (where he had read about Cellino searching for a new manager) bravely saying, 'I'll be going straight back to work. There's still lots to be done because I'm employed by a great club and I must continue to work. To deliver promotion you must plan. The Leeds fans deserve a promotion season and I'm ready, better than ever physically and mentally to deliver that. We need to help the squad by adding five or six quality players. I have a pre-season schedule ready to go and I have a list of players. Most I have discussed previously with Mr Cellino, and he liked my vision. I'm hurting at not knowing my future but I respect the right of the club owners to make a big decision in a time and manner that suits them. I have a burning desire to attack the new season.'

Unfortunately, one week later Evans became Cellino's seventh victim and was sacked. Evans was predictably gracious saying, 'The first thing you realise about this great football club is the size and the fans are simply stunning and wonderful people. It's been a wonderful experience and I wish the club every success and I will be the first to buy a ticket if they get back to the Premier League.' Cellino said, 'Steve completed the job he was brought in to do – to keep the team in the Championship – and his hard work here is greatly appreciated. I wish him and his assistant Paul Raynor the very best for the future. We have decided that a different approach is required in order to achieve our target to deliver the special season our supporters deserve.'

The day after Evans' departure, Leeds appointed ex-Swansea boss Garry Monk who is English. Cellino said, 'Garry is part of a new generation of coaches in England and has a lot of potential to develop, which is something we are targeting for the new season. He's very suited to continuing the growth of our young and improving team.' Garry Monk: 'I'm extremely honoured to be joining Leeds United. The passion of the fans, the history of the club and the ambition of the owner all ties in with what I want to do.' Monk immediately began assembling his own team (many of them targets of Steve Evans) and appointed his own backroom staff, including a long-awaited goalkeeping coach. But in a trademark interference from Cellino, using smoke and mirrors as only he can; while players coming in began to raise the optimism of the fans, current Football League Player of the Season Lewis Cook, one of the many crown jewels nurtured by Neil Redfearn was smuggled out through the back door and went to Bournemouth. Cellino then launched a vicious attack on one of the few remaining star youngsters at the club, Charlie Taylor. Unconfirmed reports have said that Garry Monk has had a sign put over his office door: 'Cellino Keep Out'.

Endnote

This book started with a monk and is ending with a monk, but as Leeds United begin the 2016/17 season with Massimo Cellino pledging to refund 25 per cent or possibly 50 per cent back to season ticket holders if the club fail to get into at least the play-offs, Leeds fans are left wondering how on earth this club could manage to find skint Arabs and a billionaire who appears to have just escaped from a lunatic asylum. So, as this book goes to publication, the latest head coach of Leeds United Football Club, Garry Monk, has passed through the, for now, stationary manager's revolving door and into the vacant car sat in the Leeds roller coaster station. Which way will the car go now, up or down, or just amble across? Only time will tell. Fasten your seat belts.